MW00416331

A CERTAIN IDEA OF AMERICA

A CERTAIN IDEA OF AMERICA

Selected Writings

PEGGY NOONAN

PORTFOLIO | PENGUIN

Portfolio / Penguin
An imprint of Penguin Random House LLC
penguinrandomhouse.com

All columns first published in *The Wall Street Journal* and have been edited slightly for clarity.

Book design by Alissa Rose Theodor

LIBRARY OF CONGRESS CONTROL NUMBER: 2024037311

ISBN 9780593854778 (hardcover)
ISBN 9780593854785 (ebook)

Printed in the United States of America

1 3 5 7 9 10 8 6 4 2

For Will and Alice in an auspicious year

CONTENTS

FOREWORD

This is not a book about the day to day of our national political life. It is simply about loving America and enjoying thinking aloud about it.

The columns gathered here are varied in terms of subject matter. They are about the things that endure, and things that deserve to be encouraged. A number of them are about spectacular human beings. As my editor and I read through the past few years of *Wall Street Journal* columns, if I said, "I really enjoyed writing that," or she said, "I loved this," or I said, "This was important to me," it was in. If not, out. We chose about eighty from more than four hundred. We found ourselves most attracted to themes of history and its pleasures.

The book is divided into seven parts.

"Let Us Now Praise Famous Men" is mostly about great figures and artists of the twentieth century, from Billy Graham to Oscar Hammerstein, from Queen Elizabeth II to Senator Margaret Chase Smith of the state of Maine, and from Tom Wolfe to Bob Dylan, with some side trips to the nineteenth century and the generals of the American Civil War. Looking back on a career of now fifty years, I see that from the beginning what I have loved most, what has most moved me, is writing honest praise.

"I Don't Mind Being Stern," on the other hand, is about having fun, as a public writer, taking as big a stick as you can to people and things you are certain deserve it. The U.S. Senate changing its dress code to accommodate a senator who enjoys dressing like a child? Get the stick. Vengeful Prince Harry? Ditto. We were certain a recent Broadway production of *Cabaret* deserved our stern attention, in a piece whose last line is its summation: "Life Isn't *Merde*." We castigate men who aren't gentlemen, and admonish parents who, as their personal vanity product, wind kids up to become mindless status robots. Also receiving fire are woke academics who speak garbage thoughts with garbage words. (I am sorry to use the word "woke," which is boring and sounds merely sarcastic, but the thing is that when you say it, everyone pretty much knows what you mean.) I believe we were the first to compare contemporary social justice warriors with the practitioners of the struggle sessions of the Chinese Cultural Revolution. We enjoyed pointing out that the leaders of the French Revolution were, largely, sociopaths. There's a piece written in the hours after January 6, 2021.

In "Try a Little Tenderness" we turn to love, which we posit as a very good thing. We call for artists to enter politics. We meditate, after the fire that swept the Cathedral of Notre Dame, in Paris, on the enduring presence and power of religious faith. We unabashedly love, we swoon over and wish to marry, Leo Tolstoy and *War and Peace*. We mourn for Uvalde, Texas. We talk about the endless drama of men and women, and instruct America that more happens every day in the office than business. Also we declare Taylor Swift an American phenomenon, and if you don't like it you can just shake it off.

"It Appears He Didn't Take My Advice" is two columns long. The first, on Joe Biden, was so spectacularly wrong in its central prediction that it made us laugh. Yet looking back five years, it seemed to me in its reasoning to be still oddly pertinent. The second, on Donald Trump, on the eve of the 2016 election, seems to me to have some prescience as to his central problems as a historical figure. Also in the writing of it I remember a feeling of poignance.

"On America" is about the foibles, troubles, and triumphs of our country. It includes the story of my great-aunt Jane Jane, and how, as an Irish immigrant, she came to love her new country. I'd say the general theme of this section is about keeping your poise under pressure. It includes recent college graduates, the Normandy invasion, and the spirited, against-the-grain testimony of an old-fashioned capitalist. Also included, a portrait of the dynamics that produced a political sea change: "The Protected Versus the Unprotected."

"Watch Out" contains columns about the worries that preoccupy my mind: the dark potentials of AI, skepticism as to the character and motives of its inventors; the possible use of nuclear weapons, and the ongoing dramas in Ukraine and the Mideast.

"We Can Handle It" is about working our way, as a nation, through things that roil us, from the #MeToo movement to the abortion wars, from the creation of a sane foreign policy, to the low state of the American presidency.

This collection draws its title from the famous first sentence of Charles de Gaulle's "War Memoirs," most happily translated as "All my life I have had a certain idea of France." It struck me when I read it many years ago and stayed with me because all my life I have had a certain idea of America, and from the beginning it shaped my thinking and drove my work.

What is that idea? That she is good. That she has value. That from birth she was something new in the history of man, a step forward, an advancement. Its founders were engaged in the highest form of human achievement, stating assumptions and creating arrangements whereby life could be made more: just. In the workings of its history I saw something fabled. The genius cluster of the Founders, for instance—how did it happen that those particular people came together at that particular moment with exactly the right (different but complementary) gifts? Long ago I asked the historian David McCullough if he ever wondered about this. He said yes, and the only explanation he could come up with was: "Providence." That is where my mind settles, too.

De Gaulle said his thoughts on France were driven as much by emotion as reason, and the same for me. A piece in here dated July 3, 2019, speaks of both:

> I'm not really big on purple mountain majesties. I'd love America if it were a hole in the ground, though yes, it's beautiful. I don't love it only because it's "an idea," as we all say now. That strikes me as a little bloodless. Baseball didn't come from an idea, it came from *us*—a long

cool game punctuated by moments of high excellence and utter heartbreak, a team sport in which each player operates on his own. The great movie about America's pastime isn't called *Field of Ideas*, it's called *Field of Dreams*. And the scene that makes every grown-up weep is when the dark-haired young catcher steps out of the cornfield and walks toward Kevin Costner, who suddenly realizes, That's my father.

He asks if they can play catch, and they do, into the night.

The great question comes from the father: "Is this Heaven?" The great answer: "It's Iowa."

Which gets me closer to my feelings on patriotism. We are a people that has experienced something epic together. We were given this brilliant, beautiful thing, this new arrangement, a political invention based on the astounding assumption that we are all equal, and that where you start doesn't dictate where you'll wind up. We've kept it going, father to son, mother to daughter, down the generations, inspired by the excellence and in spite of the heartbreak. Whatever was happening, depression or war, we held high the meaning and forged forward. We've respected and protected the Constitution.

And in the forging through and holding high we've created a history, traditions, a way of existing together.

We've been doing this for 243 years now, since the first Fourth of July and in spite of all the changes that have swept the world.

It's all a miracle. I love America because it's where the miracle is.

I would say of the above, welcome to my deepest heart.

You'll see some of the U.S. Civil War here. It has been a lifelong preoccupation and followed my interest in Abraham Lincoln, whose life has gripped me since childhood. He is the only American president who was both a political and literary genius—literally, genius—and about him clung an air of the mystical. He was completely human (homely ways, off-color jokes, depressions, a writer of angry letters) and yet there was something almost supernatural in his ability to be fair, to be just, to be merciful toward his tormentors (the angry letters were thrown in a drawer). What a figure. Tolstoy thought him the greatest man in history.

Religious faith is a constant subtext here because it's my constant subtext.

Anyway, America. With all her harrowing flaws (we have always been a violent country, for instance) she deserves from us a feeling of profound protectiveness. Our great job as citizens is to shine it up a little, make it better, and hand it on, safely, to the generation that follows, and ask them to shine it up and hand it on. I think that is often what I was trying to do. When you see this I will have been a weekly columnist in *The Wall Street Journal* for just shy of a quarter century. I am grateful I haven't run out of opinions.

All of these columns have appeared in *The Wall Street Journal*. The titles of some have been changed though not the dates, and some words and references have been added or replaced to enhance clarity but not alter meaning.

CHAPTER 1

LET US NOW PRAISE FAMOUS MEN

On great figures and artists,
most, but not all, of the twentieth century.

BILLY GRAHAM, THE ECUMENICAL EVANGELIST

February 22, 2018

You know the miraculous life of Louis Zamperini, whose story was told in Laura Hillenbrand's epic, lovely book, *Unbroken.* Louis was the delinquent, knockabout son of Italian immigrants in Torrance, California, who went on to run for America in the 1936 Berlin Olympics, then joined the Army Air Corps before Pearl Harbor. He crashed in the Pacific, drifted in a raft on open sea for forty-seven days, came near death—shark attacks, storms, strafing by Japanese bombers—and survived, only to be captured by enemy troops. He spent two years in Japanese prison camps—beaten, tortured, brutalized as much as a person can be and still live.

He came back a hero, shocked to be alive. But his life went from rise to descent—rage, alcoholism, destruction. He couldn't focus enough to make a living, couldn't stop the downhill slide. His wife, Cynthia, announced she was leaving. One day a neighbor told them of something going on in town, in L.A. An evangelist named Billy Graham had set up a tent and invited the public. Cynthia grabbed at the straw, but Louie refused. He wasn't going to watch some con man screaming. Cynthia argued for days and finally fibbed. Billy Graham, she said, talks a lot about science. Louie liked science. So he went, grudgingly, and they sat in the back. The following quotes are from *Unbroken.*

This is what Billy Graham looked like: "His remarkably tall blond hair fluttered on the summit of a remarkably tall head, which in turn topped a remarkably tall body. He had a direct gaze" and "a southern sway in his voice." Studio chiefs saw a leading man and offered him a movie contract. Graham laughed and said he wouldn't do it for a million a month. He was thirty-one and had been traveling the world for years.

This is what he hid: He was wearing out. "For many hours a day, seven days a week, he preached to vast throngs, and each sermon was a workout, delivered in a booming voice, punctuated with broad gestures of the hands, arms, body. He got up as early as five, and he stayed in the tent late into the night, counseling troubled souls." His weight dropped and there were circles under his eyes. "At times he felt that if he stopped moving his legs would buckle, so he took to pacing his pulpit to keep himself from keeling over."

It cost him to be Billy Graham. He wanted to end his crusades, but their success convinced him "Providence had other wishes."

This is what Billy Graham was not like: Elmer Gantry. Louie expected "the sort of frothy, holy-rolling charlatan that he'd seen preaching near Torrance when he was a boy. What he saw instead was a brisk, neatly groomed man two years younger than himself." This man was . . . serious. "He asked his listeners to open their Bibles to the eighth chapter of John."

This is what Billy Graham said: "Here tonight, there's a drowning man, a drowning woman . . . a drowning boy, a drowning girl that is lost in the sea of life."

He spoke of the Pharisees surrounding Jesus that day in the temple and presenting the woman taken in adultery. Moses in the law commanded us, they said, that she should be stoned. What say you? Jesus stooped down and wrote with his finger on the ground, as if he hadn't heard. They pressed; he wrote. He lifted himself and said, "Let him who is without sin cast the first stone." They were convicted by their own conscience and left. Jesus, alone with the woman, asked, "Has no one condemned thee?" No man, she said. He said, "Neither do I condemn thee. Go now and sin no more."

But what was Jesus writing on the ground? Graham suggested Christ was enacting the writing of the facts of our individual lives: "God takes down your life from the time you were born to the time you die." He will see the truth. "You're going to say, 'Lord, I wasn't such a bad fellow.'"

Louie felt something tighten. He felt "a lurking, nameless uneasiness," like "the shudder of sharks rasping their backs along the bottom of the raft."

And so began his conversion. He went on to a life of greatness, helping boys as lost as he'd once been.

That is the importance of Billy Graham. We talk about the "friend of presidents" who "moved among the powerful," but he was a man who wanted to help you save your soul whoever you were, in whatever circumstance. And there would have been millions.

"Louis wasn't the only one in the tent," Laura Hillenbrand said this week, by phone: "Without Reverend Graham, Louie would not have lived."

"What reached into Louis's soul," she added, "was Graham's ability to reach into the individual, the person in front of him—of God being interested in him personally." Louis had to come to terms with two huge things, the mystery of his suffering (why did this injustice happen?) and the mystery of his survival (so many others are gone). But you didn't have to float on a raft and be tortured to suffer: "Everyone suffers. Louis was no different from anyone else in the tent that night."

He's still no different from anyone else in the tent.

Here I want to say, I think there was something different and special going on between Catholics and Billy Graham. They saw, as Louis Zamperini, raised Catholic, saw, his earnestness, his confidence in his message. They saw him swimming against the modern tide, as they often felt they were. And maybe they looked and imagined the cost.

I asked the archbishop of Philadelphia, Charles Chaput, if he saw this also. He emailed back: "When I was growing up, back in the 1950s, relations between Catholics and Protestants were still wary." But Catholic families "felt that Billy Graham was the Protestant preacher they could feel a real kinship with. He had the ability to reach across all the fractures in Christianity and speak to the common believing heart." Archbishop Chaput compared him to C. S. Lewis. "In a sense, he spoke the same kind of 'mere' Christianity that Lewis did so well, but with an American accent."

As the big thing to be desired now is that we hold together as a nation and not split apart, Graham's ecumenical force should be noted among his achievements.

Throughout his life Billy Graham had an air of "I'm not important, God is important." It didn't seem like a line but a conviction. He said once, "I am not going to Heaven because I have preached to great crowds. . . . I am going to Heaven just like the thief on the cross who said in that last moment, 'Lord, remember me.'"

And Christ said, "This day you will be with me in Paradise."

Graham's son asked what he wanted on his gravestone. He thought and said, "Preacher."

Since Wednesday morning one of his quotes was all over social media: "Someday you will read or hear that Billy Graham is dead. Don't you believe a word of it. I shall be more alive than I am now. I will just have changed my address. I will have gone into the presence of God."

Rest in peace, American preacher man.

THE WISDOM OF OSCAR HAMMERSTEIN

March 29, 2018

Let's unfurrow the brow and look at something elevated. It's a small thing, a half-hour television interview from sixty years ago, but it struck me this week as a kind of master class in how to be a public figure and how to talk about what matters. In our polarized moment it functions as both template and example.

In March 1958, the fierce young journalist Mike Wallace—already famous for opening an interview with the restaurateur Toots Shor by asking, "Toots, why do people call you a slob?"—decided to bore in on Oscar Hammerstein II. (For the record, Shor responded that Wallace had him confused with Jackie Gleason.) Hammerstein was the fabled lyricist and librettist who with composer Richard Rodgers put jewels in the crown of American musical theater—*Oklahoma!, South Pacific, The King and I,* and *Carousel,* whose latest Broadway revival is about to open. He was a hero of American culture and a famous success in a nation that worshiped success.

Wallace was respectful but direct and probing. He asked Hammerstein if critics who'd called his work sentimental didn't have a point.

Hammerstein said his critics were talented, loved the theater, and there was something to what they'd said. But he spoke of sentiment "in contradistinction to sophistication": "The sophisticate is a man who thinks he can swim better than he can and sometimes drowns himself. He thinks he can drive better than he really can and sometimes causes great smashups. So, in my book there's nothing wrong with sentiment because the things we're sentimental about are the fundamental things in life: the birth of a child, the death of a child or of anybody, falling in love. I couldn't be anything but sentimental about these basic things."

What, Wallace asked, was Hammerstein's message in *South Pacific*?

Hammerstein said neither he nor Rodgers had ever gone looking for vehicles by which to deliver messages. They were attracted to great stories and wanted to tell them onstage. But "when a writer writes anything about anything at all, he gives himself away." He inevitably exposes his beliefs and hopes. The love stories in *South Pacific* were shaped by questions of race. The main characters learned that "all this prejudice that we have is something that fades away in the face of something that's really important." That thing is love.

Does this reflect his views on interracial marriage?

Hammerstein, simply: "Yes."

The King and I, he said, is about cultural differences. The Welsh governess and the Siamese children know nothing of each other at the start: "There again, all race and color had faded in their getting to know and love each other." On the other hand, *Allegro*, about disillusionment and professional achievement, carries a warning: "After you're successful, whether you be a doctor or a lawyer or a librettist, there is a conspiracy that goes on in which you join—a conspiracy of the world to render you less effective by bestowing honors on you and taking you away from the job of curing people, or of pleading cases, or writing libretti and . . . putting you on committees." He added he was "a fine one to talk": he couldn't stop joining committees.

Is he religious? Here Hammerstein told a story. A year ago he was rushing to work and jaywalked. A policeman called out; Hammerstein braced for a dressing down. But the officer recognized him and poured out his appreciation for his work. Hammerstein thanked him and moved to leave, but the policeman had a question. "He said, 'Are you religious?' And I said, 'Well, I don't belong to any church,' and then he patted me on the back and he said, 'Ah, you're religious all right.' And I went on feeling as if I'd been caught, and feeling that I *was* religious. He had discovered from the words of my songs that I had faith—faith in mankind, faith that there was something more powerful than mankind behind it all, and faith that in the long run good triumphs over evil. If that's religion, I'm religious, and it is my definition of religion."

Then to politics.

Wallace: "You are an active liberal."

Hammerstein: "Yes, I guess I am."

What connection does this have with your work?

"I think it must have a connection, because it expresses my feelings, my tendencies," Hammerstein said. "As I've said before, a writer gives himself away if he's writing honestly."

Wallace: "Would you agree that most of our writers and directors on Broadway and television in Hollywood are liberal and that there is a liberal complexion to their work?"

"I think I would, yes," Hammerstein replied, honestly and with no defensiveness.

Wallace's office had just spoken to "a militant dissenter" from liberalism, Ayn Rand, author of the recently published novel *Atlas Shrugged*. She said, "The public is being brainwashed by the so-called liberal or leftist philosophies, which have a stranglehold on the dissemination of ideas in America." How did Hammerstein respond?

He didn't like her adding the word "leftist," "because you can be a liberal without being a leftist, and many and most liberals are." Beyond that, her criticism was an example of what's working. "I think it's fine that there is a Miss Rand who comes out stoutly for the conservative. I think it's fine that we have all kinds of thinkers in the world. . . . I admit that the majority of writers in this country are on the liberal side."

But he added, of Rand, "*We need her to hold us back, and I think she needs us to pull her forward.*"

Italics mine. Because liberals and conservatives do need each other, and the right course can sometimes be found in the tug between them.

Wallace: "The public does rarely get anything but a liberal viewpoint from Hollywood or from television, from Broadway," and the charge can be "safely made that there is a certain intolerance of conservative ideas among liberals."

Hammerstein, again undefensive: "I think so, too."

What's to be done about it? Nothing, said Hammerstein: "Just be yourself, that's all." If the public likes Miss Rand, "there will be a Miss Rand trend." Let the problem work its way out in a free country.

Hammerstein said he tries sometimes to vote Republican "just for the sake of switching—just for the sake of telling myself I'm not a party man," which he doesn't want to be. "But somehow or other I always wind up voting Democratic." Balancing the budget bores him. "I have an idea that the more liberal Democratic tendency—to borrow and owe money is healthier for us." Most big corporations borrow, and they make progress with the money. When the U.S. borrows money, Hammerstein said, he felt "the people in the lower income bracket get the most out of it. But I'm no economist—this is merely a guess."

We're all guessing, and working on instinct and experience. Moral modesty and candor are good to see.

In our public figures, especially our political ones, they are hard to find. I offer Hammerstein's old words as an example—a prompter—of what they sound like.

THE MYSTERY AND GRACE OF PAUL SIMON

March 28, 2024

Easter's coming, Holy Week's here, and Passover is a few weeks away, so it's a good time to look at the work of a great artist who's brought considerable beauty into the world, Paul Simon. Alex Gibney's two-part MGM+ documentary on the making of his most recent album is also beautiful—moving, mellow, sweet, and deep. It tells of Mr. Simon's life and touches on three big themes—the nature of creativity and where it comes from; that tricky thing called a career, which carries a talent forward into the world and keeps it there, or not; and, centrally, an ongoing spiritual event in Mr. Simon's life that sounds like an ongoing miracle, or at least has pronounced supernatural aspects.

Mr. Simon, now eighty-two, is one of the greatest American songwriters of the twentieth century, and you carry his songs in your head—"Bridge Over Troubled Water," "Scarborough Fair," "American Tune," "Mrs. Robinson." It was classic after classic. "People used to say, 'Oh, you have your finger on the pulse,'" Mr. Simon says in the documentary. "And I would think, no, I don't have my finger on the pulse, I just have my finger out there, and the pulse is running under it, for the time being." How long it lasts is a mystery, knowing the pulse is there and feeling its vibrations is a gift, putting your hand out there is the effort.

He grew up in the New York City borough of Queens, where his heroes were Mickey Mantle, JFK, Lenny Bruce, and Elvis. He met neighborhood boy Art Garfunkel in sixth grade, and they began to sing together, Mr. Simon writing the music and Mr. Garfunkel harmonizing. Mr. Simon says something arresting about America when he was coming up: "My culture was radio. It wasn't like I was singing the music of Queens, you know? We didn't have people sitting around on the porches in Queens singing fables about what it was like in Queens in the old days."

What he worked with was AM radio Top 40—the Everly Brothers, the Cleftones. America was becoming less local and regional even then, more a national entity projecting a national sound that generation after generation would imitate, recapitulate, expand on.

When Simon & Garfunkel first went on Dick Clark's *American Bandstand*, Mr. Simon was asked where he was from. "Macon, Georgia," he spontaneously lied. Because it sounded like a real place with a real meaning, not just someplace waves were passing through. I mention this because I think that's a very American longing, to come from somewhere real, discrete, and vividly itself.

He took his guitar into the bathroom at his parents' house to write. "The tile made an echo and the water was kind of a white-noise sound." He felt a flow of creative energy and wondered what it was. "One second ago that thought was not here and now I'm weeping. How'd that happen? And how can I do it again?"

Simon & Garfunkel knew huge recording success, would, in the coming decades, break up, reunite, part. Popularity fluctuated; Mr. Simon's career went hot and not-hot. There's a powerful section on a lukewarm period. Mr. Simon, solo, looking for the different sounds of the world, goes to Jamaica and South Africa. In the latter, in 1985, he is surrounded by singers and musicians and music he doesn't know. They form the elements of what would become his masterpiece, *Graceland*. You hear the blunt, raucous accordion riff that opens "The Boy in the Bubble," and it sounds so big. Later, when Mr. Simon started writing the lyrics he found that his subject matter was unrelated to the world he'd just visited—he was writing about the Mississippi River, about Elvis Presley's Graceland. Confused, he went there for the first time and realized he was writing about a father and son on a journey of repair. He accepted it, because creativity is a mystery. "I really love the mystery."

Once he told Dick Cavett he didn't know why he wrote "Where have you gone, Joe DiMaggio? / Our nation turns its lonely eyes to you," but he wasn't perturbed not to understand. Someday it would mean something. I came to be a shorthand way of saying Americans have a sense of lessened greatness, that our heroes are in the past.

Now to the supernatural event. Mr. Simon and his wife, the musician Edie Brickell, had been living in Texas for a few years when, on January 15, 2019, he had a dream that said, "You're working on a piece called *Seven Psalms*." He hadn't written anything in a few years, hadn't wanted to, but the dream was so strong that he got up and wrote it down. "I had no idea what that meant." Gradually, information came—chords, a sound. Then he started to wake up two or three times a week between 3:30 and 5:00 a.m. and words would come. "I'd write them down and if I tried to add to them—'Oh, that's a good verse, I'll write a second verse'—it would stop." He thought, whatever it is, "it's coming to me and that's all, I just have to wait, and when it comes, write it down."

In the documentary he sings one of the songs that came of the process:

I've been thinking about the great migration
One by one they leave the flock
I've been wondering about their destination
Meadow grass on a jagged rock
The Lord is my engineer
The Lord is the earth I ride on
The Lord is the face in the atmosphere
The path I slip and slide on

It's beautiful. He alters the lyrics slightly on the final album, but they're beautiful, too.

Throughout all this, another major event. He suddenly lost hearing in his left ear. Within a month it was almost gone. He couldn't hear his music the same, his voice sounded different; it used to come from here and now it was there. He fell into depression, got out of bed, searched for remedies and workarounds. In time he thought maybe the whole thing—the dream, the words and sounds, the songs, the deafness—was part of the same whole, one he was meant to grapple with. Maybe it was supposed to be hard. Why not? The whole album was about an "argument" he is having with himself, which he later calls a "debate," "about belief or not." "Maybe it isn't supposed to be so easy. Maybe you're supposed to have an obstacle." Maybe the struggle helps you know what you know in a deeper way.

Wynton Marsalis, another great artist and Mr. Simon's close friend, told him, as he recorded, to "leave the struggle in there."

There are more spiritual references in the documentary—he speaks of the psalms of David and makes biblical references—and once you see them you realize they've always been there in Mr. Simon's work. All writers reveal their obsessions and preoccupations, and half the time they're not even conscious of it. And no one knows where anyone's going or what's going on with them, but Paul Simon is speaking the language of conversion and I think he's going to graceland.

HATS OFF TO TOM WOLFE

May 17, 2018

"You can take off your hats now, gentlemen, and I think perhaps you had better." That was Stephen Vincent Benét in 1941, in the *Saturday Review of Literature,* on the work of Scott Fitzgerald, who had recently died.

I thought of it on the death this week of Tom Wolfe. Not that he was ignored or forgotten, but we are coming to terms with his greatness in a purer, less guarded way than in the past.

He picked up American journalism and shook it hard, then he picked up the novel and shook that, too. He saw what was happening all around us, and he said that's not "what's happening," that's *history*—the social and cultural story of the great Hog-stomping Baroque America of the second half of the twentieth century, which was begging to be captured and finally was, by him, in a way no one else would or could.

He invented characters that presented us to ourselves. He had two masterpieces, *The Right Stuff* in nonfiction and *The Bonfire of the Vanities* in fiction. He issued one of the great literary manifestos: *Stop your navel gazing, get out your notebook, there's a world exploding out there.*

His words entered the language. He fearlessly, brazenly faced up to America's blood wars, its ethnic and racial rivalries, its merry bitterness. "Yo, Gober!" "He's another Donkey, same as me."

On top of that he strutted through the world like some crazed, antique peacock—the faded vanilla suits, the high-collar shirts, the polka-dot ties, the socks and handkerchief, the spats.

What a figure! When I heard the news, I thought of last November, at the New York Public Library's annual gala. When I walked in he and Sheila, his warm, elegant wife, were seated alone as the party raged around them.

I kissed them hello, they invited me to sit, and, twenty minutes later, after talk of Donald Trump, toward whom he was equal parts fair-minded, amused, and amazed, I left to join friends. Halfway through the room I turned back. Tom was gazing, bemused, at the crowd. "That's Dickens," I said to a friend. "That's Zola." There should have been a line waiting to meet him, to say, "I shook Tom Wolfe's hand."

I saw him now and then over many years and thought of him as Paul McHugh, a professor and psychiatrist who was his close friend, did. "He was warmhearted," he said. Tom Wolfe had killer eyes but was not cold. There was sweetness there, and sympathy. He wrote of social status, and, as Dr. McHugh said, "he was especially great at deflating those whose position led them to the bullying of others."

He worked himself hard. Dr. McHugh would call him and say, "I know I'm interrupting you." Tom would reply, "Thank God!"

He suffered and was gallant. He'd had scoliosis when young, and an injury the past decade had left him with a spinal misalignment. He was bent sharply at the waist, his trunk tilted right. He was often in pain. His famous walking stick with the wolf's head wasn't only for fun and show, he needed it.

Imagine caring so much about how you presented yourself to the world, and facing that challenge. Imagine presenting yourself anyway, in part because it gives the world delight.

We met more than twenty years ago when we were thrown together as seatmates at a Manhattan think-tank dinner. The auspices were not good. I'd recently tangled with a close friend of his, and to make it worse I'd been in the wrong and knew it. Beyond that I was awed. I never told him, but my first book was half an homage to him: *Bonfire* and his manifesto, *Stalking the Billion-Footed Beast,* filled my soul. His prose had an anarchic, liberating impact. In one chapter I realized my puny self was in the thick of history. I set myself to describing the audio experience of Air Force Two, its curious, soft pulsating sound. GARRRUUUMMMM. "The engines weaving in and out; the air conditioned hum; the soft murmurings of power: I'm flying." My editor was alarmed. Cut that: "People will think you're imitating Tom Wolfe!" "I *am* imitating Tom Wolfe! It's my *homage*!" He laughed. We kept it.

At the dinner, uncomfortable and awed, I turned earnest. Nothing's more boring than that! Still, we were together, and did our best. At one point he started talking about what was happening in neuroscience. He was amused by the new pill that affects sexual mood—I think he said "sexual readiness"—it's flying off the shelves! I said yes, but the pill that will be more popular, and which they'll eventually make, will be the one that makes you fall back in love, because that will solve everyone's problems. "He's responsible and sweet but it's just not enough!" "I don't love my wife anymore!" That's the pill that will really sell.

We giggled. He gave me a scrutinizing look and said, "You're quite a woman." I answered solemnly, as if considering the proposition obvious and the burden heavy: "Yes, I am." He threw back his head, and we were off to the races.

The last time I saw him was almost three months ago, at the wedding of a brilliant young woman and a handsome man. The wedding party was in a fashionable restaurant in downtown New York. We were seated at a red leather banquette, where we had a Writer Moment. I looked out at the boisterous crowd—laughing, gesturing, talking over the din. I said, "Tom, this sound of the voices hitting the ceiling, the laughter—this reminds me of the description in *Bonfire* of a grand Park Avenue party or reception: 'Their swimming teeth.'"

Tom got a look of immediate interest, a flush of approval. "Did I say that?"

"You did."

He laughed, like *Oh, that was good.*

I said I remember reading it and thinking, "Oh, I am in a presence." He pressed my hand and held it for a moment.

Once the aged Tolstoy was in his sitting room, a fire in the fireplace. His daughter came in and said, "Papa, listen." She read a page of a description of a great battle. He listened and said, "Oh, that's good. Who is that?" She said, "Papa, it's you. *War and Peace*."

All writers forget. And the greatest and most prolific forget most.

This was a great man. And I see him now as I did a dozen years ago, again at a New York Public Library dinner. We met as we were leaving, walked through the lobby, parted at the door.

It was something to see that man going down the broad imposing steps, tricked out in the white suit, a flowing black cape, a big, broad-brimmed black hat worn at a tilt, the stick, walking carefully but with a certain flair, a certain élan, because he knew he was being watched because he was, let's face it, Tom Wolfe. And I was watching, as he disappeared into the night, into the teeming city, going northward toward home.

Goodbye, Tom Wolfe. Oh, it was good to have him here, wasn't it?

THOUGHTS ON THEODORE ROOSEVELT AND JOHN HAY AFTER THE RUSSIAN INVASION OF UKRAINE

March 24, 2022

John Hay had a warm mind and a cool heart. The secretary of state to presidents William McKinley and Teddy Roosevelt (1898–1905) had two baseline gifts necessary for diplomatic achievement but not always seen together, a quick apprehension of the size and meaning of events and a subtlety and sympathy in the reading of human beings. A biographer, John Taliaferro, wrote, "His manners, his mind, and his conduct as a spokesman for a nation finding its voice on the world stage were nonpareil and pitch-perfect."

As a young man Hay had been literary secretary to Abraham Lincoln; no one had worked closer with him day by day. He was in the White House the night Lincoln was shot and at his bedside the morning he died in the boardinghouse near Ford's Theatre. In the years afterward he held high Lincoln's standard in books and speeches, but it wasn't until the summer of 1905, when Hay himself was dying, that he fully understood what Lincoln had been to him.

He had a dream, he wrote in his diary, that he had been called to the White House for a meeting with Roosevelt, but when he walked in the president was Lincoln. "He was very kind and considerate, and sympathetic about my illness. He said there was little work of importance on hand. He gave me two unimportant letters to answer. I was pleased that this slight order was within my power to obey. I was not in the least surprised at Lincoln's presence in the White House. But the whole impression of the dream was one of overpowering melancholy." At what was gone, and surely what Hay had lost.

History is human. We know this but our knowledge gets lost in considering other factors such as landmass, economic strength, weaponry, and energy sectors.

Here we get to our subject. In Hay's years as America's leading diplomat, no country vexed the patient public servant more, no nation drove him more to distraction, than Russia. I went back to Mr. Taliaferro's excellent 2013 biography, *All the Great Prizes*, to quote some passages, and saw that I'd written in the margins, "It didn't start with communism." It didn't start with Vladimir Putin. Russia has long bedeviled.

In the first years of the twentieth century the Russians were pushing to expand east, to extend their sphere and dominate trade and rail lines in Chinese Manchuria. They wanted to tax there. They wanted to secure the deepwater port at Port Arthur, where they had a naval base. They were moving to annex Manchuria. Japan felt its interest threatened—if Russia took Manchuria, it would move next on Korea.

When Hay protested Russia's aggression, Russia responded with hurt feelings—how could you accuse us, we'd never hurt you. In time he told Roosevelt, "Dealing with a government with whom mendacity is a science is an extremely difficult and delicate matter."

The Russo-Japanese War of 1904–05 was a human disaster, with land battles bigger than Antietam and Gettysburg. Near the end, at the battle of Mukden, an estimated 330,000 Russian troops went up against 270,000 Japanese, with more than 160,000 casualties. Russia lost that battle, as it had most of its fleet at Port Arthur.

America maintained neutrality. "We are not charged with the cure of the Russian soul," Hay wrote to Roosevelt. But all the way through he communicated with both sides, once comforting the Japanese ambassador, who had burst into tears. Privately Hay was disgusted by Russia's cavalier aggression, and Roosevelt, who had just taken up jujitsu in his daily workout and felt a special rapport with the Japanese ambassador, was privately rooting for the underdog. He wrote his son Theodore III, "For several years Russia has behaved very badly in the Far East, her attitude toward all nations, including us, but especially toward Japan, being grossly overbearing."

At one point President Roosevelt was so angry with Russia's conduct that he was tempted to "go to an extreme." Hay, who didn't unload much unloaded.

"Four years of constant conflict with [the Russians] have shown me tha you cannot let up a moment on them without danger to your midriff. The bear that *talks* like a man is more to be watched than Adam Zad"—a reference to Kipling's Adam-zad, the bear that walks like a man.

They were both blowing off steam. But Hay never wrote of any other country with the asperity he did of the Russians, and ever after he and Roosevelt called Russia "the bear that walks like a man."

In the end Japan won and Russia was humiliated.

Here we see our parallels to today, which are obvious. Russia wanted something and went forward alone. A disapproving world expected it to crush little Japan and was shocked when it didn't. As was Russia, which had overestimated its military and underestimated Japan's spirit.

More than that, the war changed Russia. It spurred the 1905 revolution, which Lenin later called "the great rehearsal" for 1917. There were huge worker demonstrations, massive strikes, military mutinies. It was bloody. The people, peasants to urban intellectuals, rebelled, and the government almost fell, holding on only through new repressions and promises of reform.

Day by day the people of today's Russia will come to hear about what has happened in Ukraine, will feel and absorb its consequences, will feel some embarrassment at what has happened on the international stage—all led by a leader who is detached from his people. They aren't going to like it.

Something else happened in the Russo-Japanese War, and that was Tolstoy, the greatest man of Russia, its genius of literature and moral inquiry. He took to *The Times* of London for an essay. "Bethink yourselves," he said to his countrymen. "Again war," he said. "Again sufferings necessary to nobody, utterly uncalled for; again fraud, again the universal stupefaction and brutalization of men.

"If there be a God, He will not ask me when I die (which may happen at any moment) whether I retained . . . Port Arthur, or even that conglomeration which is called the Russian Empire, which he did not confide to my care, but He will ask me what I have done with that life which He put at my disposal." He will ask if I have fulfilled his law and loved my fellow man.

"Yesterday I met a reservist soldier accompanied by his mother and wife. All three were riding in a cart." The soldier had been drinking, the wife crying. "Goodbye," called the soldier, "off to the Far East."

"Art thou going to fight?" Tolstoy asked.

"Well, some one has to fight!"

"No one need fight," said Tolstoy.

The soldier reflected for a moment. "But . . . where can one escape?"

That, Tolstoy said, is the heart of the matter. What journalists and officials mistake for patriotism—"for the faith, the Czar, the Fatherland"—is simply a spirited admission that one is trapped.

The families of the boys sent to fight, Tolstoy said, will think what he himself thinks: "What do we want with this Manchuria, or whatever it is called? There is sufficient land here."

We end where we began. Do you know what American Tolstoy revered? Lincoln. Tolstoy thought him the greatest man in history.

Greatness sees greatness. I wonder who will be the Tolstoy, in Russia, of today?

THESE GENERALS WERE THE CLOSEST OF ENEMIES

May 24, 2018

On Memorial Day we think of those who served. Here let's look at an old story about a military man's affections. It's the story of Lo Armistead and Win Hancock—close friends, career officers who'd served side by side in the U.S. Army. Then history took one of its turns and they wound up on opposite sides at Gettysburg, where one was killed by the other's troops. It is one of the most moving tales of the Civil War, and is warmly told in Michael Shaara's classic novel, *The Killer Angels.*

It's a good story to have in our minds as coming years unfold.

In June 1863, 155 years ago, General Robert E. Lee's seventy-thousand-man Army of Northern Virginia slipped across the Potomac River and invaded the North.

Brigadier General Lewis "Lo" Armistead, forty-six, was with him. Lo was an abbreviation of his nickname, Lothario, wryly bestowed because that's what he wasn't. He was quiet, considered shy, twice widowed, and from a family of fighters. Armisteads had served in all of America's wars. Now and then something broke through his composure: Everyone in the Army knew he'd left West Point after breaking a dinner plate over fellow cadet Jubal Early's head. Shaara: "He was an honest man, open as the sunrise." And he was brave.

He was eventually based in Southern California, where his quartermaster, Winfield Scott Hancock, became his close friend.

Armistead was seven years older and from Virginia, while Hancock was from Pennsylvania, but they had much in common. Hancock had also attended West Point, though he graduated. Both had served in the Mexican War, both been lauded for gallantry and promoted to higher rank. Hancock was humorous and liked to paint. Years later, in his memoirs, Ulysses S. Grant would remember Hancock as "a man of very conspicuous personal appearance. . . . His genial disposition made him friends, and his personal courage and his presence with his command in the thickest of the fight won him the confidence of troops serving under him."

By the end of the Civil War he too had a nickname: "Hancock the Superb."

When the war came the officers of the U.S. Army had to decide where they stood. Hancock stood firm with the Union; Armistead went with the Confederacy. We don't know all Armistead's thinking but Shaara suggests some of it in his portrayal of the thoughts of Lieutenant General James Longstreet, also Armistead's friend and under whom he served. Longstreet did not think much of "the Cause." To Longstreet, "the war had come as a nightmare in which you chose your nightmare side."

Shaara suggests Armistead saw it pretty much the same. But, unlike many on his side, Longstreet wasn't in denial as to the war's cause. "The war was about slavery, all right," he said, in Shaara's telling. That wasn't why he fought, "but that was what the war was about."

When the war came, Armistead, Hancock, and others had a gathering to say goodbye. Shaara imagines a soldier's farewell: "Goodbye, good luck, and see you in Hell." But to Armistead it was more than that: "They had been closer than brothers." Tears were shed. In Shaara's story, Armistead tells Hancock, "Win, so help me, if I ever lift a hand against you may God strike me dead." In other sources, Armistead says, "Goodbye. You can never know what this has cost me."

It was the last time they would see each other.

Some time afterward Armistead sent Almira, Hancock's wife, a package to be opened in the event of his death.

Two years into the war, Gettysburg. Armistead heard that Hancock was there and asked Longstreet if he might see him. Sure, said Longstreet, if you can find his position, get a flag of truce and go on over. (This was not completely unheard of in that war: Opposing officers would find each other in field glasses and wave hello or tip their hats.)

But everything was too chaotic, nobody knew where they were, and it didn't happen.

July 3 was Pickett's Charge. Armistead was one of Major General George Pickett's brigade commanders.

Lee judged the Union Army to be reinforced on the wings but soft in the center. That center was a long sloping field leading to a clump of trees at a ridge. He would send in fifteen thousand men and split the Union lines. It would be hard—a mile uphill, over open ground, with Union artillery trained on them behind a low stone wall. But the Confederate artillery would smash the Union artillery before the charge commenced. And then they'd break the Union line, and the Union.

It was of course one of the epic miscalculations in modern military history.

At some point Armistead heard who was up there waiting at the stone wall. It was the Second Corps. It was led by Win Hancock. Armistead knew: He wouldn't break.

The charge began, Armistead led his brigade out of the woods and onto the field. Quickly the Union artillery opened up. Shells came raining down; canisters of metal balls whirled through the air. Explosions, musketry. Union men were out in the open, kneeling and firing. Men fell all around. The smoke thickened and the troops could barely see, so Armistead put his black felt hat on the tip of his sword, held it up and called, "Follow me."

Troops fell, gaps closed. About thirty yards from the wall, "unable to advance, unwilling to run," the charge stalled and stopped. Armistead knew it was over. He was hit in the leg but kept going. He reached the wall and made it to the other side. He was hit again and doubled over, then hit yet again. He sat down.

A Union officer came over. Armistead asked for General Hancock. The officer apologized: Hancock had been hit.

Armistead asked the officer to give him a message: "Tell General Hancock that General Armistead sends his regrets."

Armistead died in a Union hospital tent.

Pickett, amazingly, survived, but was bitter about Lee to the end. His division sustained 60 percent casualties. Of thirteen colonels, seven died and six were wounded. The Confederate Army would never recover.

Longstreet was with Lee at Appomattox. Soon after the war he became a Republican—and supported his friend Grant in his efforts to rebuild the South. Naturally they never forgave him.

Hancock survived his wounds and the war. In 1880 he ran for president as a Democrat. He lost to Republican James A. Garfield of Ohio, who'd fought at Shiloh. It was close—he lost the popular vote by only nine thousand. But Hancock the Superb, hero of the Union Army, swept the South.

In time it became known what was in the package Lo Armistead sent Almira Hancock. It was his personal Bible.

All these stories are part of our history and should never be lost. If we lose them we lose ourselves, and we lose, too, part of the gift we give our immigrants, which is stories that explain the thing they have joined.

The stories should be told plain but with heart, too.

We've overcome a great deal. We see this best when we don't deny our history but tell the whole messy, complicated, embarrassing, ennobling tale.

HISTORY GIVES GEORGE H. W. BUSH HIS DUE

December 6, 2018

I feel it needs to be said again: George Herbert Walker Bush should have been awarded the Nobel Peace Prize for his leadership during the collapse of the Soviet Union. It was an epic moment in modern world history, and a close-run thing. "One mishap and much could unravel," former Canadian Prime Minister Brian Mulroney said, in his eulogy, of those days when the wall was falling, the Warsaw Pact countries rising and the Soviet Union trying to keep its footing as it came to terms with its inevitable end. Patience and shrewdness were needed from the leader of the West, a sensitive, knowing hand.

In *A World Transformed* (1998), Bush described his public approach as being marked by "gentle encouragement." It caused him some trouble: "I had been under constant criticism for being too cautious, perhaps because I was subdued in my reaction to events. This was deliberate." He didn't want to embarrass or provoke. He reminded Mikhail Gorbachev, at the December 1989 Malta summit, that "I have not jumped up and down on the Berlin Wall."

It was Bush's gift to be sensitive even to Soviet generals who were seeing their world collapse around them. He knew that a humiliated foe is a dangerous foe—and this foe had a nuclear arsenal. He slowly, carefully helped ease Russia out of its old ways and structures, helped it stand as its ground firmed up, and helped divided Germany blend together peacefully, fruitfully.

You'd think the world would have been at his feet, and the prizes flying in from Oslo. It didn't happen. Why?

Here's a theory: Bush's achievement wasn't seen for what it was, in part because America in those days was still going forward in the world with its old mystique. Its ultimate grace and constructiveness were a given. It had gallantly saved its friends in the First World War, and again in the Second; it had led the West's resistance to communism. It was *expected* to do good.

Having won the war, of course it would win the peace. It seemed unremarkable that George Bush, and Brent Scowcroft, and a host of others did just that.

Bush was the last president to serve under—*and add to*—that American mystique. It has dissipated in the past few decades through pratfalls, errors, and carelessness, with unwon wars and the economic crisis of 2008. The great foreign-affairs challenge now is to go forward in the world successfully while knowing that the mystique has been lessened, and doing everything possible to win it back.

Bush came to be somewhat defensive about his reticence in those days. As a former aide I respected his caution, his sense that the wrong move could cause things to go dark at any moment. But I saw it differently: The fall of Soviet communism was a crucial event in the history of the West, and its meaning needed stating by the American president. There was much to be lauded, from the hard-won unity of the West to Russia's decision to move bravely toward new ways. Much could be said without triumphalism.

It is a delicate question, in statecraft as in life, when to speak and when not to. George Bush thought it was enough to do it, not say it, as the eulogists asserted. He trusted the people to infer his reasoning from his actions. (This was his approach on his tax increase, also.) But in the end, to me, leadership is persuasion and honest argument: *This is my thinking. I ask you to see it my way.*

Something deeply admirable, though: No modern president now considers silence to be an option, ever. It is moving to remember one who did, who trusted the people to perceive and understand his actions. Who respected them that much.

To the state funeral in the Washington National Cathedral: Its pomp and ceremony served to connect Americans to our past and remind us of our dignity. In a way, it was a resummoning of our mystique. It was, for a moment, the tonic a divided nation needed.

There was majesty—the gleaming precision of the full-dress military, the flag-draped casket coming down the aisle, the bowed heads and hands on hearts, the bells tolling, the dignified solemnity.

For those of us in the pews there was none of the sadness and anguish that accompanies the leaving of a soul gone too soon, or tragically. This was a full life happily lived, and we were there to applaud, to see each other and say, "Remember that time?"

There was a sense of gratitude that the old man had, the past week, gotten his due. For decades the press and others had roughed him up—"wimp," "lapdog." His contributions had not been fully appreciated. Now they were. We were happy but not triumphalist.

We were reminded: *History changes its mind*. Nothing is set. A historical reputation can change, utterly. Sometimes history needs time and distance to see the landscape clearly.

And history is human. German Chancellor Angela Merkel, the seniormost world leader, was there. Back home her party was in the middle of a battle to choose her successor, and she couldn't afford to be gone. But when she heard of Bush's death she said she had to come to Washington. She told reporters that without Bush she "would hardly be standing here." She had grown up in East Germany.

There was something else. She had told Bob Kimmitt, a former U.S. ambassador to Germany, that Bush had treated her "like a somebody when I was not." Meeting with the obscure junior minister in the Oval Office in 1991, the president treated the young woman with great personal and professional respect. And so there she was this week, because history is human and how you treat people matters.

Two other points about the funeral. Its unembarrassed religiosity and warmly asserted Christianity were beautiful, and refreshing. The burial rite was from the Episcopal Church's *Book of Common Prayer*, and it was a great and moving moment when the presiding bishop, the Most Reverend Michael Bruce Curry, met the flag-draped coffin at the Great West Doors and said, "With faith in Jesus Christ, we receive the body of our brother George for burial." Such simple, humble, egalitarian words. "Our brother George." The frozen chosen done themselves proud.

And there was a consistent message in the speeches. George Bush in his ninety-four years asked for and received everything—a big, loving family, wealth, position, power, admiration. But the lesson of that life was clear: He worked for it, he poured himself into it. He gave it everything he had. He made sacrifices to be who he was.

We gave a lot of attention to his life this week, in part because we want to remind ourselves that such fruitful lives are possible. We want to show the young among us what should be respected and emulated, and that public service can be a calling, and that calling brilliantly met.

This was a good man, a brave one who proved himself solid when major edifices of the world were melting away. He was kind and gentle.

And he loved America.

We were lucky to have him—the steady one, the sensitive one. The diplomat.

ON MARGARET CHASE SMITH

December 3, 2020

History can sometimes help us through current moments by showing what's needed and providing inspiration.

This year marks the seventieth anniversary of a great act by a great lady. Margaret Chase Smith was a U.S. representative from 1940 to 1949 and a senator from 1949 to 1973. Her name is always followed by "the first"—the first woman to serve as a senator from Maine, first to serve in both the House and Senate, first to have her name placed in nomination for the presidency at a major party convention.

She was generally considered a moderate to liberal Republican, and sometimes called a progressive one. She wanted to provide citizens the help they needed to become fully integrated into society and productive within it.

She was independent and made this clear early. She was initially the only member from Maine to support Lend-Lease and extension of the draft. She survived these votes because she understood her state: It was isolationist but also patriotic, against war but for preparedness, and Mainers didn't like partisanship messing with foreign policy. She was for civil rights, supported Social Security and Medicare. She had a strong sense of where she was from, and felt the civic romance of it. She told biographer Patricia L. Schmidt that she loved Maine's small-town church spires, and her dream was to see that each town had the money to buy a spotlight so the white spires could be seen for miles at night.

She faced criticism from the right. No, she'd blandly state on being questioned, union leaders hadn't endorsed her in the last election, but she couldn't help it if union members loved her.

She was by nature honest and humorous. Her dignity and simplicity led people to think her a blue blood, but her roots were modest. Her mother worked in a shoe factory, her father as a hotel clerk and barber. She got her first job at thirteen in a five-and-dime, didn't go to college, and became a telephone operator. She was proud of all this and liked to speak of her roots, not to brag about her steep climb but as a kind of affirmation: Look what's possible in America.

She'd married a local politician who became a congressman, Clyde Smith. When he died in 1940 she filled the remaining months in his term and was reelected in the first of many landslides. There were Mrs. Smith Goes to Washington clubs.

She never asked anyone to vote for her because she was a woman, but because she was the better candidate. Still, she thought women brought particular "sensibilities" to office: "The thing that concerns women more than anything else is the betterment of social conditions of the masses. Women are needed in government for the very traits of character that some people claim disqualify them."

She could be wry. NBC's Robert Trout once asked what she'd do if she woke up in the White House. "I think I'd go right to Mrs. Truman and apologize. And then I'd go home." She thought a lot about how other people heard things. When she spoke to grade-school children, she always explained that, though it is true she sat on the floor of the Senate, she wasn't really sitting on the floor.

But it is her "Declaration of Conscience" speech for which she is best remembered. It was 1950 and she was increasingly disturbed by Senator Joe McCarthy's anticommunist crusade. In February he'd made his speech in Wheeling, West Virginia, charging that communists had infiltrated the U.S. government at the highest levels. He claimed to have 205 names of known communists; in later statements he put the number at 57 and 81.

The base of the party found his opposition to the communist swamp in Washington electrifying. His wildness and disrespect for norms was seen as proof of authenticity: *He's one of us and fighting for us.*

Smith was anticommunist enough that Nikita Khrushchev later described her as "blinded by savage hatred," and she was certain communism would ultimately fail. But you don't defeat it with lies.

She always listened closely when McCarthy spoke. Once he said he was holding in his hand "a photostatic copy" of the names of communists. She asked to see it. It proved nothing. Her misgiving increased.

She didn't want to move against him. She was new to the Senate; he was popular in Maine. She waited for her colleagues. They said nothing.

Finally she'd had enough. On June 1, 1950, she became the first Republican to speak out. On the way to the chamber Joe McCarthy suddenly appeared. "Margaret," he said, "you look very serious. Are you going to make a speech?"

"Yes," she said, "and you will not like it."

He has some intelligence network, she thought. It left her rattled.

She took her seat. McCarthy was two rows behind her. When she was recognized she said the Senate needed to do "some soul-searching." The Constitution "speaks not only of the freedom of speech but also of trial by jury instead of trial by accusation." Those "who shout the loudest about Americanism" are ignoring "some of the basic principles of Americanism," including the right to hold unpopular beliefs and to independent thought. Exercising those rights "should not cost one single American citizen his reputation or his right to his livelihood, nor should he be in danger of losing his reputation or livelihood merely because he happens to know someone who holds unpopular beliefs. Who of us does not? Otherwise none of us could call our souls our own."

People are tired of "being afraid of speaking their mind lest they be politically smeared as 'Communists' or 'Fascists.' . . . Freedom of speech is not what it used to be in America."

She took on both parties, accusing the Democrats of showing laxness and "complacency" toward "the threat of communism here at home," and the Republicans of allowing innocent people to be smeared.

She feared a fiery McCarthy rebuttal. He quietly left the room. She was praised in some quarters—Bernard Baruch said if a man had given that speech he'd be the next president—and damned in others. Her colleagues didn't like being shown up by a woman.

McCarthy got her dumped from a subcommittee. The Maine press didn't like that and pushed back: "They Done Our Girl Dirt."

Her speaking slot at the 1952 Republican convention was pulled. She told biographers that at first she was given twenty-five minutes in a prominent spot, then fifteen. Finally House Minority Leader Joe Martin told her she could have five minutes. "And you have to represent a minority."

"What do you mean, 'a minority'?" Smith asked. "You represent the women," he said. She passed.

Yet she had three more landslides to come. Maine admired her independence and integrity. She didn't lose a reelection bid until 1972. She was almost seventy-five. Times had changed.

What are we saying?

When history hands you a McCarthy—reckless, heedlessly manipulating his followers—be a Margaret Chase Smith. If your McCarthy is saying a whole national election was rigged, an entire system corrupted, you'd recognize that such baseless charges damage democracy itself. You wouldn't let election officials be smeared. You'd stand against a growing hysteria in the base.

You'd likely pay a price. But years later you'd still be admired for who you were when it counted so much.

RICHARD NIXON'S EXAMPLE OF SANITY IN WASHINGTON

March 31, 2022

This extended moment of history reminds me of Washington in the years before and during the Civil War. There was a kind of hysterical intensity among our political class in those days, on all sides. The instability was so dramatic—Representative Preston Brooks caning Senator Charles Sumner on the floor of the Senate in 1856, poor Mary Todd Lincoln with her rage and manias, and her husband telling her that if she continues like this she'll wind up in the asylum. Those are famous examples, but you can't pick up a book about those days and not see what looks like real and widespread personal destabilization. There was a lot of self-medicating, as they say. The journals and diaries of Mary Chesnut, who resided in the heart of the Washington establishment as the country broke apart and in capitals of the Confederacy as it formed, tell constantly of the officers and politicos coming to her home to drink into the night, and the ladies and their laudanum. Something strange had been let loose as things broke apart.

I started thinking things were entering Civil War territory during the Brett Kavanaugh hearings in 2018 and the demonstrations around it—the hissing mobs in a Senate office building, where 293 were arrested; the screams as the Judiciary Committee chairman began his opening statement; the harassing of senators in elevators; the surrounding of the Supreme Court and scratching on its big bronze doors. I know the charges against Justice Kavanaugh were grave, I know they incited passion on both sides, but this looked to me not like activism, which to achieve anything must have at its core seriousness, maturity, and discipline, but like untreated mental illness.

And then of course the insurrection of January 6, the prime example of this new, strange era.

Connected are Ginni Thomas's texts to White House chief of staff Mark Meadows in the days after the 2020 election. They capture two characteristics of radicals on both sides, now and maybe forever. The first is that they have extreme respect for their own emotions: If they feel it, it's true. The other is that they tend to be stupid, in the sense of having little or no historical knowledge or the sense of proportion such knowledge brings.

The texts were revealed last week by Bob Woodward of *The Washington Post* and Robert Costa of CBS News, and you have seen them. In the days after the election, Mrs. Thomas warned Mr. Meadows of "the greatest Heist of our History." There's proof: "Watermarked ballots in over 12 states have been part of a huge Trump & military white hat sting operation in 12 key battleground states." There will be justice: "Biden crime family & ballot fraud co-conspirators . . . are being arrested & detained for ballot fraud right now & over coming days, & will be living in barges off GITMO to face military tribunals for sedition." "Do not concede," she warned him. "It takes time for the army who is gathering for his back."

This is a person who lives in the heart of the Washington establishment and had no proof for any of the wild things she was saying. But when you're a conspiracist, every way you look there's a grassy knoll. Naturally the chief of staff wrote back. "This is a fight of good versus evil." "Evil always looks like the victor until the King of Kings triumphs. Do not grow weary in well doing. The fight continues." He appears to be patronizing her and speaking in a way thoroughly in line with Sinclair Lewis and the great American tradition of hucksters wrapping their con in the language of Christian faith.

But it's worth noting the focus of their obsession, the continued belief in some quarters that Donald Trump really won the 2020 election. Joe Biden won not closely but by seven million votes, and every challenge was thrown out of court, including by Trump-appointed judges.

Here we should remember the man who may well have had a presidential election stolen from him, but who ended a stop-the-steal movement before it could take off. It was 1960, Vice President Richard Nixon versus Senator John F. Kennedy. It was the closest popular vote in the twentieth century, with Kennedy receiving 34.2 million votes and Nixon 34.1 million, a margin of barely one-sixth of a percentage point. Widespread fraud was suspected in Illinois and Texas, which had enough electoral votes to be decisive.

Nixon's biographers haven't usually agreed with his political views—they've mostly been fascinated liberals—but virtually all speak with respect of this chapter in his life. The best treatment is in John Farrell's very fine *Richard Nixon: The Life*. "In Chicago, election fraud was a work of art," Mr. Farrell writes. On that nail-biting election night Mayor Richard J. Daley called Kennedy in Hyannisport and said, "Mr. President, with a little bit of luck and the help of a few close friends, you're going to carry Illinois."

As for Texas, everyone knew what Robert Caro later established, that Lyndon B. Johnson, Kennedy's vice presidential nominee, had the state wired, with credible charges of ballot-box fraud going back to 1948.

Theodore White, the journalist who helped invent the mythos around JFK, wrote in 1975 that no one will ever know who won in 1960, but, in Illinois and Texas, Democratic "vote-stealing had definitely taken place on a massive scale."

Nixon believed the election was stolen. President Dwight D. Eisenhower and Senate Minority Leader Everett Dirksen wanted him to challenge the results. Nixon thought it could take months and might not succeed, but his thoughts went deeper than that. In the Cold War, the nuclear age, unity at home and abroad was needed. Young democracies looked up to us. If they thought our elections could be stolen it would hurt the world's morale.

The *New York Herald Tribune* had launched an investigative series, but Nixon talked the reporter into stopping it: "Our country cannot afford the agony of a constitutional crisis."

In Evan Thomas's brisk *Being Nixon: A Man Divided*, he reports that the GOP wise man Bryce Harlow urged Nixon to challenge, but Nixon said no: "It'd tear the country to pieces. You can't do that."

So he didn't. On January 6, 1961, Nixon presided over the formal certification of his opponent's election. "This is the first time in one hundred years that a candidate for the presidency announced the result of an election in which he was defeated and announced the victory of his opponent," he said. "In our campaigns, no matter how hard-fought they may be, no matter how close the election may turn out to be, those who lose accept the verdict and support those who win."

For once his colleagues gave that complicated man his due, with a standing ovation that wouldn't stop until Nixon took a second bow.

History went on and took its turns. Nixon came back and won the presidency in 1968. But when you read all this you wonder, Why can't self-professed patriots love America like that now—maturely, protectively? And how important it is to know something of history, to know it so well you can almost trust it. Instead of just feeling what you feel and making a hash of things.

ON THE DEATH OF A QUEEN

September 8, 2022

"For the British people, Victoria was more than an individual, more even than the queen," Robert K. Massie wrote in *Dreadnought: Britain, Germany, and the Coming of the Great War.* "She was—and had been as long as most of them could remember—a part of the fabric of their lives. She embodied history, tradition, government, and the structure and morality of their society. They trusted her to remain there, always to do her duty, always to give order to their lives. She did not disappoint them. In return, they gave her their allegiance, their devotion—and their esteem."

We all knew it was coming yet it feels like a blow. A mighty presence has passed, one who meant more to us perhaps than we'd noticed.

The reign of Queen Elizabeth II surpassed Victoria's (1837–1901) in September 2015. For the vast majority of her people, she was the only monarch they had ever known. Her life spanned almost a century, through wars, through empire and its decline, through every cultural and political shift. And in all that time she was a symbol of continuity, stability, and soundness.

There will be, mostly but not only in Britain, a surge of sentiment as if a big page has been turned and we very much don't want it to turn—we don't want to get to the end of that book, don't want to close it.

Her virtues were old-school virtues.

- *She accepted her life with grace.* When she became queen at twenty-five she recognized it as her duty and destiny. She was a member of a particular family and the heir to a particular throne. She had a duty to the people of her country and would sacrifice a great deal—privacy, leisure, some faint sense of control of one's life—to meet it. She represented the permanent over the merely prevalent.

Sally Bedell Smith, in her great biography *Elizabeth the Queen: The Life of a Modern Monarch*, quoted the British journalist Rebecca West, who observed that the monarch is "the emblem of the state, the symbol of our national life, the guardian of our self-respect." But it was more than that too; you didn't have to be English to appreciate what she was doing.

- *She did what she said she'd do.* After her father's death, she met with the leaders of Britain at St. James's Palace. In a clear voice she declared, "By the sudden death of my dear father, I am called to assume the duties and responsibilities of sovereignty. . . . I shall always work, as my father did throughout his reign, to advance the happiness and prosperity of my peoples. . . . I pray that God will help me to discharge worthily this heavy task that has been lain upon me so early in my life." She did, and everyone watching over the years could see it.

- *She gave it everything she had.* She was conscientious, serious-minded, responsible. Every day but Christmas and Easter Sunday and wherever she was, she directed her energies to the red leather dispatch boxes of official government papers, Foreign Office cables, budget documents, intelligence reports. She was deskbound as long as needed, often working into the evening. After that the private audiences, public events, consultations. She didn't flag.

- *It wasn't about her.* The important thing was the institution, the monarchy, and its responsibility to its subjects. She wanted to be a queen the country adhered to and was proud of, so she maintained dignity. She knew her role. She didn't show moods or take sides, never tried to win the crowd, didn't attempt to establish a reputation for wit or good nature. She was in her public dealings placid, as a great nation's queen would be. "She has been, as someone once said, the light above politics," Ms. Smith said Thursday on CNN. "Even when I'd watch her at royal events she would hesitate to clap or smile because she didn't want to show favoritism. She has wanted to be a force for everybody and a glue for the nation, and that sort of exterior has been important."

- *She was a woman of faith.* At her 1953 coronation in Westminster Abbey, the most important moment happened outside of television range. It was when the archbishop of Canterbury poured holy oil and anointed the new queen, "making a sign of the cross on the palms of each of her hands, her forehead, and exposed upper chest," Ms. Smith wrote. (Victoria hadn't allowed her archbishop to touch her chest.) Elizabeth felt that the anointing "sanctified her before God to serve her people." Her friends said it was the anointing, not the crowning, that made her queen.

- *She understood her role.* She was the longest reigning monarch in British history, a continuous thread to the past. Decades passed but the thread remained and never broke, which suggested things would hold together, and everything in the end would be all right. She understood that in the tumultuous twentieth century the idea of continuity itself was a gift to her country. She had to be reliable, and was.

- *Because of all this, when she entered the room, Britain entered the room.* Majesty entered, something old and hallowed and rich in meaning, something going back to tribes that painted themselves blue and forward to the Magna Carta. It was mysterious, but I saw it once: She entered a hall full of voices and suddenly, silence. It was only a few years ago, but I realized that in a time when personal stature is mindlessly thrown off or meanly taken, hers had only increased.

There is something so touching in the way she had begun in the past few years to laugh and smile so often, to show her joy, her simple pleasure in being there. You saw it in pictures taken this week, which showed her seeing off an old prime minister and seeing in a new one, wearing a plaid skirt and long gray cardigan, holding her cane and laughing merrily. I think of how moved I was by the clip a few months ago of the queen and Paddington Bear, in which she divulged what she kept in her purse—a marmalade sandwich. The royal band outside struck up Freddie Mercury, and she kept time with a spoon on her teacup. I didn't know when I saw it why it moved me so much, and realized: because my mind was saying, Don't go old friend, we'll miss you.

The great of Britain have been talking for years about how sad it will be when she departs. They're about to be taken aback by how deep and pervasive the mourning is. Britain is braced for hard times; people won't easily lose such a figure of stability and continuity. "King Charles" will sound strange on the tongue.

And they loved her.

Now I am imagining the royal funeral, the procession, the carriages of state going slowly down the Mall, the deep crowds on each side. The old will come in their chairs and the crowd will kindly put them in front, the best view, to wave goodbye to their friend, with whom they had experienced such history together.

Requiescat in pace, Elizabeth Regina.

A GREAT MAN GOT ARRESTED AS PRESIDENT

April 6, 2023

We need a palate cleanser. It is Easter (whose theme is resurrection and salvation), Passover (freedom and remembering), and Ramadan (devotion). So let us go back to affectionate days and men of stature.

It has been noted that the first and only previous American president to be arrested was Ulysses S. Grant. He was arrested in 1872, while president, for "fast driving" his two-horse carriage not far from the White House. The arresting officer, William West, was a Union Army veteran, a black man a few years on the police force. There had been complaints men were speeding their horses in the "aristocratic" part of town. One day Officer West stopped the president, whom he recognized, and gave him a warning. "Your fast driving, sir . . . is endangering the lives of the people who have to cross the street." The president apologized.

But the next night, patrolling at Thirteenth and M Streets, West saw a slew of carriages barreling down the street at high speed, with the president in the lead.

West held up his club. Grant got control of his horses and asked, abashed, if he'd been speeding. In 1908, when the story broke in Washington's *Sunday Star*, West said Grant had the look of a schoolboy caught in a guilty act. He reminded Grant of his promise to stop speeding. West told Grant, "I am very sorry, Mr. President, to have to do it, for you are the chief of the nation and I am nothing but a policeman, but duty is duty, sir, and I will have to place you under arrest."

Grant did something he hadn't done much, which was surrender. He invited West into his carriage and drove to the station house. On the way they talked about the war. West had been at the evacuation of Richmond.

Grant said he admired a man who does his duty. At the station house Grant put up twenty dollars and stayed long enough to be amused by friends, also hauled in, who were protesting their arrests. Days later word reached him that West's job might be in danger. Grant dispatched a quick message to the chief of police, complimenting West on his fearlessness and making clear he hoped no harm would come to him. None did.

In coming years they'd greet each other on the street, talk about horses. West served another twenty-five years in the department, distinguishing himself in detective work. He didn't tell the story of arresting the president until he'd retired. The Metropolitan Police Department confirmed the account a century later.

Last year at this time we wrote about Grant, recounting his role in the most history-drenched Holy Week in U.S. history, the seven days in 1865 that spanned the end of the Civil War, the stillness at Appomattox, and the assassination of Abraham Lincoln.

More can be said. A thing that always fascinates is a quality Grant had that left close observers balancing in their minds two different and opposite thoughts. One: There is nothing special in this plain, quiet, undistinguished fellow. The other: He is marked by destiny; something within him encompasses the epic working out of fate, even of nations.

The obscure former soldier and unsuccessful farmer would become, over two or three years, the only indispensable man in the Union after Lincoln. Then, all worlds conquered, he would lose everything in a cascade of misfortunes that yielded . . . a final and transcendent human triumph.

That famous story, from Ron Chernow's still-splendid *Grant:*

On Christmas Eve in 1883, Grant, hale and prosperous at sixty-one, was dropped off at his Manhattan town house. Pivoting to give the driver a holiday tip, he slipped on the ice, fracturing his hip. Pleurisy followed; arthritis "crept up his legs"; he was bedridden and then had trouble walking. Grant had earlier formed a business partnership with the "Young Napoleon of Finance," twenty-nine-year-old Ferdinand Ward, a financial genius who was alas, the Sam Bankman-Fried of his day. His profits were revealed as nonexistent; in the spring of 1884 Grant found out he was ruined, broke, his public reputation severely damaged. A few months later—"When sorrows come they come not single spies, but in battalions"—he bit into a piece of peach and cried aloud in pain, thinking he'd swallowed a wasp. The feeling of fire in his throat wouldn't go away, and months later he was told it was cancer.

Now he summoned everything he had to do that he'd long refused to do, write his memoirs. He did it for money, so his wife and family would be secure.

He wrote sitting up in a chair, his legs on a facing chair, with a wool cap on his head, a shawl at his shoulders, "a muffler around his neck concealing a tumor the size of a baseball." After he ate or drank he required opiates, but opiates clouded his mind so he wrote long days without eating or drinking. Yet the words flowed, "showing how much thought and pent-up feeling lay beneath his tightly buttoned façade." He wrote 275,000 words of "superb prose" in less than a year.

The first sentence—"My family is American, and has been for generations, in all its branches, direct and collateral"—has the compressed beauty of his battlefield dispatches. He died on July 23, 1885, three days after he finished the manuscript. The unexpected masterpiece became a publishing phenomenon.

Mark Twain, who published it, watched Grant's funeral procession for five hours from the windows of his office on Union Square. Afterward he joined William Tecumseh Sherman for drinks and cigars at the Lotos Club. They talked about the marvel and mystery of Grant's personality. Sherman thought his close friend had been a mystery even to himself. He had no peer as a military genius—"Never anything like it before"—but he wasn't steeped in the literature of war, of strategy and grand tactics. He was nothing like the purified, prissy Grant emerging in the newspapers. "The idea of all this nonsense about Grant not being able to stand rude language and indelicate stories!" He roared at off-color tales. "Grant," said Sherman, "was no namby pamby fool; he was a MAN—all over—rounded & complete."

Twain confessed a regret. In helping supervise and edit Grant's memoirs he had never pressed Grant on his struggle with alcohol. His enemies had called him a drunk; his friends had acknowledged wartime binges. Sherman himself had said of their friendship, "He stood by me when I was crazy, and I stood by him when he was drunk." But Twain hadn't thought to probe, and knew now he should have, for the people would have appreciated it, and understood.

Why do we remember greatness? What purpose is there in remembering?

To remind us who we've been. To remind us what's still lurking there in the national DNA.

So we know what greatness *looks* like. So we can recognize it when it's within our environs. Because human greatness will never completely go away, even though you may look north, east, south, and west and be unable to see it. You're not sure it's anywhere around. But it will be there.

Maybe it's there. Look closer. Maybe that's a seed. Help it grow.

BOB DYLAN, A GENIUS AMONG US

June 18, 2020

Summer begins and it may be a hard one. Lots of pain in this big place. The cultural upheaval continues, the plague marches on, a bitter election looms. This is a good time to think about something noble and inspiring, the life and work of Bob Dylan. He has an album out this week, his first with original material since 2012, called *Rough and Rowdy Ways*.

Mr. Dylan wrote his most famous anthem, "Blowin' in the Wind," in 1962. He has been operating at the top of American culture and embedded in the national consciousness for almost sixty years. You have to go back to Robert Frost and Mark Twain to find such a span of sustained literary productivity and importance.

Like Twain and Frost his great subject is America. Like them he is a genius: He did work of high artistic merit that had never been done before and won't be replicated. For me, having known his work since I was young, his songs are grave, wistful, rollicking, full of meaning, and true. Also, obviously, prophetic, as if he were picking up big clear waves of themes in the electrical static all around us. "There's a battle outside and it is ragin' / It'll soon shake your windows and rattle your walls / For the times they are a-changin'."

That was true when he wrote it and is true today. Great art is always about right now. It time-travels. Mr. Dylan's music never settles down into an era, it's dynamic, it's like hearing the past in active conversation with the future.

There are two things you have to do if you have big ambitions and want to create something important that lasts. The first is the daily work and trying to keep it at a height that satisfies you. That's hard. If you succeed, the second is dealing with the effects of the work, managing a career. That's tricky. It involves making big, real-time decisions about paths and ways of being. You have to figure out if an opportunity is a true opening or an easy way out; if a desire for security has the potential to become a betrayal of yourself and the thing God gave you, your gift.

Mr. Dylan seems to have handled all this by following to an almost radical degree the dictates of his essential nature and talent, and doing the work as he envisions it day to day. You can wind up being a hero one decade and a joke the next when you choose that route, and that's what happened to him. But, in the end, this: In October 2016, he became the first writer of songs to win the Nobel Prize for Literature.

What a great figure.

In his autobiography, *Chronicles*, Mr. Dylan writes of how one night, when he was starting out playing the clubs in New York in the 1960s, he stumbled on a man who'd been stabbed to death. The blood made interesting patterns in the snow. This reminded Mr. Dylan of old photos of the Civil War. He began to study the war, deeply. Its meaning would shape him: "Back there, America was put on the cross, died and was resurrected. There was nothing synthetic about it. The godawful truth of that would be the all-encompassing template behind everything that I would write."

He loves the mythic, fabulous figures of U.S. history. On the first page of his autobiography he writes of meeting Jack Dempsey. "Don't be afraid of hitting somebody too hard," the old boxer, taking him for a bantamweight, advised him. On *Rough and Rowdy Ways*, Mr. Dylan sings of William Tecumseh Sherman and George Patton, "who cleared the path for Presley to sing / who carved out the path for Martin Luther King." It's as if it's all a continuum in which America's outsize and spectacular beings clear the way and pave the path for the renegades and revolutionaries who will follow.

Mr. Dylan has the soul of a worker, a craftsman who has learned his craft. He spoke of this in February 2015, when he received the Person of the Year award from MusiCares Foundation. *Rolling Stone* later printed a transcript taken, the magazine said, from Mr. Dylan's notes.

"These songs didn't come out of thin air," he said. He learned how to write lyrics by listening to folk songs over and over. He studied them, absorbed them, sang "The Ballad of John Henry," the steel-driving man with the hammer in his hand. "If you had sung that song as many times as I did you'd have written 'How many roads must a man walk down?' too." He said his intention was "extending the line," continuing the music he loved by internalizing it and turning it into his own words, thoughts, and stories.

In a *New York Times* interview last weekend, the historian Douglas Brinkley asked Mr. Dylan about the musical tributes he'd done to John Lennon. Is there anyone else he wants to write a ballad for?

Some public figures "are just in your subconscious for one reason or another," he said. "None of those songs with designated names are intentionally written. They just fall down from space. I'm just as bewildered as anybody else as to why I write them."

Writers are often asked how they get their ideas, and the language with which they express them. The truth is they don't know. Why *did* your mind yield up that thought in those words? Walker Percy thought when he got something right the Holy Spirit had snuck into him.

Mr. Dylan doesn't know where it comes from. Sometimes you write "on instinct," he told Mr. Brinkley. "Kind of in a trance state." His recent songs are like that: "The lyrics are the real thing, tangible, they're not metaphors. The songs seem to know themselves and they know that I can sing them, vocally and rhythmically. They kind of write themselves and count on me to sing them."

Mr. Dylan more and more speaks of fellow artists—fellow workers—with great tenderness. He reminds me of what Pope John Paul II said, that artists know a special pain because they imagine a work and see it in their heads but can never execute it perfectly, can never achieve what they'd imagined, and forever carry the anguish of an unmet dream.

Mr. Dylan looked up to Nina Simone, "an overwhelming artist." When she recorded his songs, it "validated" him. "Johnny Cash was a giant of a man, the Man in Black." When Mr. Dylan was criticized, Cash defended him in letters to magazines. In Cash's world nobody told a man what to do, especially an *artist*. Little Richard was a man of "high character": "He was there before me. Lit a match under me." Why didn't people appreciate his gospel music? "Probably because gospel music is the music of good news and in these days there just isn't any. Good news in today's world is like a fugitive, treated like a hoodlum and put on the run. Castigated. All we see is good-for-nothing news. . . . On the other hand, gospel news is exemplary. It can give you courage."

We can forget: There are geniuses among us. They're doing their work and bringing their light. Remembering this is encouraging.

Also Bob Dylan needed freedom to be Bob Dylan. Lose that and you lose everything. But isn't it good that he's here? Rock on, Bob Dylan. Your work adorns us.

CHAPTER 2

I DON'T MIND BEING STERN

One of life's pleasures is taking a stick to people and things that deserve it.

THE SENATOR'S SHORTS AND AMERICA'S DECLINE

September 21, 2023

For years I've had a thought whose expression I could never get right, but it applies to our subject this week, so here goes:

Since the triumphant end of World War II, America has come to greatly enjoy the idea of its preeminence. We're "the leader of the free world," we dominate science, medicine, philanthropy. We teach emerging nations the ways of democratic governance; we have the biggest economy and arsenal; we win all the medals, from the Nobel Prizes to the Olympics. This has been the way of things for nearly eighty years, and for much of that time we brought to the task of greatness a certain earnestness of style. We had a lot of brio and loved our wins, but we also applauded for the other teams from the Olympic stands, and our diplomats and political figures—JFK, Reagan—walked through the world with a natural but also careful dignity.

Which was good, because preeminence entails obligations. You have to act the part. You have to present yourself with dignity. You have to comport yourself with class.

For some time—let's say since the turn of this century—we've been at a point in our power where we still love to insist on the preeminence—USA! USA!—while increasingly ignoring the responsibilities.

That is the thought I want to express: We want to be respected but no longer think we need to be respectable.

We are in a crisis of political comportment. We are witnessing the rise of the classless. Our politicians are becoming degenerate. This has been happening for a while but gets worse as the country coarsens. We are defining deviancy ever downward.

Two examples from the past two weeks. One is the congresswoman who was witnessed sexually groping and being groped by a friend in a theater, seated among what looked like a thousand people of all ages. The other is the candidate for Virginia's House of Delegates who performed a series of live sex acts with her husband on a pornographic website, and the videos were then archived on another site that wasn't password-protected. She requested cash for each sexual act, saying she was "raising money for a good cause." Someone called it a breakthrough in small-donor outreach.

It was within this recent context that Senate Majority Leader Chuck Schumer did something that isn't in the same league in terms of shock but nonetheless has a deep institutional resonance. He quietly swept away a centuries-old tradition that senators dress as adults on the floor of the Senate. Business attire is no longer formally required. Mr. Schumer apparently doesn't know—lucky him, life apparently hasn't taught him—that when you ask less of people they don't give you less; they give you much less. So we must brace ourselves.

His decision is apparently connected to the desires of Senator John Fetterman of Pennsylvania, who enjoys parading around in gym shorts and a hoodie. Why would his desires receive such precedence?

Because he has political needs. He must double down on his brand. He imagines that dressing like a slob deepens his perceived identification with the working class. But this kind of thing doesn't make you "authentic," it just makes you a different kind of phony. Mr. Fetterman, born into affluence and privilege, reacted to criticism of Mr. Schumer's decision with an air of snotty entitlement. He mocked critics, making woo-woo monster sounds to reporters and telling a House critic to "get your s— together." He said Republicans were "losing their minds" and ought to have better things to do.

Here are reasons John Fetterman, and all senators, should dress like an adult.

It shows respect for colleagues. It implies you see them as embarked on the serious business of the nation, in which you wish to join them.

It shows respect for the institution. "Daniel Webster walked there." And Henry Clay, "Fighting Bob" La Follette, Arthur Vandenberg, and Robert Taft. The U.S. Senate is the self-declared world's greatest deliberative body.

It shows a mature acceptance of your role, suggesting you've internalized the idea of service. You are a public servant; servants by definition make sacrifices.

It reflects an inner discipline. It's not always easy or convenient to dress like a grown-up. You've got to get the suit from the cleaners, the shoes from the cobbler. The effort means you bothered, took the time, went to the trouble.

It reflects an inner modesty. You'd like to be in sneaks and shorts but you admit that what you'd like isn't the most important thing. It shows that thoughts of your own comfort aren't number 1 in your hierarchy of concerns. Also, you know you're only 1 of 100, and as 1 percent of the whole you wouldn't insist on officially lowering standards for the other 99.

It bows to the idea of "standards" itself, which implies you bow to other standards too, such as how you speak and what you say.

It shows you understand that America now has a problem with showing respect. We can't take a seat on a plane without causing an incident, can't be in a stadium without a fight. You would never, given that context, move for standards to become more lax.

It shows you admit to yourself that you're at an age and stage when part of your job is to model for the young how to behave, how to be. It shows you're not a selfish slob who doesn't know what time it is.

It shows you don't think you're better than others or deserving of greater rights. News reporters outside the hearing room operate under a general dress code; citizens who testify before Congress do so in business dress. The old dress code still applies to Senate staffers. They don't show up in torn undershirts and sandals. Why are you better than they are? Conversely, why would their dressing like you make anything in America better?

It shows, finally, that you understand that as a high elected official of the United States you owe the country, and the world, the outward signs of maturity, judgment, and earnestness. That isn't asking too much. It is a baseline minimum.

Also, the least people could do in public life now is make everything look a little better, not a little worse.

I hope Mr. Fetterman's colleagues don't join him in taking another brick out of the Capitol facade but quietly rebuke him, and Mr. Schumer, by very clearly not joining in, by showing up for work in your sober, serious best.

I leave you with a picture of some dark day in the future. China moves on Taiwan, and perhaps the White House, whoever's in it, bobbles, or is unsure, or makes immediate mistakes. Everything is uncertain, anxiety high.

All of us, and much of the world, will look for voices in Congress who ca steady things—voices of deliberation and calm. And we'll turn our lonely eyes and see . . . the congresswoman from the theater, the senator in his play clothes.

That will be a bad moment.

How people bear themselves has implications greater than we know. It's not about "sartorial choice." It's about who we need you to be—and who you *asked* to be when you first ran.

LIFE ISN'T *MERDE*

April 25, 2024

I wish to protest the current ugliness. I see it as a continuing trend, "the uglification of everything." It is coming out of our culture with picked-up speed, and from many media silos, and I don't like it.

You remember the 1999 movie *The Talented Mr. Ripley*, from the Patricia Highsmith novel. It was fabulous—murders, mayhem, a sociopath scheming his way among high-class expats on the Italian Riviera. The laid-back glamour of Jude Law, the Grace Kelly-ness of Gwyneth Paltrow, who looks like a *Vogue* magazine cover decided to take a stroll through the streets of 1950s Venice, the truly brilliant acting of Matt Damon, who is so well-liked by audiences I'm not sure we notice anymore what a great actor he is. The director, Anthony Minghella, deliberately showed you pretty shiny things while taking you on a journey to a heart of darkness.

There's a new version, a streaming series from Netflix, called *Ripley*. I turned to it eagerly and watched with puzzlement. It is unrelievedly ugly. Grimy, gloomy, grim. Tom Ripley is now charmless, a pale and watchful slug slithering through ancient rooms. He isn't bright, eager, endearing, only predatory. No one would want to know him! Which makes the story make no sense. Again, Ripley is a sociopath, but few could tell because he seemed so sweet and easy. In the original movie, Philip Seymour Hoffman has an unforgettable turn as a jazz-loving, prep-schooled, in-crowd snob. In this version that character is mirthless, genderless, hidden. No one would want to know him either. Marge, the Paltrow role in the movie, is ponderous and plain, like a lost 1970s hippie, which undercuts a small part of the tragedy: Why is the lovely woman so in love with a careless idler who loves no one?

The ugliness seemed a deliberate artistic decision, as did the air of constant menace, as if we all know life is never nice.

I go to the number 1 program on Netflix this week, *Baby Reindeer*. People speak highly of it. It's about a stalker and is based on a true story, but she's stalking a comic so this might be fun. Oh, dear, no. It is again unrelievedly bleak. Life is low, plain, and homely. No one is ever nice or kind; all human conversation is opaque and halting; work colleagues are cruel and loud. Everyone is emotionally incapable and dumb. No one laughs except for the morbidly obese stalker, who cackles madly. The only attractive person is the transgender girlfriend, who has a pretty smile and smiles a lot, but cries a lot too and is vengeful.

Good drama always makes you think. I thought, Do I want to continue living?

I go to the *Daily Mail* website, once my guilty pleasure. High jinks of the rich and famous, randy royals, fast cars and movie stars, models, and rock stars caught in the drug bust. It was great! But it seems to have taken a turn and is more about crime, grime, human sadness, and degradation—child abuse, mothers drowning their babies, "Man Murders Family, Self." It is less a portal into life's mindless, undeserved beauty than a testimony to its horrors.

I go to the new *Cabaret*. Who doesn't love *Cabaret*? It is dark, witty, painful, glamorous. The music and lyrics have stood the test of time. The story's backdrop: The soft decadence of Weimar is being replaced by the hard decadence of Nazism.

It is Kander and Ebb's masterpiece, revived again and again. And this revival is hideous. It is ugly, bizarre, inartistic, fundamentally stupid. Also obscene but in a purposeless way, without meaning.

I had the distinct feeling the producers take their audience to be distracted dopamine addicts with fractured attention spans and no ability to follow a story. They also seemed to have no faith in the story itself, so they went with endless pyrotechnics. This is *Cabaret* for the empty-headed. Everyone screams. The songs are slowed, because you might need a moment to take it in. Almost everyone onstage is weirdly hunched, like a gargoyle, everyone overacts, and all of it is without art.

On the way in, staffers put stickers on the cameras of your phone, "to protect our intellectual property," as one said.

It isn't an easy job to make the widely admired Eddie Redmayne unappealing, but by God they did it. As he's a producer I guess he did it, too. He takes the stage as the Emcee in a purple leather skirt with a small green cone on his head and appears further on as a clown with a machine gun and a weird goth devil. It is all so childish, so plonkingly empty.

Here is something sad about modern artists: They are held back by a lack of limits.

Bob Fosse, the director of the classic 1972 movie version, got to push against society's limits and Broadway's and Hollywood's prohibitions. He pushed hard against what was pushing him, which caused friction; in the heat of that came art. Directors and writers now have nothing to push against because there are no rules or cultural prohibitions, so there's no friction, everything is left cold, and the art turns in on itself and becomes merely weird.

Fosse famously loved women. No one loves women in this show. When we meet Sally Bowles, in the kind of dress a little girl might put on a doll, with heavy leather boots and harsh, garish makeup, the character doesn't flirt, doesn't seduce or charm. She barks and screams, angrily.

Really it is harrowing. At one point Mr. Redmayne dances with a toilet plunger, and a loaf of Italian bread is inserted and removed from his anal cavity. I mentioned this to my friend, who asked if I saw the dancer in the corner masturbating with a copy of what appeared to be *Mein Kampf*.

That's what I call intellectual property.

In previous iterations the Kit Kat Klub was a hypocrisy-free zone, a place of no boundaries, until the bad guys came and it wasn't. I'm sure the director and producers met in the planning stage and used words like "breakthrough" and "a *Cabaret* for today," and "we don't hide the coming cruelty." But they *do* hide it by making everything, beginning to end, lifeless and grotesque. No innocence is traduced because no innocence exists.

How could a show be so frantic and outlandish and still be so tedious? It's almost an achievement.

And for all that there is something smug about it, as if they're looking down from some great, unearned height.

I left thinking, as I often do now on seeing something made ugly: *This is what purgatory is going to be like.* And then, no, this is what hell is going to be like—the cackling stalker, the pale sociopath, Eddie Redmayne dancing with a plunger.

Why does it all bother me?

Because even though it isn't new, uglification is rising and spreading as an artistic attitude, and it can't be good for us. Because it speaks of self-hatred, and a society that hates itself, and hates life, won't last. Because it gives those who are young nothing to love and feel soft about. Because we need beauty to keep our morale up.

Because life isn't *merde,* in spite of what our entertainment geniuses say.

GET READY FOR THE STRUGGLE SESSION

March 7, 2019

The Chinese Cultural Revolution was a bitter thing, a catastrophe comparable in its societal effects, and similar in its historical feel, to the terrors of Stalin and the French Revolution. No one knows how many died; historians say up to two million. But what I find myself thinking of these days is the ritual humiliations, the "struggle sessions."

In the mid-1960s Mao Zedong, suspicious of those around him, wary of the moves of erstwhile Soviet allies, damaged by a disastrous famine his policies had caused, surveyed the scene and decided it was time for a little mayhem. The problem wasn't his disastrous ideology, it was, he wrote, "feudal forces full of hatred towards socialism . . . stirring up trouble, sabotaging socialist productive forces." The party had been "infiltrated" by pragmatists and revisionists. He wrote—it is the epigraph of Frank Dikötter's *The Cultural Revolution: A People's History, 1962–1976*—"Who are our friends? Who are our enemies? That is the main question of the revolution."

He would find and purge his foes, the usual suspects: intellectuals and other class enemies, capitalist roaders, those who clung to old religions or traditions. In *Mao's Last Revolution,* Roderick MacFarquhar and Michael Schoenhals tell of a Ministry of Higher Education official brought up on charges of enjoying a "bourgeois lifestyle." He'd been seen playing mah-jongg.

Mao unleashed university and high school students to weed out enemies and hold them to account. The students became the paramilitary Red Guards. They were instructed by the party to "clear away the evil habits of the old society" and extinguish what came to be known as "the four olds"—old ideas and customs, old habits and culture. "Sweep Away All Monsters and Demons," the state newspaper instructed them.

With a vengeance they did.

In the struggle sessions the accused, often teachers suspected of lacking proletarian feeling, were paraded through streets and campuses, sometimes stadiums. It was important always to have a jeering crowd; it was important that the electric feeling that comes with the possibility of murder be present. Dunce caps, sometimes wastebaskets, were placed on the victims' heads, and placards stipulating their crimes hung from their necks. The victims were accused, berated, assaulted. Many falsely confessed in the vain hope of mercy.

Were any "guilty"? It hardly mattered. Fear and terror were the point. A destroyed society is more easily dominated.

The Chinese Catholic Margaret Chu, a medical-lab assistant, was dragged into the office of her labor camp in 1968 and made to answer invented charges. "Their real motive was once and again to force me to admit all my alleged crimes," she wrote decades later. "'I did not commit any crimes,' I asserted." She was accused again, roughed up. She denied her guilt again. "Immediately two people jumped on me and cut off half my hair."

She was tortured, left in handcuffs for 100 days, and imprisoned for years. While being tortured she sometimes prayed for death so her suffering would stop.

The Cultural Revolution lasted roughly a dozen years and died with Mao in September 1976. In time a party congress denounced it as what it was: ruinous.

So I ask you to entertain an idea that has been on my mind. I don't want to be overdramatic, but the spirit of the struggle session has returned and is here, in part because of the internet, in part because of the extremity of our politics, in part because more people are lonely. "Contention is better than loneliness," as my people, the Irish, say, and they would know.

The air is full of accusation and humiliation. We have seen this spirit most famously on the campuses, where students protest harshly, sometimes violently, views they wish to suppress. Social media is full of swarming political and ideological mobs. In an interesting departure from democratic tradition, they don't try to win the other side over. They only condemn and attempt to silence.

The spirit of the struggle session is all over Twitter. On literary Twitter social-justice warriors get advance copies of new books and denounce them for deviationism—as insensitive, racist, appropriative, anti-LGBTQ. Books on the eve of publication have been pulled, sometimes withdrawn by authors who apologize profusely. Everyone's scared. And the tormentors are not satisfied by an apology. They're excited by it and prowl for more prey.

A few weeks ago a young woman on Twitter thought aloud: "What if public libraries were open late every night and we could engage in public life there instead of having to choose between drinking at the bar and domestic isolation." This might get people off their screens and help them feel "included and nourished."

A nice idea. Maybe some local official would pick it up. Instead there was a small onslaught of negative reaction. "Libraries are already significantly underfunded and they struggle to make do with what they've got." "Before you suggest this understand that librarians are maxed out—our facilities are understaffed, we're underpaid." The idea would only work in "mainly affluent urban & suburban communities with already well-funded libraries whose wealth insulates them." A woman soon to marry a librarian warned of "what this would do to the lives of the people who work there."

After being batted about, the young woman apologized: "I made insensitive tweets abt public libraries & the individuals that staff them. I apologize for those tweets. I have much to learn abt the difficult challenges public librarians face, the services they provide, & how much they strive to meet the needs of communities they serve."

She abased herself for having had a pretty idea. But that is dangerous when thought-cops are out there, eager to perceive insufficient class loyalty.

Senator Kirsten Gillibrand understood the mood of things when she self-abased all over television after she announced for president. Once a Blue Dog Democrat, now a progressive, she nervously expressed remorse at her past deviationism. Her previous conservative stands, she said, were "callous." "They certainly weren't empathetic." "I did not think about suffering in other people's lives." She was "embarrassed" and "ashamed" of past stands. "I was not caring about others. . . . I was wrong."

At least no one cut her hair. Maybe that will be in the 2024 cycle.

Joe Biden understands the moment. He quickly apologized last week after calling Vice President Mike Pence "a decent guy." Progressive Cynthia Nixon denounced Mr. Pence as "America's most anti-LGBT elected leader" and asked Mr. Biden to "consider how this falls on the ears of our community." "You're right, Cynthia," he quickly responded.

All the Democratic candidates have apologized for something. Elizabeth Warren is abjectly sorry she took a DNA test.

Leaders of great liberal newspapers are in constant fear because so many of their readers—and writers—are more doctrinaire in their views, and angry. The struggle session is in the internal chat room.

There's a feeling in the air, isn't there? We're all noticing pieces of the story here and there, in this incident and that. But maybe it has an overall meaning. And maybe that meaning isn't good.

I don't know if we're a crueler, more aggressive country than in the past. We're certainly a louder one, and more anonymous in our cruelties.

And none of it portends good.

THE LEFT IS OVERPLAYING ITS HAND

July 8, 2021

The word now is "radicalized." So many people feel pushed to the edge and are pushing back. Go to social-media sites and search "school-board meeting," adding descriptors like "explosive," "outrage," and "chaos." Parents are rising up. New York Democrats just picked an anti-crime former cop as their mayoral nominee. Other signs that suggest a spirit of having been radicalized: Longtime alliances based on natural affinity are loosening. Conservatives by nature support and respect the military. That's changing among some of them, or at least becoming less reflexive, under the pressure of charges of political correctness and a woke brass. Conservatives have begun detaching from traditional support for corporations over the idea they're too woke, too big, and feel no particular loyalty to America, which made them, when the China market beckons.

There's a sense in America of a continuing political realignment, that it didn't all start and end in 2015–16. I think that what happened last summer, when the streets erupted and statues toppled, is being answered now with a pushback—a quieter one but no less consequential.

In connection with that, a small but possibly telling piece from a man of the left, journalist Kevin Drum, a veteran of *Mother Jones* and *Washington Monthly*, who posted some thoughts on July 3 on his blog at Jabberwocking .com. What he said is the obvious, but it wouldn't be obvious to all his readers, and those to whom it is obvious wouldn't want it said.

He titled the piece bluntly: "If You Hate Culture Wars, Blame Liberals."

"It is not conservatives who have turned American politics into a culture war battle," he writes. "Since roughly the year 2000, according to survey data,

Democrats have moved significantly to the left on most hot button social issues, while Republicans have moved only slightly right."

He cites data on issues from abortion and religion to guns, same-sex marriage, immigration, and taxes. The numbers suggest "the obvious conclusion that over the past two decades Democrats have moved left far more than Republicans have moved right." He's not personally unhappy with this, but Democrats should be concerned they're moving further away from median voters.

He refers to the work of David Shor, "a data geek who identifies as socialist but is rigorously honest about what the numbers tell us." Mr. Shor told *New York* magazine a few months ago that Democrats in 2020 gained roughly seven points among white college-educated voters. Support among blacks declined by a point or two, and Hispanic support dropped by eight or nine. This followed last summer's defund-the-police movement. The Democrats had, in Mr. Shor's words, "raised the salience of an ideologically charged issue that millions of nonwhite voters disagreed with us on."

In the past four years, Mr. Shor said, "white liberals have become a larger and larger share of the Democratic Party." But whites are "sorting on ideology" more than nonwhite voters. "We've ended up in a situation where white liberals are more left wing than Black and Hispanic Democrats on pretty much every issue: taxes, health care, policing, and even on racial issues or various measures of 'racial resentment.'"

"Black conservatives and Hispanic conservatives," Mr. Shor notes, "don't actually buy into a lot of these intellectual theories of racism. They often have a very different conception of how to help the Black or Hispanic community than liberals do." His conclusion: "If we polarize the electorate on ideology—or if nationally prominent Democrats raise the salience of issues that polarize the electorate on ideology—we're going to lose a lot of votes."

Mr. Drum agrees: However those on the left feel about the Democrats' "leftward march," the party "has been pulled far enough left that even lots of non-crazy people find us just plain scary. . . . Democrats have stoked the culture wars by getting more extreme on social issues and Republicans have used this to successfully cleave away a segment of both the non-college white vote and, more recently, the non-college nonwhite vote."

Why, then, is it still conventional wisdom on the left and in the mainstream media that it is conservatives who are culture warmongers? Because "for most people, losing something is far more painful than the pleasure of gaining something of equivalent value. And since conservatives are 'losing' the customs and hierarchies that they've long lived with, their reaction is far more intense than the liberal reaction toward winning the changes they desire."

Mr. Drum speculates that "the whole woke movement in general" has turned off many moderate voters. "Ditto for liberal dismissal of crime and safety issues."

The white activist class won't like hearing this, he says, but moving to the left, while galvanizing the progressive base, "risks outrunning the vast middle part of the country, which progressive activists seem completely uninterested in talking to."

He ends: "And for God's sake, please don't insult my intelligence by pretending that wokeness and cancel culture are all just figments of the conservative imagination. Sure, they overreact to this stuff, but it really exists, it really is a liberal invention, and it really does make even moderate conservatives feel like their entire lives are being held up to a spotlight and found wanting."

Good on him for speaking truth to rising power.

The cultural provocations that are currently tearing us apart do, certainly and obviously, come from progressives. And the left seems to have no prudent fear of backlash. They don't seem to believe public opinion counts for much anymore.

Randi Weingarten, president of the American Federation of Teachers, made this clear in her big speech this week to union members. She said parents who are rising up against the teaching of what is called critical race theory aren't opposing, as they perceive it, a radical and destructive theory in which they fear to see their children indoctrinated. No, they are bullies, "culture warriors" who are trying to stop teachers "from teaching students accurate history."

It was a very aggressive speech. It threw a match in the gasoline. You wouldn't give it unless you thought a big political party is fully with you and fully has your back. That of course is the Democratic Party, of which the teachers unions (though not all teachers) are a major subsidiary, and in which they have major power, including financial power.

That may be good for the teachers unions. I'm not sure it will prove, in a time of pushback, an unalloyed good for the Democrats.

I end with what I think is the left's misreading of its position. They act as if they've got everyone on the run, including those who show their movement the greatest respect in corporate suites and private offices. But I think something unspoken is going on. As a journalist based in New York, you meet a lot of executives, corporate leaders, people in the arts and education. They publicly support the woke regime, speak the lingo, are on board with the basic assumptions, and much early support was sincere. But they have grown indignant at and impatient with the everyday harassments of woke ideology. Deep down, many of them would like to see the left knocked back on their heels. I think the left is overplaying its hand.

AMERICA NEEDS MORE GENTLEMEN

January 18, 2018

I used to think America needed a parent to help it behave. Now I think it needs a grandparent. Our culture has been so confused for so long on so many essentials, and has gotten so crosswise on the issue of men and women, that we need more than ever the wisdom of the aged.

That was my thought as I read this week's sexual-harassment story, about the thirty-something TV star, the girl in her twenties, and their terrible date.

The woman in the story, recounted on the website Babe.net, went unnamed, and it doesn't feel right to add to the man's social-media misery. Nor is it necessary to assign blame since they were both such hapless representatives of their sex.

They had one thing in common: They were impressed by his celebrity. He deploys it to get what he wants, she wanted to be close to it. They met at an industry party, flirted by text; he asked her to his apartment and took her to a restaurant where he rushed her through dinner. They returned to his home, where he immediately made overt sexual advances, which she accepted but did not want. She seems to have had no sense that any outward show of respect was due her. Taken aback by how quickly he was moving, she tried to slow things via "nonverbal cues." Among them was allowing him to perform oral sex on her, and performing it on him, which in fairness he may have interpreted as an indication of enthusiasm. She is an articulate person but was for some reason unable to say, "Stop, this is not what I want. I have to leave." At no point does she allege he threatened her, either physically or professionally, or tried to bar the door.

He was boorish, a slob, what used to be called a wolf. He wished to use her sexually and didn't understand her reservations. Isn't that what first dates are for?

Is he a creep? Of course. She has been accused of trying to jump onto the #MeToo movement, painting herself as a victim, and exhibiting no sense of "agency." (Though she is at least competent at revenge.) She expects us to understand why she didn't walk out. Why did she stay, and expect such a gross figure suddenly to show sensitivity? In his interactions as she reports them, he never pretended not to be a pig.

Here is why we're discussing this. All the stories we've read the past few months about predators—not those accused of rape and sexual assault, which are crimes, but of general piggishness, grabbiness, manipulation, and power games—have a common thread. The men involved were not gentlemen. They acted as if they'd never heard of the concept.

We have lost track of it. In the past forty years, in the movement for full equality, we threw it over the side. But we should rescue that old and helpful way of being. The whole culture, especially women, needs The Gentleman back.

A person of the cultural left would say that is a hopelessly patriarchal thing to say. But one thing the #MeToo movement illustrates is that women are often at particular risk in the world, and need friends and allies to stand with them. That would be men. And the most reliable of them are gentlemen.

There are a million definitions of what a gentleman is, and some begin with references to being born to a particular standing. But in America any man could be one who had the guts to withstand the demands.

The dictionary says a gentleman is a chivalrous, courteous, honorable man. That's a good, plain definition. The Urban Dictionary says, "The true gentleman is the man whose conduct proceeds from good will . . . whose self control is equal to all emergencies, who does not make the poor man conscious of his poverty, the obscure man of his obscurity, or any man of his inferiority or deformity." That's good, too.

A website called Gentleman's Journal offers a list of twenty traits that make a man a gentleman. I liked "A gentleman always walks a woman home." He doesn't pack her off alone to an Uber downstairs, in the back of which she weeps as she sends her friends horrified texts, which is what happened with the Hollywood star and the girl. I liked "A gentleman ruins his lover's lipstick, not her mascara." And "If a woman comes with baggage, a gentleman helps her unpack it."

A gentleman is good to women because he has his own dignity and sees theirs. He takes opportunities to show them respect. He is not pushy, manipulative, belittling. He stands with them not because they are weak but because they deserve friendship. Once, at a gathering of women in media, I spoke of a columnist who years before had given me helpful critiques of my work and urged me on. "A gentleman is an encourager of women."

It goes deeper than memorizing and repeating certain behaviors, such as standing when a woman or an older person enters the room. That is a physical expression of inner regard. Being a gentleman involves not only manners but morals. The nineteenth-century theologian John Henry Newman—an Anglican priest who became a Catholic cardinal—said a gentleman tries not to inflict pain. He tries to remove the obstacles "which hinder the free and unembarrassed action of those about him." He is "tender toward the bashful, gentle toward the distant, and merciful toward the absurd. . . . He is never mean or little in his disputes, never takes unfair advantage."

David Gandy, a fashion model, wrote a few years ago in London's *Telegraph* that his work had taught him "being a gentleman isn't about what you do or what you wear, it's about how you behave and who you are." A gentleman "holds chivalry and politeness in great regard. He holds the door for people; he gives up his seat; he takes off his coat to a lady on a cold evening." These are old-fashioned actions, but a gentleman still holds to them "even though the world has changed."

Yes, a gentleman does.

A man once told me it's hard to be a gentleman when fewer of the women around you seem interested in being ladies. But that's when you should step up your gentleman game. We are all here to teach and inspire.

By the way, I notice there are definitions of what a gentleman is and how you can be one all over the internet.

Someone must be looking for this information. That's good.

The age of social media has worked against the ideas of decorum, dignity, and self-control—the idea of being a gentleman. You can, anonymously, be your lowest, most brutish self, and the lowering spreads like a virus.

But you can't judge a nation by its comment threads, or let's hope so. You can judge it by its struggle to maintain standards. For inspiration we end with Hollywood, with Jimmy Stewart in *The Philadelphia Story*. The character played by Katharine Hepburn makes a pass at him, and he notes he could have taken advantage of the moment but she'd been drinking and "there are rules about that."

Here's to the rules, and the gentlemen who help keep them alive.

REFLECTIONS ON IMPEACHMENT, TWENTY YEARS LATER

November 29, 2018

December marks the twentieth anniversary of Bill Clinton's impeachment. There are many recent retrospectives on the scandal that led to it, including former Independent Counsel Ken Starr's mildly indignant *Contempt* and Alex Gibney's superb documentary series *The Clinton Affair.*

As I look back twenty years on, I'm more indignant about some aspects, less about others.

I didn't believe the story when I first heard it—presidents and staffers don't carry on like that. When I came to see that it was true, I was angry. I wrote angrily in these pages.

I see it all now more as a tragedy than a scandal. I am more convinced than ever that Mr. Clinton made the epic political miscalculation of the twentieth century's latter half. He had two choices when news of the affair was uncovered: Tell the truth and pay the price, or lie and hope to get away with it.

If he'd told the truth, even accompanied by a moving public apology, the toll would have been heavy. He would have taken a hellacious political beating, with a steep slide in public approval and in stature. He would have been an object of loathing and ridicule—the goat in the White House, a laughingstock. Members of his party would have come down on him like a ton of bricks. Newt Gingrich and the Republicans would have gleefully rubbed his face in it every day. There would have been calls for impeachment.

It would have lasted many months. And he would have survived and his presidency continued.

Much more important—here is why it is a tragedy—it wouldn't have dragged America through the mud. It only would have dragged *him* through the mud. His full admission of culpability would have averted the false testimony in a criminal investigation that became the basis for the Starr report and the two articles of impeachment the House approved.

The American people would've forgiven him for the affair. We know this because they'd already forgiven him when they first elected him. There had been credible allegations of affairs during the 1992 campaign. Voters had never thought highly of him in that area. His nickname the day he was inaugurated was Slick Willie.

If he had chosen the path of honesty, Americans wouldn't have backed impeaching him, because they are adults and have also made mistakes and committed sins. They would have been more like the grand-jury member who spoke comfortingly to Monica Lewinsky as she wept near the end of her testimony: "Monica, none of us in this room are perfect. We all fall and we all fall several times a day. The only difference between my age and when I was your age is I get up faster." That is the sound of an American looking in the face of remorse.

And we know Mr. Clinton would have been forgiven because in September 1998—after the Starr report was released, amid all the mud and lies and jokes about thongs and cigars—a Gallup poll asked, "Based on what you know at this point, do you think that Bill Clinton should or should not be impeached and removed from office?" Sixty-six percent answered "should not be."

Bill Clinton, political genius, didn't understand his country's heart.

And so he lied: "I want you to listen to me. . . . I did not have sexual relations with that woman, Miss Lewinsky"—and the year of hell, the cultural catastrophe, followed. That's what it was, a year in which eight-year-olds learned about oral sex from the radio on the way home from school, and ten-year-olds came to understand that important adults lie, angrily and consistently, and teenagers knew that if the president can do it, I can do it. It marked the end of a certain mystique of leadership, and it damaged the mystique of American democracy. All of America's airwaves were full of the sludge—phone sex and blue dresses. The scandal lowered everything.

It was a tragedy because, in lying and trying to protect himself, Mr. Clinton was deciding not to protect America. And that is the unforgivable sin, that he put America through that, not what happened with Monica.

Mr. Clinton's foes made the catastrophe worse. The independent counsel was obliged by law to "advise the House of Representatives of any substantial and credible information . . . that may constitute grounds for an impeachment." The Starr report ran 452 pages and contained an astonishing level of sexual detail, of prurient, gratuitous specificity. Congress could have withheld it from the public or released an expurgated version. It didn't have to be so humiliating. But Mr. Clinton's enemies made sure it was.

Almost immediately on receiving the Starr report, Congress voted to release it in full, "so that the fullest details of his sins could be made public," as Ken Gormley writes in his comprehensive 2010 history of the scandal, *The Death of American Virtue: Clinton vs. Starr.* They put it up on the web. Its contents wound up on every screen in America, every newspaper, every television and radio.

Lawmakers released the videotape of Mr. Clinton's grand-jury testimony, so everyone could see the handsome presidential liar squirm.

Mr. Starr's staffers said they needed extremely detailed, concrete specificity to make the American people understand what happened. At the time I assumed that was true in a legal sense. Now I look back and see mere bloodlust and misjudgment.

I see the desire to rub Mr. Clinton's face in it just as he'd rubbed America's face in it.

Top to bottom, left to right, a more dignified government, one that cared more about both America's children and its international stature, would have shown more self-restraint and forbearance. And there might have been just a little pity for the desperate, cornered liar who'd defiled his office.

It wouldn't have so ruined the life of a woman who, when her relationship with the president commenced, was only twenty-two. She paid a steeper reputational price than anyone. Charles Rangel, at the time a senior Democratic congressman, said on television that she was a "young tramp." The White House slimed her as a fantasist. She went into hiding, thought about suicide.

And in the end, twenty years later, she put the Clintons to shame.

Publicly for two decades she has reacted with more style and dignity than they, said less and with less bitterness and aggression, when they were the ones with all the resources, and a press corps eager to maintain good relations with them because Hillary would surely one day be president.

Monica told her side and kept walking, and even refrained from blaming her shaming on the Clintons. Feminists abandoned and derided her. She took it all on her back and bore it away. In my book, after all this time, she deserves respect.

Sometimes America gets fevers. They don't so much break as dissipate with time. Twenty years ago we were in a fever. Others will come. The thing to do when it happens is know it's happening, notice when the temperature is high, and factor it in as you judge and act, realizing you're not at your best. Twenty years ago, almost none of our leaders were.

THE UVALDE POLICE SCANDAL

June 2, 2022

The great sin in what happened in Texas is that an eighteen-year-old with murder in his heart walked into a public school and shot to death nineteen kids and two teachers. The great shock is what the police did—their incompetence on the scene and apparent lies afterward. This aspect has rocked the American people.

Uvalde wasn't an "apparent law-enforcement failure." It is the biggest law-enforcement scandal since George Floyd, and therefore one of the biggest in U.S. history. Children, some already shot, some not, were trapped in adjoining classrooms. As many as nineteen cops were gathered in the hall just outside. The *Washington Post* timeline has the killer roaming the classrooms: "The attack went for so long, witnesses said, that the gunman had time to taunt his victims before killing them, even putting on songs that one student described to CNN as 'I-want-people-to-die music.'"

Students inside were calling 911 and begging for help. The officers failed to move for almost an hour.

Everyone in America knows the story. Finding out exactly how and why it happened is the urgent business of government. We can't let it dribble away into the narrative void and settle for excuses. "People are still shaken up." "Probes take time." "We're still burying the children." We can't let the idea settle in that this is how it is now, if bad trouble comes you're on your own. It is too demoralizing.

We can't let it settle in that the police can't be relied on to be physically braver than other people. An implicit agreement in going into the profession is that you're physically brave. I don't understand those saying with nonjudgmental empathy, "I'm not sure I would have gone in." It was *their job* to go in. If you can't cut it, then don't join and get the badge, the gun, and the pension.

The most focused and intense investigating has to be done now, when it's still fresh and raw—before the nineteen cops and their commanders fully close ranks, if they haven't already, and lawyer up.

Those officers—they know everything that happened while nothing was done for an hour. A lot of them would have had to override their own common sense to stand down under orders; most would have had to override a natural impulse toward compassion. Many would be angry now, or full of reproach or a need to explain.

Get them now.

Within moments of the massacre's ending, the police were issuing strange claims. They said the shooter was confronted by a school guard and shots were exchanged. Not true. They said the shooter was wearing body armor. He wasn't. They said he was "barricaded" inside the classroom. Is that the right word for a guy behind a single locked door? They said a teacher left open the door the shooter used to enter. Videotape showed otherwise. They didn't admit what happened outside the school as parents pleaded with the police to do something and tried to fight past the cordon so at least *they* could do something. *The Washington Post* had a witness who heard parents tell the police, "Do your f— job!" The police said they were. A man yelled, "Get your f— rifles and handle business!" Those parents were patronized and pushed around.

Even accounting for the fog of war there's something next-level about the spin and falsehoods that occurred in Uvalde.

The commander on scene, school district police chief Pete Arredondo, hasn't given a public statement on what went wrong. Why is he allowed not to tell the public what happened? He didn't take reporters' questions until cornered Wednesday by CNN's Shimon Prokupecz. Mr. Arredondo was evasive. Reports he's stiff-arming investigators are wrong, he said; he's in touch with them and he'll have more to say but not now. Then, in fatherly tones: "We're not going to release anything. We have people in our community being buried. So we're going to be respectful."

A better form of respect would have been stopping the guy who left them grieving their dead children.

What I fear is a final report issued in six months or a year that will hit all the smarmy rhetorical notes—"a day of epic tragedy for our brothers and sisters in a small Texas town"—but fail, utterly, to make clear who was responsible for the lost hour.

All this has made Governor Greg Abbott look particularly bad. He gave the imprimatur of his office to early police fictions. In his first news conference following the massacre he was strangely insistent on their sterling valor: "They showed amazing courage by running toward gunfire."

Only after videos of the parents being pushed around by the cops made their way to social media did he make an about-face. In a later news conference he talked of free funerals and mental health resources. Pressed finally on what was already becoming a police scandal, he said he'd been "misled" by authorities and was "livid." Glad he talked about his emotions. We don't do that enough in America.

But who misled him? Do they still have a job?

You wonder what his first briefing was like.

Governor: "I need the truth: What went down?"

Burly police official in Stetson: "Within minutes we stormed the school like Iwo Jima—took out the enemy under a hail of fire, carried the women and children to safety. Fixed bayonets. Knives in our teeth. Trust me."

Governor: "Got it, thanks!"

There is only one way to handle such a mistake: Know it won't disappear. Lead a swift and brutal investigation, talk about it every day, keep the heat on. When people know you're playing it straight, they're generous. When they know you aren't—there's an election in November and they'll let you know.

I close with a thought tugging around my brain. I think I am seeing a broad and general decline in professionalism in America, a deterioration of our pride in concepts like rigor and excellence. January 6 comes and law enforcement agencies are weak and unprepared and the U.S. Capitol falls to a small army of mooks. Afghanistan and the departure that was really a collapse, all traceable to the incompetence of diplomatic and military leadership. It's like everyone's forgotten the mission.

I'm not saying, "Oh, America was once so wonderful and now it's not." I'm saying we are losing old habits of discipline and pride in expertise—of peerlessness. There was a kind of American gleam. If the world called on us—in business, the arts, the military, diplomacy, science—they knew they were going to get *help*. The grown-ups had arrived, with their deep competence.

America now feels more like people who took the Expedited Three-Month Training Course and got the security badge and went to work and formed an affinity group to advocate for change. A people who love to talk, endlessly, about sensitivity, yet aren't sensitive enough to save the children bleeding out on the other side of the door.

I fear that as a people we're becoming not only increasingly unimpressive but increasingly unlovable.

My God, I've never seen a country so in need of a hero.

AMERICA HAS LOST THE THREAD

September 16, 2021

I want to say something that struck me hard after the ceremonies marking 9/11 last Saturday. The grief felt and expressed had to do with more than the memories of that day twenty years ago. It also had to do with right now.

It had to do with a sense that we are losing the thread, that America is losing the thread. We compared—we couldn't help it, it is in the nature of memory—the America of now with the America of twenty years ago, and we see a deterioration. We feel disturbance at this because we don't know if we can get our way back. The losing of the thread feels bigger than ideology, bigger certainly than parties. It feels like some more fundamental confusion, an inability to play the role of who we are, and to be comfortable in who we are.

Certainly, most obviously and geopolitically we lost the thread in Afghanistan. We went there twenty years ago to make quick work of mass murderers who'd attacked us, and those who'd harbored and helped them. But we didn't get the man who gave us 9/11, he escaped, and attention turned elsewhere, to Iraq, and we just stayed and walked in circles and came up with new words to rationalize the mission and it all turned into a muddle of confused intentions. Ten years in it was like the drunken song, "We're Here Because We're Here."

Having lost the thread in the war we then with an almost magical consistency lost the thread in the ending of it. It was a frantic calamity of ill-thought-through actions and mistaken agendas. The horrifying part was that it couldn't have proceeded without a willful ignoring of reality.

Evidence of a lost thread: 9/11 was a deeply communal event. We were all in it together, wounded together, and mourning together. We dug deep, found our best selves, and actually saw the best selves in others. The spontaneous community of those who showed up at the hospital to give blood, of those on the top floors of the towers who gathered to try to lead people out, of those on the plane who banded together to storm the pilot's door—"Let's roll." It wasn't just you, you were part of something.

The country we are experiencing now is one of people in different groups ganging up on each other. We all see this. It's all division, driven by identity politics, race, gender, class. Twenty years ago we were grateful for cops, now we denigrate them and they leave and we argue about why they left. A rising generation of voters who were children when 9/11 happened and who became conscious of history during the 2008 economic crisis see (and have been well taught!) the imperfections, mistakes, and sins of their own country but have no human memory of the abuses of other systems, of how damaging deep socialism, and communism, have been. The passion of their emerging beliefs will engender opposing passions. They already are.

Just about every large business in America is now run by its human resources department because everyone appears to be harassing and assaulting each other, or accusing each other. Is this the sign of a healthy country?

Following the trauma and drama of 9/11 we started discovering in some new way our nation's meaning—what it was in history, meant in history, meant to us. We talked about it. We saw: The first thing the firemen did after the towers fell was put up the flag.

Twenty years in our history is treated as all sin, sin, sin. We're like mad monks flagellating ourselves. We are going through a nonstop condemnation of our past and our people and their limits and ignorance. It isn't healthy. Reflection and honest questioning are, but not this. And so much of it comes from our most successful and secure, our elites and establishments. Regular people look and think, "But if our professors and media leaders and tech CEOs hate us, who is going to help us think our way out of this mess?" And they know someone has to, because they know in a way elites can never understand, because they have grown so used to security, that no nation can proceed in the world safely and fruitfully when at bottom it hates itself.

Watching the ceremonies last weekend it was understandable if you thought, We started out rediscovering our love and wound up obsessed with our sins. We started out together and wound up more divided than ever, driven apart by opportunists who set us at each other's throats.

And of course it all plays out in a million political and cultural issues. The pandemic came, a once-in-a-lifetime occurrence (we hope), and somehow that shared experience became another opportunity for division. Government had to be deft and persuasive and honest about what it didn't know and didn't have, and often failed. But government can always regulate, spend, and tax. We're no deficit hawks in this corner but doesn't U.S. public debt going toward thirty trillion dollars feel a little . . . high? And dangerous?

When a country has lost the thread it gets a mob breaking into the U.S. Capitol going for the ballots that will ensure and formalize a presidential election. When it's lost the thread it can no longer maintain a rough consensus—it doesn't even *want* a rough consensus—on how we vote.

And there are the million goofy things that are insignificant and yet somehow feel . . . telling. The Met Gala the other night showed the elite of a major industry literally losing the thread. Google the pictures. It was a freak show. There was no feeling of a responsibility to present to the world a sense of coherence or elegance, to show a thing so beautiful it left the people who saw it aspiring to something they couldn't even name. All this was presided over by a chic and cultivated woman who is cunning and practical. If freaky is in she's going freaky deaky to the max. Follow the base, even if it's sick. Do not lead. Leading is impossible now.

That's what I see with leaders all over America's business life. What follows the lost thread is go-with-the-flow. Even when you know it isn't going anywhere good. Especially when it's going nowhere good.

What are regular people doing? My sense is they're trying to hide from the national, figuring they'll make strong what they can make strong—the family, the school, the local. They're not trying to "maintain control" or "retreat," they're just trying to make things work. But what does it mean for a country when its most sober and thoughtful people are essentially trying to hide from it? To hide from the accusations and division and the growing air of freakishness, from the whole cultural revolution and the woke regime, trying to enforce boundaries between "that" and "us." And knowing all the while that, as they say, you may be through with the culture but the culture isn't through with you.

I feel certain this whole story will have some effect on, maybe a big effect on, the next election and the one after that. Just people feeling, knowing, that we've lost the thread, need to get it back, and wondering what we can do to help make that happen.

THE HALF-MADNESS OF PRINCE HARRY

January 12, 2023

Prince Harry's book is odd. There's even something half-mad about it.

He opens with a dramatic meeting at Frogmore Cottage, his former mansion on the grounds of Windsor Home Park. It is just after the death of Prince Philip, Harry's paternal grandfather. For months Harry has been estranged from his father, Charles, and his brother, William—a "full-scale public rupture." Harry has flown in from America and requested a meeting. The day is overcast, chilly. Charles and William arrive late looking "grim, almost menacing," and "tightly aligned." "They'd come ready for a fight." Harry is tongue-tied, vulnerable, leaves heartbroken. "I wanted peace. I wanted it more than anything."

You feel such sympathy. What could have driven them so far apart? Why are Charles and William so cold?

Then you realize, wait—Philip died just a month after the Oprah interview in which Harry rather coolly portrayed his family as remote and hapless puppets and implied they were racist.

Harry forgets, in the opening, to tell us that part. But you can see how it might have left Charles and William a little indignant.

This is the book's great flaw, that Harry doesn't always play it straight, that he thinks "my truth" is as good as *the* truth. There are other flaws, and they grate. There's a heightened-ness to his language—he never leaves a place; he flees it "in fear for our sanity and physical safety." He often finds his wife "sobbing uncontrollably" on the floor and the stairs, mostly over what he fails to realize are trivial things. He is grandiose: "My mother was a princess, named after a goddess." "How would I be remembered by history? For the headlines? Or for who I actually was?" Lord, he was an attractive man fifth in line for a largely ceremonial European throne; it would hardly remember him at all. (Unless he wrote a scalding book and destabilized the monarchy!) He repeatedly points out that he's a Windsor and of royal blood. His title means a lot to him. He is exhibitionistic: "My penis was oscillating between extremely sensitive and borderline traumatized." (Frostbite.)

There are gaps in his knowledge base that wouldn't be irritating if he weren't intent on establishing that he's giving you the high-class rarefied inside dope. "Never complain, never explain" has been an expression of the old American upper class since forever, and I'm sure the British one, too. It isn't special to the Windsors. "An heir and a spare" is old Fleet Street tabloidese. It doesn't mean, as he suggested on book tour, that he was bred for body parts.

Famous families often have internal communication problems. The children of those families learn much of what they know from the many books written about the clan. They internalize and repeat observations and stories that aren't quite right but are now given their insider imprimatur.

Harry's anecdotes tend to undermine the institution of the monarchy. When he was a teenager Britain's biggest tabloid told the palace it had evidence he was doing drugs. In fact, as Harry tells us candidly, he did do drugs when he was young. The palace, no doubt knowing this, opted to "play ball" with the newspaper and not deny all aspects of the story. This made Harry feel thrown under the bus.

His father, he believes, used him as a "sacrifice," to appease a powerful editor and bolster his own sagging reputation. "No more the unfaithful husband, Pa would now be presented to the world as the harried single dad coping with a drug-addled child." He reports that Charles and his wife, Camilla, were jealous of William and Kate's "drawing attention away from them." His stories of jealousy sound like projection. But they also make the book feel less like "Clown Turns on Circus" than something more deadly, especially just before Charles's coronation this May.

Harry accuses the tabloids of violating his privacy, and no doubt they often did. What is almost unbelievable is that he is so unmoored and destabilized by this inevitable aspect of fame, especially royal fame. He implies he left Britain primarily because of the newspapers and their criticism of his wife.

But the odd, half-mad thing about this book is that in it he violates his own privacy, and that of others, more than Fleet Street ever could.

He is careful throughout to say he is telling his story in order to help others, those who've struggled with mental illness or been traumatized by war. It is hard to know another person's motives; it can be hard to know your own. But I don't think this book is about others. I think it's about his own very human desire for revenge, to hurt those who've hurt him. And to become secure in a certain amount of wealth. And to show his family and Fleet Street that their favorite ginger-haired flake could make his own way, set up his own palace, break free, fly his own standard, become the duke of Netflix. This book is classic Fredo: "I can handle things. I'm smart. Not like everybody says, like dumb, I'm smart and I want respect!"

It is all so contradictory. He says he wants reconciliation but writes things that alienate, he says he reveres the monarchy and isn't trying to bring it down but he has gone beyond removing bricks from the facade and seems to be going at the bearing walls.

I close with a thought on privacy. Prince Harry violates his own. He tells us too much about himself and others.

Once there was a reigning personal style of public reticence about private pain. You didn't share it with everybody, and you didn't use it for advantage or as a weapon: *I have known pain, you must bow before me.* The forces of modernity have washed away the old boundary between public and private. It isn't good. It's making us less human even as we claim to be more sensitive.

But fully mature people still have a sense of their own privacy, they keep to themselves what is properly kept to oneself. Privacy isn't some relic of the pre-tech past, as I said once, it is connected to personhood. It has to do with intimate things—the inner workings of your head and heart, of your soul. You don't just give those things away. Your deepest thoughts and experiences are yours, held by you; they are part of your history. They are part of your dignity. You share them as a mark of trust. This is true intimacy, not phony intimacy but the real thing.

If you tell all the strangers your secrets what do you tell your intimates?

A friend said the other day, "Most of the forces in the world are pushing toward exhibitionism and calling it honesty. The assumption is if you keep things to yourself you have something to hide." But you aren't reserved out of shame, you are reserved out of a sense of your own value and self-respect. And it doesn't leave you alone; it means you are part of something larger, a whole world of distinct souls.

You shouldn't violate your own privacy, not for attention or admiration, and not for money. It's a mistake. And it won't heal you.

THE SEXUAL-HARASSMENT RACKET IS OVER

November 23, 2017

I find myself thankful for something that is roiling our country. I am glad at what has happened with the recent, much-discussed, and continuing, sexual-harassment revelations and responses. To repeat the obvious, it is a watershed event, which is something you can lose sight of when you're in the middle of it. To repeat the obvious again, journalists broke the back of the scandal when they broke the code on how to report it. For a quarter century we had been stuck in the He Said/She Said. Anita Hill and Clarence Thomas gave their testimonies, each offered witnesses, and the fair-minded did their best with the evidence at hand while sorting through all the swirling political agendas. In the end I believed Mr. Thomas. But nobody knows, or rather only two people do.

What happened during the past two years, and very much in the past few months, is that reporters and news organizations committed serious resources to unearthing numbers and patterns. Deep reporting found not one or two victims of an abuser but, in one case, that of Bill Cosby, at least thirty-five. So that was the numbers. The testimony of the women who went on the record, named and unnamed, revealed patterns: the open bathrobe, the running shower, the "Let's change our meeting from the restaurant to my room/your apartment/my guesthouse." Once you, as a fair-minded reader, saw the numbers and patterns, and once you saw them in a lengthy, judicious, careful narrative, you knew who was telling the truth. You knew what was true. Knowing was appalling and sometimes shocking, but it also came as a kind of relief.

Once predators, who are almost always repeat offenders, understood the new way of reporting such stories, they understood something else:

They weren't going to get away with it anymore. They'd never known that. And they were going to pay a price, probably in their careers. They'd never known that either.

Why did this happen now? It was going to happen at some point: Sexual harassment is fairly endemic. Quinnipiac University released a poll this week showing that 60 percent of American women voters say they've experienced it. Maybe the difference now is that the Clintons are gone—more on that in a moment. And maybe there's something in this: Sexual harassment, at least judging by the testimony of recent accusers, has gotten weirder, stranger, more brutish. The political director of a network news organization invites you to his office, trains his eyes on you, and masturbates as you tell him about your ambitions? The Hollywood producer hires an army of foreign goons to spy on you and shut you up? It has gotten weird out there. These stories were going to blow up at some point.

Sexual harassment is not over because sin is not over. "The devil has been busy!" a journalist friend said this week as another story broke. But as a racket it will never be the same.

Some great journalism, some great writing and thinking, has come of this moment. Ronan Farrow's *New Yorker* pieces have been credible and gutsy on all levels. Masha Gessen's piece in the same magazine last week warned of moral panic, of a blurring of the lines between different behaviors and a confusion as to the boundaries between normal, messy human actions and heinous ones. Rebecca Traister of *New York* magazine has argued that it is a mistake to focus now on the question of punishments, that maybe the helpful thing is to focus on what's going on in our society that predators think they can get away with this.

Caitlin Flanagan in *The Atlantic* wrote the most important political piece in "Bill Clinton: A Reckoning." What is striking about this moment, she argued, is not the number of women who've come forward with serious allegations. "What's remarkable is that these women are being believed." Most didn't have police reports or witnesses, and many were speaking of things that had happened years ago. "We have finally come to some kind of national consensus about the workplace; it naturally fosters a level of romance and flirtation, but the line between those impulses and the sexual predation of a boss is clear."

What had impeded the ability of victims to be believed in the past? The Bill Clinton experience. He was "very credibly" accused, as Ms. Flanagan wrote, of sex crimes at different points throughout the 1990s—Juanita Broaddrick said he violently raped her; Paula Jones said he exposed himself to her; Kathleen Willey said she went to him for advice and that he groped and assaulted her. These women "had far more credible evidence" than many recent accusers. "But Clinton was not left to the swift and pitiless justice that today's accused men have experienced." He was rescued instead by "a surprising force: machine feminism."

That movement had by the '90s devolved into a "partisan operation." Gloria Steinem in March 1998 wrote a famous *New York Times* op-ed that, in Ms. Flanagan's words, "slut-shamed, victim-blamed, and age-shamed" the victims and "urged compassion for and gratitude to the man the women accused." This revealed contemporary feminism as "a weaponized auxiliary of the Democratic Party." Ms. Steinem characterized the assaults as "passes," writing, "Even if the allegations are true, the President is not guilty of sexual harassment."

Ms. Steinem operated with the same logic as the skeeviest apologist for Roy Moore: *Don't credit any charges. Gotta stick with our team.*

Ms. Flanagan: "The widespread liberal response to the sex-crime accusations against Bill Clinton found their natural consequence 20 years later in the behavior of Harvey Weinstein: Stay loudly and publicly and extravagantly on the side of signal leftist causes and you can do what you want in the privacy of your offices and hotel rooms."

The article called for a Democratic Party "reckoning" on the way it protected Bill Clinton. It was a great piece.

I close with three thoughts.

The first springs from an observation Tucker Carlson made on his show about ten days ago. He marveled, briefly, at this oddity: Most of the accused were famous media personalities, influential journalists, entertainers. He noted that all these people one way or another make their living in front of a camera.

It stayed with me. What *is* it about men and modern fame that makes them think they can take whatever they want when they want it, and they'll always get away with it, even as word, each year, spreads: *Watch out for that guy.*

Second, if the harassment is, as it seems to me, weirder and more over the top now than, say, forty years ago, why might that be?

Third, a hard and deep question put quickly: An aging Catholic priest suggested to a friend that all this was inevitable. "Contraception degenerates men," he said, as does abortion. Once you separate sex from its seriousness, once you separate it from its life-changing, life-giving potential, men will come to see it as just another want, a desire like any other. Once they think that, then they'll see sexual violations as less serious, less charged, less full of weight. They'll be more able to rationalize. It's only petty theft, a pack of chewing gum on the counter, and I took it.

In time this will seem true not only to men, but to women.

This is part of the reason I'm thankful for what I'm seeing. I experience it, even if most women don't, or don't consciously, as a form of saying no, this is important. It is serious.

KIDS, DON'T BECOME SUCCESS ROBOTS

March 14, 2019

A few thoughts on the college admissions scandal in which wealthy and accomplished parents allegedly lied, cheated, and bribed to get their kids admitted to elite universities.

I bet your reaction was like mine: an electric sense of "I didn't know that was going on!" followed by an immediate "Of course that was going on!" Because there's a lot of crazy money in dizzy hands, and there's a lot of status involved in where your kids go to school.

It must be stressed that this is a scandal not of kids but of adults, fully functioning and wildly successful ones who knew what they were doing.

Here is something I think is part of the story. In the past decade or so I've observed a particular parenting style growing prevalent among the upper middle class and wealthy. It is intense. They love their kids and want the best for them, they want to be responsible, but there's a degree to which one wonders if they don't also see them as narcissistic extensions of themselves. They are hyper-attentive, providing meticulous academic grooming—private schools, private tutors and coaches, private classes in Chinese language and cello. They don't want their children fat—that isn't "healthy," by which they mean "attractive." They communicate the civilized opinions of the best people and signal that it would be best to hew to them.

They aim their children at the best colleges, which are, to them, basically brands. The colleges too market themselves that way—"Well, we *are* Harvard." Get in there and you're branded, too.

I believe a lot of parents do all this not only so their children will do well but so they will look good.

They are status monkeys creating success robots.

Which in one way is odd. Their family has already arrived! But there is something sick about America that no matter how much success you have it's not enough, you must have more. And everyone must know you have it.

An apparently laudable goal becomes an extreme competition.

If their child succeeds they were successful parents. If they were successful parents their status is enhanced in a serious way: Everyone respects successful parents! There is no one who doesn't! Magazine profiles of celebrities stress close families, happy children.

If Billy gets into Yale his parents won the race. If he does not, well, maybe they were average parents, or maybe not so good. Or maybe Billy isn't that bright. ("Neither is his father," the neighbors whisper.)

The kids pick up through cues the family ethos: The purpose of an education is to look good. When—this is old-fashioned, but let's say it anyway—the purpose of an education is to enrich a mind, to help the young discover great thought, to teach history and science, to spur a sense of purpose and vocation.

An irony is that success robots, once wound up and pushed forward, often struggle. The president of an elite college told me recently that the most surprising thing about recent classes is the number of students who ask for and need psychological services. They seem, said the president, unusually dependent on their parents.

A traditional reason for going away to college is to get away from your parents, to function and flourish on your own. But that's hard when you've been so closely guided, so aimed toward achievement, even as its ultimate meaning was never quite explained to you.

I'll tell you where I saw success robots. I go to schools a lot, have taught at universities and seen a ton of great kids and professors who've really sacrificed themselves to teach. A few years ago I worked for a few months at an Ivy League school. I expected a lot of questions about politics, history, and literature. But that is not what the students were really interested in. What they were interested in—it was almost my first question, and it never abated—was networking. They wanted to know how you network. At first I was surprised: "I don't know, that wasn't on my mind, I think it all comes down to the work." Then I'd ask, "Why don't you just make friends instead?" By the end I was saying, "It's a mistake to see people as commodities, as things you can use! Concentrate on the work!" They'd get impatient. They knew there was a secret to getting ahead, that it was networking, and that I was cruelly withholding successful strategies.

In time I concluded they'd been trained to be shallow, encouraged to see others as instruments. They didn't think great work would be rewarded, they thought great connections were. And it was what they'd implicitly been promised by the school: Get in here and you can network with the cream of the crop, you'll rise to the top with them.

Here is a school that is an antidote to that. Three years ago I went to a smallish school that enrolls mostly students who are the first in their families to go to college. It was Tennessee Technological University in Cookeville. A lot of the kids are local, a racial and ethnic mix, immigrants and children of immigrants. They were so mature—gracious, welcoming, quick with smart questions on presidents and policy. At a reception I complimented a young woman on her pretty cocktail dress. She smiled and said, "I got it from the clothes closet." I shook my head. The Clothes Closet, she explained, is where students go to get something to wear to a job interview or an event like this one. People contribute what they've got, the students can always put something nice together. In time they contribute clothes, too.

Cheryl Montgomery, the college's director of development, laughed when I called her about it this week and told me that the closet, which had literally been a closet, is now in an office renovated to function as one. "We've got everything," she said. "Men's suits, women's professional suits and dresses, ties, belts, shoes. We don't want a student to worry, 'Am I dressed appropriately?'" Interviews are hard enough. A lot of students don't have anyone in their lives to help them. "Last Friday a gentleman who's a quite spiffy dresser came to see me, a very successful businessman, and he donated four sport coats, a trove of men's dress slacks, and very nice button-down shirts, all in style." When a cash donation comes in, it goes toward clothes for the unusually large and the unusually small.

I came away from Tennessee Tech thinking what I always think when I see such schools: We're going to be OK.

And now, because you'd be lost without it, my advice to students still considering college in the year 2019. Avoid elite universities if you can; they're too often indoctrination mills anyway. Aim at smaller, second-tier colleges, places of low-key harmony, religiously affiliated when possible—and get a real education. Every school has a library. Every library has books. That's what you need.

You'll be with a better class of people—harder-working, less cynical, more earnest. First-generation college students who are excited to be there and committed to study. Immigrants who feel grateful to be there. Home-schooled kids with self-possession and dignity, who see the dignity in others.

Do not network. Make friends. Learn about the lives of others.

WHAT WERE ROBESPIERRE'S PRONOUNS?

July 25, 2019

We often make historical parallels here. History doesn't repeat itself but it does rhyme, as clever people say. And sometimes it hiccups. Here is a hiccup.

We start with the moral and political catastrophe that was the French Revolution. It was more a nationwide psychotic break than a revolt—a great nation at its own throat, swept by a spirit not only of regicide but suicide. For ten years they simply enjoyed killing each other. They could have done what England was doing—a long nonviolent revolution, a gradual diminution of the power of king and court, an establishment of the rights of the people and their legislators so that the regent ended up a lovely person on a stamp. Instead they chose blood. Scholars like to make a distinction between the Revolution and the Terror that followed, but "the Terror was merely 1789 with a higher body count." From the storming of the Bastille onward, "it was apparent that violence was not just an unfortunate side effect. . . . It was the Revolution's source of collective energy. It was what made the Revolution revolutionary."

That is from Simon Schama's masterpiece *Citizens*, his history of the Revolution published in 1989, its 200th anniversary. It is erudite, elegant, and heroically nonideological.

John Adams, across the sea in America, quickly understood what was happening in France and voiced alarm. In contrast his old friend Thomas Jefferson egged on the Revolution and lent it his moral prestige. Faced with news of the guillotines, he reverted to abstractions. He was a genius with a true if hidden seam of malice, and rarely overconcerned with the suffering of others.

The Revolution had everything—a ruling class that was clumsy, decadent, inert; a pathetic king, a queen beyond her depth, costly wars, monstrous debt, an impervious and unreformable administrative state, a hungry populace. The task of the monarchy was to protect the poor, but the king had "abdicated this protective role." Instead of ensuring grain supplies at a reasonable price, Mr. Schama notes, the government committed itself to the new modern principle of free trade: "British textiles had been let into France, robbing Norman and Flemish spinners and weavers of work." They experienced it as "some sort of conspiracy against the People."

One does see parallels. But they're not what I mean.

It was a revolution largely run by sociopaths. One, Robespierre, the "messianic schoolmaster," saw it as an opportunity for the moral instruction of the nation. Everything would be politicized, no part of the citizen's life left untouched. As man was governed by an "empire of images," in the words of a Jacobin intellectual, the new *régime* would provide new images to shape new thoughts. There would be pageants, and new names for things. They would change time itself! The first year of the new Republic was no longer 1792, it was Year One. To detach farmers from their superstitions, their Gregorian calendar and its saints' days, they would rename the months. The first month would be in the fall, named for the harvest. There would be no more weeks, just three ten-day periods each month.

So here is our parallel, our hiccup. I thought of all this this week because I've been thinking about the language and behavioral directives that have been coming at us from the social and sexual justice warriors who are renaming things and attempting to control the language in America.

There is the latest speech guide from the academy, the Inclusive Communications Task Force at Colorado State University. Don't call people American, it directs: "This erases other cultures." Don't say a person is mad or a lunatic, call him "surprising/wild" or "sad." "Eskimo," "freshman," and "illegal alien" are out. "You guys" should be replaced by "all/folks." Don't say "male" or "female"; say "man," "woman," or "gender non-binary."

In one way it's the nonsense we've all grown used to, but it should be said that there's an aspect of self-infatuation, of arrogance, in telling people they must reorder the common language to suit your ideological preferences. There is something mad in thinking you should control the names of things. Or perhaps I mean surprising/wild.

I see in it a spirit similar to that of the Terror. There is a tone of "I am your moral teacher. Because you are incapable of sensitivity, I will help you, dumb farmer. I will start with the language you speak."

An odd thing is they always insist they're doing this in the name of kindness and large-spiritedness. And, yet, have you ever met them? They're not individually kind or large-spirited. They're more like messianic schoolmasters.

Offices and schools are forced to grapple with all the new gender-neutral pronouns. Here a handy guide from a website purporting to help human resources departments in midsize businesses. It is headlined "Gender Neutral Pronouns—What They Are & How to Use Them."

> He/She—Zie, Sie, Ey, Ve, Tey, E
> Him/Her—Zim, Sie, Em, Ver, Ter, Em
> His/Her—Zir, Hir, Eir, Vis, Tem, Eir
> Himself/Herself—Zieself, Hirself, Eirself, Verself, Terself, Emself

It's wrong, when you meet a new co-worker, to ask his pronouns. (We don't say "preferred" pronouns—that "implies someone's gender is a preference"!) You don't want him wondering if you think he's transgender or nonbinary. Instead, introduce yourself in a way that summons his pronouns: "Hi, I'm Jim and my pronoun is he/him." Use "they" a lot. It's gender neutral. Suggested sentence: "I spoke to the marketing director and they said they'd get back to me."

This is grammatically incorrect but so what? Correct grammar, and the intelligibility it allows, is a small price to pay for inclusion and equality.

We are being asked to memorize all this, to change hundreds of years of grammar and usage, to accommodate the needs or demands of a group that perceives itself as beleaguered.

There's a funny but painful spoof of all this on YouTube. A seemingly friendly but dogmatic teacher of adult immigrants in English as a Second Language class introduces them to the sixty-three new pronouns. They are understandably flummoxed. An Asian woman announces she identifies as a girl and then shrinks in fear this might not be allowed. A confused Eastern European man asks the pronoun of his desk. The Central American asks if the new pronouns mean gay. "You're not learning English so you can be a bigot, are you?" the teacher demands.

And there are the office arguments about bathroom policy, which I gather are reaching some new peak. There can no longer be a men's room and a women's room, so we can have one expanded bathroom everyone can use. No, we'll have three. But there may be a stigma to using the third, so keep two bathrooms but remove all designations. But the women don't want to put on their makeup with men coming in and out. But the men don't want women walking in on them—that's a harassment suit waiting to happen!

It's all insane. All of it.

But we're moving forward, renaming the months and the sexes, reordering the language. You wonder how the people who push all this got so much power. But, then, how did Robespierre?

SCENES FROM THE CLASS STRUGGLE IN LOCKDOWN

May 14, 2020

I think there's a growing sense that we have to find a way to live with this thing, manage it the best we can, and muddle through. Covid-19 is not going away anytime soon. Summer may give us a break, late fall probably not. Vaccines are likely far off, new therapies and treatments might help a lot, but keeping things closed up tight until there are enough tests isn't a viable plan. There will never be enough tests, it was botched from the beginning, if we ever catch up it will probably be at the point tests are no longer urgently needed.

Meanwhile, we must ease up and manage. We should go forward with a new national commitment to masks, social distancing, handwashing. These simple things have proved the most valuable tools in the tool chest. We have to enter each day armored up.

At the same time we can't allow alertness to become exhaustion. We can't let an appropriate sense of caution turn into an anxiety formation. We can't become a nation of agoraphobics. We'll just have to live, carefully.

Here's something we should stop. There's a class element in the public debate. It's been there the whole time but it's getting worse, and few in public life are acting as if they're sensitive to it. Our news professionals the past three months have made plenty of room for medical and professionals warning of the illness. Good, we needed it, it was news. But journalists are not now paying an equal degree of sympathetic attention to those living the economic story, such as the Dallas woman who pushed back, opened her hair salon, and was thrown in jail by a preening judge. He wanted an apology. She said she couldn't apologize for trying to feed her family.

There is a class divide between those who are hard-line on lockdowns and those who are pushing back. We see the professionals on one side—those James Burnham called the managerial elite, and Michael Lind, in *The New Class War*, calls the overclass—and regular people on the other. The overclass are highly educated and exert outsize influence as managers and leaders of important institutions—hospitals, companies, statehouses.

The normal people aren't connected through professional or social lines to power structures, and they have regular jobs—service worker, small-business owner.

Since the pandemic began, the overclass has been in charge—scientists, doctors, political figures, consultants—calling the shots for the average people. But personally they have less skin in the game. The National Institutes of Health scientist won't lose his livelihood over what's happened. Neither will the midday anchor.

I've called this divide the protected versus the unprotected. There is an aspect of it that is not much discussed but bears on current arguments.

How you have experienced life has a lot to do with how you experience the pandemic and its strictures. I think it's fair to say citizens of red states have been pushing back harder than those of blue states.

It's not that those in red states don't think there's a pandemic. They've heard all about it! They realize it will continue, they know they may get sick themselves. But they also figure this way: Hundreds of thousands could die and the American economy taken down, which would mean millions of other casualties, economic ones. Or, hundreds of thousands could die and the American economy is damaged but still stands, in which case there will be fewer economic casualties—fewer bankruptcies and foreclosures, fewer unemployed and ruined.

They'll take the latter. It's a loss either way but one loss is worse than the other. They know the politicians and scientists can't really weigh all this on a scale with any precision because life is a messy thing that doesn't want to be quantified.

Here's a generalization based on a lifetime of experience and observation. The working-class people who are pushing back have had harder lives than those now determining their fate. They haven't had familial or economic ease. No one sent them to Yale. They often come from considerable family dysfunction. This has left them tougher or harder, you choose the word.

They're more fatalistic about life because life has taught them to be fatalistic. And they look at these scientists and reporters making their warnings about how tough it's going to be if we lift shutdowns and they don't think, "Oh, what informed, caring observers." They think, "You have no idea what tough is. You don't know what painful is." And, if you don't know, why should you have so much say?

The overclass says, "Wait three months before we're safe." They reply, "There's no such thing as safe."

Something else is true about those pushing back. They live life closer to the ground and pick up other damage. Everyone knows the societal costs in the abstract—"domestic violence," "child abuse." Here's something concrete. In Dallas this week police received a tip and found a six-year-old boy tied up by his grandmother and living in a shed. The child told police he'd been sleeping there since school ended "for this corona thing," KTVT-TV reported. According to the arrest affidavit, he was found "standing alone in a pitch-black shed in a blue storage bin with his hands tied behind his back." The grandmother and her lover were arrested on felony child-endangerment charges. The Texas Department of Family and Protective Services said calls to its abuse hotline have gone down since the lockdowns because teachers and other professionals aren't regularly seeing children.

A lot of bad things happen behind America's closed doors. The pandemic has made those doors thicker.

Meanwhile some governors are playing into every stereotype of "the overclass." On Tuesday Pennsylvania's Tom Wolf said in a press briefing that those pushing against the shutdown are cowards. Local officials who "cave in to this coronavirus" will pay a price in state funding. "These folks are choosing to desert in the face of the enemy. In the middle of a war." He said he'll pull state certificates such as liquor licenses for any businesses that open. He must have thought he sounded uncompromising, like General George Patton. He seemed more like Patton slapping the soldier. No sympathy, no respect, only judgment.

Michigan Governor Gretchen Whitmer called anti-lockdown demonstrations "racist and misogynistic." She called the entire movement "political." It was, in part—there have been plenty of Trump signs, and she's a possible Democratic vice presidential nominee. But the clamor in her state is real, and serious. People are in economic distress and worry that the foundations of their lives are being swept away. How does name-calling help? She might as well have called them "deplorables." She said the protests may only make the lockdowns last longer, which sounded less like irony than a threat.

When you are reasonable with people and show them respect, they will want to respond in kind. But when they feel those calling the shots are being disrespectful, they will push back hard and rebel even in ways that hurt them.

This is no time to make our divisions worse. The pandemic is a story not only about our health but our humanity.

BRING 'EM TO JUSTICE

January 7, 2021

How do we deal with all that happened yesterday?

We remember who we are. We are a great nation and a strong one; we have, since our beginning, been a miracle in the political history of man. We have brought much good. We are also in trouble, no point not admitting it.

We regain our confidence. We've got through trouble before. We love this place and will keep it. We have a Constitution that's gotten us this far and will get us further.

We lower the boom. No civilized country can accept or allow what we saw Wednesday with the violent assault on the U.S. Capitol. This was an attack on democracy itself. That is not just a phrase. Rule by the people relies on adherence to law and process. The assault and siege was an attempt to stop the work of democracy by halting the peaceful transfer of presidential power, our crowning glory for more than two centuries.

This was a sin against history.

When something like this happens it tends to be repeated. It is our job to make sure it is not.

And so we should come down like a hammer on all those responsible, moving with brute dispatch against members of the mob and their instigators.

On the rioters: Find them, drag them out of their basements, and bring them to justice. Use all resources, whatever it takes, with focus and speed. We have pictures of half of them; they like to pose. They larked about taking selfies and smiling unashamed smiles as one strolled out with a House podium. They were so arrogant they were quoted by name in news reports. It is our good luck they are idiots. Capitalize on that luck.

Throw the book at them. Make it a book of commentaries on the Constitution. Throw it hard.

They have shamed and embarrassed their country in the eyes of the world, which is not only a painful fact but a dangerous one. The world, and the young—all of us—need to see them pay the price.

Now to the devil and his apprentices.

As for the chief instigator, the president of the United States, he should be removed from office by the Twenty-Fifth Amendment or impeachment, whichever is faster. This, with only a week and a half to go, would be a most extraordinary action, but this has been an extraordinary time. Mike Pence is a normal American political figure; he will not have to mount a new government; he appears to be sane; he will in this brief, strange interlude do fine.

The president should be removed for reasons of justice—he urged a crowd to march on Congress, and, when it turned violent, had to be dragged into telling them, equivocally, to go home—and prudence. Mitt Romney had it exactly right: "What happened here . . . was an insurrection, incited by the president of the United States." As for prudence, Mr. Trump is a sick, bad man and therefore, as president, a dangerous one. He has grown casually bloody-minded, nattering on about force and denouncing even his own vice president as a coward for not supporting unconstitutional measures. No one seems to be certain how Mr. Trump spends his days. He doesn't bother to do his job. The White House is in meltdown. The only thing that captures his interest is the fact that he lost, which fills him with thoughts of vengeance.

Removing him would go some distance to restoring our reputation, reinforcing our standards, and clarifying constitutional boundaries for future presidents who might need it.

As for his appointees and staff, the garbage they talk to rationalize their staying is no longer acceptable to anyone. "But my career." Your career, in the great scheme of things, is nothing. "But my future in politics." Your future, even if your wildest schemes are fulfilled, is a footnote to a footnote. There are ways to be a footnote honorably. "But my kids." When they are twenty they will read the history. You want them proud of your role, not petitioning the court for a name change.

It was honorable to arrive with high hopes and idealistic commitments. It is not honorable to stay.

As for the other instigators, a side note.

True conservatives tend to have a particular understanding of the fragility of things. They understand that every human institution is, in its way, built on sand. It's all so frail. They see how thin the veil is between civilization and chaos, and understand that we have to go through every day, each in our way, trying to make the veil thicker. And so we value the things in the phrase that others use to disparage us, "law and order." Yes, always, the rule of law, and order so that the people of a great nation can move freely on the streets and do their work and pursue their lives.

To the devil's apprentices, Senators Josh Hawley and Ted Cruz. They are clever men, highly educated, well-credentialed, endlessly articulate. They see themselves as leading conservative lights, but in this drama they have proved themselves punks practicing punk politics. They are like people who know the value of nothing, who see no frailty around them, who inherited a great deal—an estate built by the work and wealth of others—and feel no responsibility for maintaining the foundation because Pop gave them a strong house, right? They are careless inheritors of a nation, an institution, a party that previous generations built at some cost.

They backed a lie and held out the chimera of some possible Trump victory that couldn't happen, and hid behind the pretense that they were just trying to be fair to all parties and investigate any suspicions of vote fraud, when what they were really doing was playing—coolly, with lawyerly sophistication—not to the base but to the sickness within the base. They should have stood up and told the truth, that democracy moves forward, that the election was imperfect as all elections are, and more so because of the pandemic rules, which need to be changed, but the fact is the voters of America chose Biden-Harris, not Trump-Pence.

Here's to you, boys. Did you see the broken glass, the crowd roaming the halls like vandals in late Rome, the staff cowering in locked closets and barricading offices? Look on your mighty works and despair.

The price they will pay is up to their states. But the reputational cost should be harsh and high.

Again, on the president: There have been leaders before who, facing imminent downfall, decide to tear everything down with them. They want to go out surrounded by flames. Hitler, at the end, wanted to blow up Germany, its buildings and bridges. His people had let him down. Now he hated them. They must suffer.

I have resisted Nazi comparisons for five years, for the most part easily. But that is like what is happening here, the same kind of spirit, as the president departs, as he angrily channel surfs in his bunker.

He is a bad man and not a stable one and he is dangerous. America is not safe in his hands.

It is not too late. Removal of the president would be the prudent move, not the wild one. Get rid of him. Now.

PSYCHOS IN THE C-SUITE

December 1, 2022

It is my impression we're making more psychopaths. I can't back this up with statistics because doctors don't write "total psycho" on the diagnosis line. Psychopathy isn't a diagnostic category and is largely viewed as part of a cluster of antisocial personality disorders. But doctors commonly use the term and it has defined characteristics. The American Psychological Association calls it a chronic disposition to disregard the rights of others. Manifestations include a tendency to exploit, to be deceitful, to disregard norms and laws, to be impulsive and reckless, and, most important, to lack guilt, remorse, and empathy.

The APA has reported that 15 percent to 25 percent of prison inmates show characteristics of psychopathology, far more than in the general adult population.

But that's where I see growth. Subtle psychopaths, the kind who don't stab you, are often intelligent, charming, and accomplished. I believe two are currently in the news. (I confine myself to the business sphere, leaving out the equally rich field of politics.)

Elizabeth Holmes was just sentenced to eleven years in federal prison for defrauding investors in her famous Theranos scam. People used to ask why she did it. By now that's clear. She did it to be important. She wanted to be admired. She wished to be thought a genius, a pioneer. She no doubt wanted money, though part of her con was to live relatively modestly—she wore the same black turtleneck and trousers most days. She wanted status, then and now, as Tom Wolfe said, the great subject of American life. And she seemed to think she deserved these things—that she *merited* them, simply by walking in. One thing you pick up as you read John Carreyrou's great reporting, in these pages and his book, is that she seemed not at all concerned with the negative effects of her actions on others. She didn't seem to care that investors lost hundreds of millions, people lost jobs, the great men she invited on her board were humiliated.

Sam Bankman-Fried's cryptocurrency-trading firm, FTX, collapsed last month. We're still in the why-did-he-do-it phase—*Was it deliberate deception? Untidy bookkeeping? Visionaries often leave the details to others!* We make mysteries where there aren't any. He had a great life while it worked! He made himself famous, rich, admired—friend of presidents and prime ministers, the darling of a major political party. To the Democrats he was the biggest thing since George Soros.

But somehow a valuation of $32 billion was, in a matter of weeks, turned into, or revealed as, nothing. FTX filed for bankruptcy on November 11, and FTX's new CEO, John Ray, said he believed gross negligence was involved and a "substantial portion" of FTX customers' assets may be "missing or stolen." Soon after, the crypto firm BlockFi filed for bankruptcy in New Jersey and Bermuda.

A peculiarity of subtle psychopaths is that, while they don't seem to feel shame, they are preoccupied with being thought of as highly moral. Ms. Holmes was simply trying to help sick people get their blood tested more easily. This was part of her origin myth—a relative's illness made her sensitive to the needs of the suffering. Mr. Bankman-Fried gave away millions and became the public face of a movement called effective altruism. He was just trying to help the less fortunate live better lives! And he was so modest about it, eschewing material things, clad in rough sandals, a thin T-shirt, shorts. Like the young Saint Francis, stripping himself naked that his robes might be sold for the poor.

I don't know if Elon Musk fits in this category. I hope he's an eccentric genius with a moral core and not a psychopath. We'll find out! It's good he's in space. His buying Twitter has excited lots of people, frightened others. If he merely changes that public square from an entity of the left to an open entity, good. We'll see how content moderation goes. But many conservatives see him as a kind of savior. Is he? Saviors by definition save others.

Does he strike you as preoccupied by the needs of other people? Evince an old-fashioned interest in the public weal? He offers to buy the site, changes his mind, tries to back out, is forced to honor his agreement, takes over. In the ensuing chaos he tweets out memes of a whore tempting a monk, to illustrate, strangely, his invitation to Donald Trump to rejoin the site. He tweets out photos of his bedside table—two life-size handgun replicas and scattered cans of Diet Coke. It looked as if a school shooter lived there.

"He stands for free speech." Mr. Bankman-Fried stood for selflessness and "responsible" regulation of crypto. Ms. Holmes stood for thinking outside the box and breaking through false limits. They all believe in something.

My fear with Mr. Musk is that if a scientific paper came out saying eating baby parts will add half a century to your life, he'd tweet, *We can grow the babies in discarded ship containers and eat them—for the squeamish, God didn't make them, I did, so there's no soul or anything.*

But again, most interesting in psychopaths is the lack of remorse. They don't like being caught—that upsets them—but they don't mind causing others harm. It's their superpower. They're not hemmed in by what limits you.

Which is a conscience. People often refer to their consciences—they say things like "My conscience is clear." It's not an unknown entity to them. But they seem to think it's something they were born with, like a sense of smell. When actually a conscience has to be formed and developed or it doesn't work.

Every major faith in the world has thoughts here. In Catholic teaching, says Father Roger Landry, Columbia University's Catholic chaplain, the traditional definition of "conscience" is "a judgment of the practical reason applying moral principles to concrete circumstances leading to the conclusion to do or not do something."

"Many people today confuse their conscience with their opinion or even with their feelings about what is the right thing to do or avoid," he said in an email. "Many think that if their intentions were good, and they desired a good outcome, then the action would be morally fine. But, as is obvious, sometimes we will feel good about doing something wrong ('I stole, but he was rich'; 'I insulted her, but she deserved it.')." A conscience must be informed "with the truth that comes from God—the Ten Commandments, the Beatitudes, corporal and spiritual works of mercy, other passages in Sacred Scripture, the moral teachings of the Church." These things "illumine our eyes so that we may see things more clearly.

"Conscience can make erroneous judgments, either because it identifies wrong principles (e.g., personal autonomy as the supreme value), or has the right principles in a disordered rank (prioritizing not hurting others' feelings over helping the person give up drugs)." But to form a conscience we have a duty "to tune into God's frequency rather than our own echo chamber, or the confused noise that can come from culture."

We need better consciences. If we got them, we'd have fewer psychopaths.

AMERICA'S UNIVERSITIES ARE SELF-DESTRUCTING

December 14, 2023

Fareed Zakaria opened his CNN show last weekend with a commentary that seemed to me a signal moment in the DEI/woke/identity-politics wars. I don't know how Mr. Zakaria would characterize his political views, but there was a quality of something building within him that finally came out. It was an earnest commentary that perhaps took some daring.

"When one thinks of America's greatest strengths, the kind of assets the world looks at with admiration and envy, America's elite universities would long have been at the top of that list," he said. "But the American public has been losing faith in these universities for good reason." He scored the three presidents who'd come under fire in the House for their "vague and indecisive answers when asked whether calling for the genocide of Jews would violate their institutions' codes of conduct." Their performance was understandable if you understand that our elite universities "have gone from being centers of excellence to institutions pushing political agendas." Those agendas, "clustered around diversity and inclusion," began in good faith, "but those good intentions have morphed into a dogmatic ideology and turned these universities into places where the pervasive goals are political and social engineering, not academic merit.

"In the humanities, hiring for new academic positions now appears to center on the race and gender of the applicant, as well as the subject matter, which needs to be about marginalized groups. A white man studying the American presidency does not have a prayer of getting tenure at a major history department in America today. . . . New subjects crop up that are really political agendas, not academic fields.

"Out of this culture of diversity has grown the collection of ideas and practices that we have now all heard of—safe spaces, trigger warnings, and microaggressions." Schools have instituted speech codes "that make it a violation of university rules to say things that some groups might find offensive. Universities advise students not to speak, act, even dress in ways that might cause offense to some minority groups." When the George Floyd protests erupted, universities publicly aligned their institutions to those protests. "In this context, it is understandable that Jewish groups would wonder: Why do safe spaces, microaggressions, and hate speech not apply to us? If universities can take positions against free speech to make some groups feel safe, why not us? Having coddled so many student groups for so long, university administrators found themselves squirming, unable to explain why certain groups (Jews, Asians) don't seem to count in these conversations."

The House testimony "was the inevitable result of decades of the politicization of universities. America's top colleges are no longer seen as bastions of excellence but partisan outfits." They should "abandon this long misadventure into politics . . . and rebuild their reputations as centers of research and learning."

This was a realistic and straightforward assessment of where the universities are and what they should do. It would be helpful if all on the sane left would drop their relative silence, rise up, and end the misadventure.

I make two points connected to Mr. Zakaria's larger statement. He emphasized the decreasing number of Americans who have confidence in our elite universities. I have been reading Edmund Wilson's 1940 classic, *To the Finland Station: A Study in the Acting and Writing of History*. It famously offers a portrait of the groundbreaking French historian Jules Michelet (1798–1874), a father of modern historiography. The whole section reads like a tribute to the idea of learning, of understanding, of telling. It is not too much to say it is a kind of paean to the idea of the university.

What a scholar Michelet was, what a searcher for truth. His early life, in Wilson's words, was "sad, poor and hard." Natural brilliance drove him to and through the academy. He received honors, tutored princesses, but he was really a historian. He longed to know the facts of the past and to understand them. Appointed to the civil service, he was put in the Record Office. He was in charge of the archives of all of France. Wilson: "No one had really explored the French archives before; the histories had mostly been written from other histories" and by hired hands. Over the coming decades Michelet would write the first serious, documented, comprehensive history of France from its beginning through the 1789 revolution.

Michelet said there came to him in the archives "the whispers of the souls who had suffered so long ago and who were smothered now in the past." His approach was rational and realistic, not romantic, though there was plenty of color and sweep in his work. The story of Joan of Arc interested him because her story was fully documented—"incontestable"—and because he saw her as the first modern hero of action, "contrary to passive Christianity."

Michelet said the historian is one who, "taking history as something more than a game, makes the effort in good faith to enter into the life of the past." He treated history as the crowded, jagged thing it is, Wilson observes, and he didn't simplify. He saw the story of France, and history in general, as complex, braided, intertwined, and driven in the end more by the masses than their leaders.

The idea of this man—a true scholar who attempts to find the honest truth—seems inapplicable to the current moment. And the reason is the three words he uses—"in good faith"—to define how the historian must act. In the DEI/woke regime, the good faith of the scholar is sacrificed to political fashion. In going all in on the regime, those who run the universities negate their own worth. Faculty and professors, administrators and department heads, lower their own standing. Because they are not now seen as people of the mind, of the intellect, but as mere operatives, enforcers. They thus give up their place of respect in the public imagination.

Regular people used to imagine what a university looks like—rows of gleaming books, learned professors, an air of honest inquiry. That isn't now a picture the public can see. Now it's something else, less impressive, less *moving*. Less important to our continuance as a people.

The elites who run our elite colleges are killing their own status. They are also lowering the esteem in which college graduates are held. Your primary job as a student is *taking in*. You read, learn, connect this event with that, apply your imagination, empathize, judge. It is a spacious act—it takes time to absorb, reflect, feel—which is why you're given four whole years to do it. But if the public senses that few are studying like independent scholars in there, not enough are absorbing the expertise of their field, that they've merely been instructed to internalize a particular worldview and parrot it back . . .

Well, if that's the case, who needs them? Is it even worth having them around in the office? The people of a country have a greater stake in all this than universities and their students understand. And the elite schools are lowering their own standing more than they know.

DEMOCRACY IS NOT YOUR PLAYTHING

May 18, 2017

This will be unpleasantly earnest, but having witnessed the atmospherics the past ten days it's what I think needs saying:

Everyone, get serious.

Democracy is not your plaything.

This is not a game.

Almost four months into his administration the president of the United States has produced a building crisis that is unprecedented in our history. The question, at bottom, is whether Donald Trump has demonstrated, in his first hundred days, that he is unfit for the presidency—wholly unsuited in terms of judgment, knowledge, mental capacity, personal stability. That epic question is then broken down into discrete and specific questions: Did he improperly attempt to interfere with an FBI criminal investigation, did his presidential campaign collude with a foreign government, etc.

But the epic question underlies all. It couldn't be more consequential and will take time to resolve. The sheer gravity of the drama will demand the best from all of us. Are we up to it?

Mr. Trump's longtime foes, especially Democrats and progressives, are in the throes of a kind of obsessive delight. Every new blunder, every suggestion of an illegality, gives them pleasure. "He'll be gone by autumn."

But he was duly and legally elected by tens of millions of Americans who had legitimate reasons to support him, who knew they were throwing the long ball, and who, polls suggest, continue to support him. They believe the press is trying to kill him. "He's new, not a politician, give him a chance." What would it do to them, what would it *say* to them, to have him brusquely removed by his enemies after so little time? Would it tell them democracy is a con, the swamp always wins, you nobodies can make your little choices but we're in control? What will that do to their faith in our institutions, in democracy itself?

These are wrenching questions.

But if Mr. Trump is truly unfit—if he has demonstrated already, so quickly, that he cannot competently perform the role, and that his drama will only get more dangerous and chaotic, how much time should pass to let him prove it? And how dangerous will the proving get?

Again, wrenching questions. So this is no time for bloodlust and delight. Because democracy is not your plaything.

The president's staffers seem to spend most of their time on the phone, leaking and seeking advantage, trying not to be named in the next White House Shake-Up story. A reliable anonymous source who gives good quote will be protected—for a while. The president spends his time tweeting his inane, bizarre messages—he's the victim of a "witch hunt"—from his bed, with his iPad. And giving speeches, as he did this week at the Coast Guard Academy: "No politician in history, and I say this with great surety, has been treated worse or more unfairly." Actually, Lincoln got secession, civil war, and a daily pounding from an abolitionist press that thought he didn't go far enough and moderates who slammed his brutalist pursuit of victory. Then someone shot him in the head. So he had his challenges.

Journalists on fire with the great story of their lives—the most bizarre presidency in U.S. history and the breaking news of its daily missteps—cheer when their scoop that could bring down a president gets more hits than the previous record holder, the scoop that could bring down the candidate.

Stop leaking, tweeting, cheering. Democracy is not your plaything.

There's a sense nobody's in charge, that there's no power center that's holding, that in Washington they're all randomly slamming into each other.

Which is not good in a crisis.

For Capitol Hill Democrats the crisis appears to be primarily a chance to showboat. Republicans are evolving, some starting to use the word "unfit" and some, as a congressman told me, "talking like they're in a shelter for abused women. 'He didn't mean to throw me down the stairs.' 'He promised not to punch me again.'"

We're chasing so many rabbits, we can't keep track—Comey, FBI, memoranda; Russia, Flynn, the Trump campaign; Lavrov, indiscretions with intelligence. It's become a blur.

But there's an emerging sense of tragedy, isn't there? Crucially needed reforms in taxing, regulation, and infrastructure—changes the country needs!—are thwarted, all momentum killed. Markets are nervous.

The world sees the U.S. political system once again as a circus. Once the circus comes to town, it consumes everything, absorbs all energy.

I asked the ambassador to the U.S. from one of our greatest allies, "What does Europe say now when America leaves the room?" You're still great, he said, but "we think you're having a nervous breakdown."

It is absurd to think the president can solve his problems by firing his staff. They are not the problem. He is the problem. They're not the A-Team, they're not the counselors you'd want, experienced and wise. They're the island of misfit toys. But they could function adequately if he could lead adequately. For months he's told friends he's about to make big changes, and doesn't. Why? Maybe because talented people on the outside don't want to enter a poisonous staff environment just for the joy of committing career suicide. So he's stuck, surrounded by people who increasingly resent him, who fear his unpredictability and pique and will surely one day begin to speak on the record.

A mystery: Why is the president never careful? He doesn't act as if he's picking his way through a minefield every day, which he is. He acts like he's gamboling through safe terrain.

Thus he indulges himself with strange claims, statements, tweets. He comports himself as if he has a buffer of deep support. He doesn't. Nationally his approval numbers are in the mid- to high 30s.

His position is not secure. And yet he gambols on, both paranoid and oblivious.

History is going to judge us by how we comported ourselves in this murky time. It will see who cared first for the country and who didn't, who kept his head and did not, who remained true and calm and played it straight.

Now there will be a special prosecutor. In the short term this buys the White House time. Here's an idea.

It would be good if top Hill Republicans went en masse to the president and said, "Stop it. Clean up your act. Shut your mouth. Do your job. Stop tweeting. Stop seething. Stop wasting time. You lost the thread and don't even know what you were elected to do anymore. Get a grip. Grow up and look at the terrain, see it for what it is. We have limited time. Every day you undercut yourself, you undercut us. More important, you keep from happening the good policy things we could have done together. If you don't grow up fast, you'll wind up abandoned and alone. Act like a president or leave the presidency."

Could it help? For a minute. But it would be constructive—not just carping, leaking, posing, cheering, and tweeting but actually trying to lead.

The president needs to be told: Democracy is not your plaything.

THE MEDIA CAN'T KEEP THEIR HEADS

June 15, 2017

What we are living through in America is not only a division but a great estrangement. It is between those who support Donald Trump and those who despise him, between left and right, between the two parties, and even to some degree between the bases of those parties and their leaders in Washington. It is between the religious and those who laugh at Your Make Believe Friend, between cultural progressives and those who wish not to have progressive ways imposed upon them. It is between the coasts and the center, between those in flyover country and those who decide what flyover will watch on television next season. It is between "I accept the court's decision" and "Bake my cake." We look down on each other, fear each other, increasingly hate each other.

Oh, to have a unifying figure, program, or party.

But we don't, nor is there any immediate prospect. So, as Ben Franklin said, we'll have to hang together or we'll surely hang separately. To hang together—to continue as a country—at the very least we have to lower the political temperature. It's on all of us more than ever to assume good faith, put our views forward with respect, even charity, and refuse to incite.

We've been failing. Here is a reason the failure is so dangerous.

In the early 1990s Roger Ailes had a talk show on the America's Talking Network and invited me to discuss a concern I'd been writing about, which was old-fashioned even then: violence on TV and in the movies. Grim and graphic images, repeated depictions of murder and beatings, are bad for our kids and our culture, I argued. Depictions of violence unknowingly encourage it.

But look, Roger said, there's comedy all over TV and I don't see people running through the streets breaking into laughter. True, I said, but the problem is that, for a confluence of reasons, our country is increasingly populated by the not fully stable. They aren't excited by wit, they're excited by violence—especially unstable young men. They don't have the built-in barriers and prohibitions that those more firmly planted in the world do. That's what makes violent images dangerous and destructive. Art is art and censorship is an admission of defeat. Good judgment and a sense of responsibility are the answer.

That's what we're doing now, exciting the unstable—not only with images but with words, and on every platform. It's all too hot and revved up. This week we had a tragedy. If we don't cool things down, we'll have more.

And was anyone surprised? Tuesday I talked with an old friend, a figure in journalism who's a pretty cool character, about the political anger all around us. He spoke of "horrible polarization." He said there's "too much hate in D.C." He mentioned "the beheading, the play in the park" and described them as "dog whistles to any nut who wants to take action."

"Someone is going to get *killed*," he said.

That was twenty hours before the shootings in Alexandria, Virginia.

The gunman did the crime, he is responsible, it's fatuous to put the blame on anyone or anything else.

But we all operate within a climate and a culture. The media climate now, in both news and entertainment, is too often of a goading, insinuating resentment, a grinding, agitating antipathy. You don't need another recitation of the events of just the past month or so. A comic posed with a gruesome bloody facsimile of President Trump's head. New York's rightly revered Shakespeare in the Park put on a *Julius Caesar* in which the assassinated leader is made to look like the president. A CNN host—amazingly, of a show on religion—sent out a tweet calling the president a "piece of s—" who is "a stain on the presidency." An MSNBC anchor wondered, on the air, whether the president wishes to "provoke" a terrorist attack for political gain. Earlier Stephen Colbert, well known as a good man, a gentleman, said of the president, in a rant, "The only thing your mouth is good for is being Vladimir Putin's c— holster." Those are but five dots in a larger, darker pointillist painting. You can think of more.

Too many in the mainstream media—not all, but too many—don't even bother to fake fairness and lack of bias anymore, which is bad: Even faked balance is better than none.

Yes, they have reasons. They find Mr. Trump to be a unique danger to the republic, an incipient fascist; they believe it is their patriotic duty to show opposition. They don't like his policies. A friend suggested recently that they hate him also because he's in their business, show business. Who is he to be president? He's not more talented. And yet as soon as his presidency is over he'll get another reality show.

And there's something else. Here I want to note the words spoken by Kathy Griffin, the holder of the severed head. In a tearful news conference she said of the president, "He broke me." She was roundly mocked for this. *Oh, the big bad president's supporters were mean to you after you held up his bloody effigy.* But she was exactly right. He *did* break her. He robbed her of her sense of restraint and limits, of her judgment. He broke her, but not in the way she thinks, and he is breaking more than her.

We have been seeing a generation of media figures cratering under the historical pressure of Donald Trump. He really is powerful.

They're losing their heads. Now would be a good time to regain them.

They have been making the whole political scene lower, grubbier. They are showing the young what otherwise estimable adults do under pressure, which is lose their equilibrium, their knowledge of themselves as public figures, as therefore examples—tone setters. They're paid a lot of money and have famous faces and get the best seat, and the big thing they're supposed to do in return is not be a slob. Not make it worse.

By indulging their and their audience's rage, they spread the rage. They celebrate themselves as brave for this. They stood up to the man, they spoke truth to power. But what courage, really, does that take? Their audiences love it. Their base loves it, their demo loves it, their bosses love it. Their numbers go up. They get a better contract. This isn't brave.

If these were only one-offs, they'd hardly be worth comment, but these things build on each other. Rage and sanctimony always spread like a virus, and become stronger with each iteration.

And it's no good, no excuse, to say Trump did it first, he lowered the tone, it's his fault. Your response to his low character is to lower your own character? He talks bad so you do? You let him destabilize you like this? You are making a testimony to his power.

So many of our media figures need at this point to be reminded: You belong to something. It's called: us.

Do your part, take it down some notches, cool it. We have responsibilities to each other.

WHERE DID THE ADULTS GO?

April 5, 2018

I want to write about something that I think is a problem in our society, that is in fact at the heart of many of our recent scandals, and yet is obscure enough that it doesn't have a name. It has to do with forgetting who you are. It has to do with refusing to be fully adult and neglecting to take on, each day, the maturity, grace, and self-discipline that are expected of adults and part of their job. That job is to pattern adulthood for those coming up, who are looking, always, for How to Do It—how to be a fully formed man, a fully grown woman.

It has to do with not being able to fully reckon with your size, not because it is small but because it is big. I see more people trembling under the weight of who they are.

Laura Ingraham got in trouble for publicly mocking one of the student gun-control activists of Parkland, Florida. She's been unjustly targeted for boycotts, but it's fair to say she was wrong in what she said, and said it because she didn't remember who she is. She is a successful and veteran media figure, host of a cable show that bears her name. As such she is a setter of the sound of our culture as it discusses politics. When you're that person, you don't smack around a seventeen-year-old, even if—maybe especially if—he is obnoxious in his presentation of his public self. He's a kid. They're not infrequently obnoxious, because they are not fully mature. He's small, you're big. There's a power imbalance.

As of this week, it is six months since the reckoning that began with the *New York Times* exposé of Harvey Weinstein. One by one they fell, men in media, often journalism, and their stories bear at least in part a general theme. They were mostly great successes, middle-aged, and so natural leaders of the young. But they treated the young as prey. They didn't respect them, in part because they didn't respect themselves. They didn't see their true size, their role, or they ignored it.

It should not be hard to act as if you are who you are, yet somehow it increasingly appears to be. There is diminished incentive for people to act like adults. Everyone wants to be cool, no one wants to be pretentious. No one wants to be grim, unhip, to be passed by in terms of style.

And our culture has always honored the young. But it has not always honored immaturity.

I have spent the past few days watching old videos of the civil rights era, the King era, and there is something unexpectedly poignant in them. When you see those involved in that momentous time, you notice: They dressed as adults, with dignity. They presented themselves with self-respect. Those who moved against segregation and racial indignity went forward in adult attire—suits, dresses, coats, ties, hats—as if adulthood were something to which to aspire. As if a claiming of just rights required a showing of gravity. Look at the pictures of Martin Luther King Jr. speaking, the pictures of those marching across the Edmund Pettus Bridge, of those in attendance that day when George Wallace stood in the schoolhouse door and then stepped aside to the force of the federal government, and suddenly the University of Alabama was integrated. Even the first students who went in, all young, acted and presented themselves as adults. Of course they won. Who could stop such people?

I miss their style and seriousness. What we're stuck with now is Mark Zuckerberg's.

Facebook's failings are now famous and so far include but are perhaps not limited to misusing, sharing, and scraping of private user data, selling space to Russian propagandists in the 2016 campaign, playing games with political content, starving journalism of ad revenues, increasing polarization, and turning eager users into the unknowing product. The signal fact of Mr. Zuckerberg is that he is supremely gifted in one area—monetizing technical expertise by marrying it to a canny sense of human weakness. Beyond that, what a shallow and banal figure. He, too, appears to have difficulties coming to terms with who he is. Perhaps he hopes to keep you, too, from coming to terms with it, by literally dressing as a child, in T-shirts, hoodies, and jeans—soft clothes, the kind five-year-olds favor. In interviews he presents an oddly blank look, as if perhaps his audiences will take blankness for innocence. As has been said here, he is like one of those hollow-eyed busts of forgotten Caesars you see in museums.

But he is no child; he is a giant bestride the age, a titan, one of the richest men not only in the world but in the history of the world. His power is awesome.

His public reputation is now damaged, and about this he is very concerned. Next week he will appear before Congress. The Onion recently headlined that he was preparing for his questioning by studying up on the private data of congressmen. The comic Albert Brooks tweeted: "I sent Mark Zuckerberg my entire medical history just to save him some time."

His current problems may have yielded a moment of promise, however. Tim Cook of Apple, in an impressive and sober interview with Recode's Kara Swisher and MSNBC's Chris Hayes, said last week something startling, almost revolutionary: "Privacy to us is a human right." This was stunning because it was the exact opposite of what Silicon Valley has been telling us since social media's inception, which is *Privacy is dead. Get over it.* Some variation on that statement has been made over and over by Silicon Valley's pioneers, and they say it blithely, cavalierly, with no apparent sense of tragedy.

Because they don't do tragedy. They do children's clothes.

Perhaps what is happening with Facebook will usher in the first serious rethinking, in terms of the law, on what has been lost and gained since social media began.

Congress next week should surprise. The public infatuation with Big Tech and Silicon Valley is over and has been over for some time. Congress should grill Mr. Zuckerberg closely on how he took what people gave him and used it. Many viewers would greatly enjoy such questioning along these lines: "Is your product, your service, one without which we can't live, like Edison's electricity? It seems to me you are a visionary, sir, and we should give you your just reward, and make you a utility!"

Mr. Zuckerberg invited Congress to regulate him. Wondering why, it has occurred to me it's because he knows Congress is too stupid to do it effectively. He buys lobbyists to buy them. He knows how craven, unserious, and insecure they are, and would have no particular respect for them. Nor would he have particular reason to.

I hope they are adults. I hope they don't showboat or yell but really probe, carefully.

More than ever, the adults have to rise to the fore and set the template for what is admirable. If we don't, those who follow us will be less admirable even than us, and those after them less admirable still. That would be a tragedy, wouldn't it?

CHAPTER 3

TRY A LITTLE TENDERNESS

Here we turn to love,
which we posit as a very good thing.

MY SUMMER WITH LEO TOLSTOY

August 31, 2023

My great memory of this summer is reading Tolstoy's *War and Peace*. In all these years I never had. In college I majored in British and American literature, so didn't have to. I expected I'd catch up with it along the way, but I didn't. For one thing it was huge, more than a thousand pages, a real commitment, and one that involved patronyms, lineages, and Russian existential gloom. Also, at some point in my forties I pretty much stopped reading fiction and was drawn almost exclusively to nonfiction—histories and biographies. From youth I had read novels hoping to find out what life is, what grown-ups do, how others experience life. Now I wanted only what happened, what did we learn, how did it all turn out.

But something got in my brain the past few months, that there were great books I hadn't read and ought to. My mind went back to something George Will wrote about William F. Buckley, that later in life he'd finally read *Moby-Dick* and told friends, *To think I might have died without having read it.*

And so in late July I picked up the Louise and Aylmer Maude translation, which I gathered isn't considered the greatest but was approved by Tolstoy himself, and finished it this week. And, well, to think I might have died without having read it.

It was stupendous. At some point I understood I hadn't made a commitment of time but entered a world. It is about *life*—parties and gossip and thwarted elopements in the night, religious faith and class differences and society, men and women and personal dreams and private shames. It is about military strategy, politics, and the nature of court life, a world that exists whether the court is that of Czar Alexander in 1812, or the White

House or a governor's office today. And of course it is about the Napoleonic wars, and Russia's triumph after Napoleon's invasion.

It begins with a whoosh: "Well, Prince, so Genoa and Lucca are now just family estates of the Buonapartes." This is Anna Pavlovna Scherer, the Perle Mesta of St. Petersburg and a favorite of the empress, at one of her grand receptions. It will be seven years before Napoleon invades her country but she had her eye on him and clocked him early: "I really believe he is Antichrist." The prince to whom she's speaking shrinks back, suggests she's excitable. "Can one be calm in times like these if one has any feeling?" she asks. "You are staying the whole evening I hope!" In the end, what she cares about is the party. So does most everyone else.

I didn't understand what good company Tolstoy is. The Russian general Pfuel, an ethnic German, is "self-confident to the point of martyrdom as only Germans are, because only Germans are self-confident on the basis of an abstract notion—science, that is, the supposed knowledge of absolute truth." A Frenchman is self-assured because he regards himself personally as irresistibly attractive. "An Englishman is self-assured, as being of the best organized state of the world." "A Russian is self-assured just because he knows nothing and does not want to know anything, since he does not believe that anything can be known."

One of Napoleon's commanders rejects better quarters and sets himself up in a peasant's hut on the field. "Marshal Davout was one of those men who purposely put themselves in most depressing conditions to have a justification for being gloomy. For the same reason they are always hard at work and in a hurry."

"Anatole, with the partiality dull-witted people have for any conclusion they have reached by their own reasoning, repeated the argument."

Tolstoy's Napoleon is a puffed-up poseur, not so much confident and bold as "intoxicated by the crimes he has committed so successfully." "His whole short corpulent figure with broad thick shoulders, and chest and stomach involuntarily protruding, had that imposing and stately appearance one sees in men of forty who live in comfort." "Only what took place within his own mind interested him. Nothing outside himself had any significance for him, because everything in the world, it seemed to him, depended entirely on his will."

A small tragedy of humanity is that "man's mind cannot grasp the causes of events in their completeness, but the desire to find those causes is implanted in man's soul." And so man, in the form of historians, makes up stories. Napoleon, at the battle of Borodino, did all he'd done in previous battles, but this time he didn't triumph. Why? Because, researchers say, he had a cold. No, Tolstoy says, that isn't it! Some historians say Moscow burned because Napoleon set it on fire for revenge. Others say the Russians lit the blaze rather than let him rule there. Nonsense, Tolstoy says: Moscow burned down because it was a city made of wood. The French soldiers who occupied it cooked and lit candles and fell asleep and stumbled about. Moscow's inhabitants had fled; there was no one to watch things and no fire department.

There are beautiful set pieces. Count Pierre, sick, starving, a prisoner of Napoleon's army, on a constant forced march without shoes, sets his entire intellect to understanding the truth of life. All he has experienced tells him "that man is created for happiness, that happiness is within him, in the satisfaction of simple human needs, and that all unhappiness arises not from privation but from superfluity." An epiphany follows: "That nothing in this world is terrible." "Life is everything. Life is God. Everything changes and moves and that movement is God. . . . To love life is to love God."

His character is transformed. Once he waited to discover good qualities in people before caring for them. Now he loved them first, "and by loving people without cause he discovered indubitable causes for loving them."

I read this in a hotel in Ireland after visiting the site of a nineteenth-century Marian apparition in the town of Knock. It was a peaceful place and felt holy. Pierre would have been comfortable there.

And so the lessons of my *War and Peace* summer.

Feeling such love for a great work did something important to me. For the first time in some years I felt freed for long periods of an affliction common to many, certainly journalists, the compulsion to reach for a device to find out what's happening, what's new. But I already knew the news. Pierre was in love with Natasha. Prince Andrei was wounded at Borodino. Princess Mary was saved by Nicholas's intervention with the serfs. That was all I had to know and it was enough, it was the real news.

Don't be afraid to visit old worlds. Man is man, wherever he is you can follow. Sometimes a thing is called a masterpiece because it is a masterpiece.

When you allow a past work of art to enter your mind and imagination you are embarked on a kind of reclamation project, a rescue mission. As you read, Nicholas and Sonya are alive, but Tolstoy himself is still alive. He isn't gone, his mind is still producing, he continues in human consciousness. You are continuing something. You should feel satisfaction in this.

THE LONELY OFFICE IS BAD FOR AMERICA

July 28, 2022

Where are we in the office wars? I think there's an armistice between the return-to-the-office side and the work-from-home forces. Perhaps hostilities will resume in the fall. Bosses are hoping the old reality will snap back as the drama of 2020–22 recedes, that people will start to feel they need to come back, or can be made to. The work-from-home people are dug in, believing they're on the winning side, that the transformation of work in America, which had been going remote for years, was simply sped up and finalized by the pandemic. In this tight job market they have the upper hand. Employers are fighting for talent: *Fire me—I'll get a better job tomorrow, and you'll get fifty hours with HR onboarding my replacement.* The balance of power will change if the slowing economy leads to layoffs and hiring freezes.

The benefits of working from home are obvious: freedom, no commute; it's easier to be there for family, the dog, the dentist appointment. Less time wasted in goofy officewide meetings. I've wondered if there is another aspect, that office life was demystified by what began in the years before the pandemic, the rise of HR complaints and accusations of bullying, bad language, and sexual misconduct. Add arguments over masks and vaccines, and maybe office life came to be seen less as a healthy culture you could be part of and more like a battlefield you wanted to avoid.

Arguments against working from home are largely intangible, and I focus on these. They are less personal, more national and societal.

I don't want to see office life in America end. The decline in office life is going to have an impact on the general atmosphere of the country. There is something demoralizing about all the empty offices, something post-greatness about them. All the almost-empty buildings in all the downtowns—it feels too much like a metaphor for decline.

My mind goes first to the young. People starting out need offices to learn a profession, to make friends, meet colleagues, find romantic partners and mates. The #MeToo movement did a lot to damage mentoring—senior employees no longer wanted to take the chance—but the end of office life would pretty much do away with it.

There will be less knowledge of the workplace, of what's going on, of the sense that you're part of a burbling ecosystem. There will be fewer deep friendships, antagonisms, real and daily relationships. Work will seem without depth, flat as a Zoom screen. Less human. Without offices you'll lose a place to escape from your home life.

My guess is the end of the office will lead to a decline in professionalism across the board. You learn things in the hall from the old veteran. You understand she's watching your progress, and you want to come through with your excellence. Without her down the hall, who will you be excellent for?

There will likely, in each company and organization, be a decline in a sense of mission. A diluting of company spirit looks to me inevitable. Spirit, mission—they come from people and are established and imparted through being together, sharing a particular space, talking to each other spontaneously and privately, encouraging and correcting.

At some point in the twentieth century, America invented big-scale office life. We were the envy of the world for it. Without it there will be less bubbling creativity, less of the chance meeting in the hall and the offhand comment that results in brains sparking off brains.

Companies may seem more communal, in a way—Zoom screens aren't explicitly hierarchical. But there will be less clarity, and less leadership. Jamie Dimon of JPMorgan Chase, who has said he wants people back in the office and experienced pushback for it, just stated in his annual report that people with ambition "cannot lead from behind a desk or in front of a screen."

It is possible working at home is changing the nature of professional ambition. A piece last month in the *Journal* by Callum Borchers cited Jonathan Johnson, CEO of Overstock.com. To foster a sense of togetherness and shared mission, he invited everyone on staff to join him for lunch every

Tuesday at the company's Midvale, Utah, headquarters. In eight months, a total of ten people attended. "Most of the time, I eat my peanut butter sandwich alone," Mr. Johnson told Mr. Borchers. "When I was 25, if I had a chance to eat my sandwich with the CEO, I'd have been there."

We're pro-ambition in this space: God gave you gifts, bring them fruitfully into the world, rise, and make things better. Then again maybe this age is making people ambitious for different things.

Here are my two greatest concerns. The first is that in my lifetime the office is where America happened each day. That's why many of our most popular TV programs were about the office, from *The Mary Tyler Moore Show* through *Mad Men*, from *ER* through *30 Rock* and *Parks and Recreation*. You can name others. Even *M*A*S*H* was about the workplace. And of course *The Office*. Without Dunder Mifflin, how would Jim have met Pam? How could the utterly ridiculous Michael Scott have entered your sympathies without your seeing him every day, and knowing him?

The primary location of daily integration in America—the coming together of all ages, religions, ethnicities, and political tendencies, all colors, classes, and conditions—has been, during the past century, the office. It is where you learn to negotiate relationships with people very different from you, where you discover what people with different experiences of life really think. You discern all this in the joke, the aside, the shared confidence, the rolled eyes. And with all this variety you manage to come together in a shared, formal mission: Get that account, sell that property, get the story, process those claims.

Daily life in America happened in the office. If it doesn't, where will America happen?

And, this being a political column, my second worry. The end of the office will contribute to polarization. Receding from office life will become another way of self-segregating. People will be exposed to less and, in their downtime, will burrow down into their sites, their groups, their online angers. Their group-driven information and facts.

I suppose what I fear is a more disembodied nation. You can see it on the TV news—the empty, echoing set where there used to be people at desks in the background, running around. You see it in big offices when you go to see an accountant or a travel agent. There is no there there.

Disembodied isn't good. This fall and winter I hope we see the buildings full and the people going in and out. I want the center of our cities to hum and thrum again.

I don't want America to look like an Edward Hopper painting. He was the great artist of American loneliness—empty streets, tables for one, everyone at the bar drinking alone. We weren't meant to be a Hopper painting. We were meant to be and work together.

A GENIUS FOR FRIENDSHIP

July 1, 2021

America is a sharply divided place. The conservative world is divided, marked by the continued estrangement of old friends. There is the divide over Donald Trump, and the connected division between those open to conspiracism and those not. There are divides between those quietly fighting over policies that will determine the Republican Party's future meaning and purpose, its reason for being, and between those who differ—polite word!—on the right moral attitude, after 1/6, toward the former president.

So let's take a look at the historian Gordon Wood's superb *Friends Divided: John Adams and Thomas Jefferson* (2017), the story of two great men whose deep friendship was sundered over politics and later repaired.

They met in Philadelphia in the Continental Congress in 1775 and invented a nation together in 1776. What allies they were, how brilliantly they worked, in spite of differences in temperament, personality, cast of mind, and background. Adams of Massachusetts was hearty, frank, abrupt. He was *ardent*, a brilliant, highly educated man who found it difficult to conceal his true thoughts. His background was plain New England. He made his own way in the world.

Jefferson of course was an aristocrat, a member of Virginia's landed gentry. He let the game come to him. Mr. Wood quotes a eulogist, who said Jefferson "kept at all times such a command over his temper that no one could discover the workings of his soul." He was serene.

Adams tended to erupt. But once past his awkwardness and shyness he was jovial and warm. Jefferson, in Mr. Wood's words, "used his affability to keep people at a distance." Their mutual friend Dr. Benjamin Rush said Adams was "a stranger to dissimulation." No one ever said that of Jefferson.

In the Continental Congress Adams found Jefferson so frank and decisive on the issue of independence "that he soon seized upon my heart." Jefferson would tell Daniel Webster that Adams in those days was a "Colossus." He was "not graceful, not elegant, not always fluent." But in debate he'd come out "with a power, both of thought and of expression which moved us from our seats."

Their friendship deepened in the late 1770s and '80s, when both were diplomats representing the new nation in Europe. Abigail Adams captivated Jefferson; she was so intelligent, well-read, and politically astute that he called her "one of the most estimable characters on earth." Abigail told Jefferson her husband had no closer friend. Jefferson was "the only person with whom my companion could associate with perfect freedom, and unreserve." When Jefferson was made minister to France and Adams to Britain, their families parted. Jefferson wrote to say it left him "in the dumps."

Jefferson later told James Madison that while Adams was vain, that was "all the ill" that could be said of him. He was a man of "rigorous honesty," "profound in his views," and "he is so amiable, that I pronounce you will love him if ever you become acquainted with him."

What blew them apart? The French Revolution. Other things too but 1789 was at the heart of it. They disagreed on what it was (a continuation of 1776, said Jefferson; a perversion of 1776, said Adams) and what it would produce (a Continent drowning in blood, said Adams, who could see a Napoleon coming; a global flowering of the spirit of liberty, thought Jefferson, who seems to have mistaken Robespierre for Paul Revere). When the Revolution's ferocity was revealed in the Terror, Adams threw it in Jefferson's face: "In France anarchy had done more mischief in one night than all the despotism of their kings had ever done in 20 or 30 years."

If it hadn't been for the Revolution, they might have gotten through the other strains in store. There were many. Adams became the second president, served one term, ran for reelection and was defeated by Vice President Jefferson in the brutal, rancorous 1800 election.

They disengaged, brooded (mostly Adams), and said bitter things in letters to others (mostly Jefferson).

What saved their friendship? Their friend Benjamin Rush, another great though insufficiently remembered Founder. He and Adams had a long correspondence. In 1809, as Jefferson's second presidential term ended, Adams teasingly asked Rush if he'd had any dreams about Jefferson. Rush had a lot of dreams and often shared them. Months later he reported he *did* have a dream, about "one of the most extraordinary events" of 1809, "the renewal of the friendship" of Adams and Jefferson. In the dream Adams wrote a short note congratulating Jefferson on his retirement.

"A Dream again!" Adams responded. "It may be Prophecy."

Rush wrote to Jefferson to soften him up. You loved Adams, he said. Of all the evils of politics, none were so great "as the dissolution of friendships."

Rush then told Adams to forget what had separated them—explanations are required of lovers, he said, "but are *never so* between divided friends."

On New Year's Day 1812, Adams sent Jefferson a friendly letter. Jefferson wrote back right away, what he later called a "rambling gossiping epistle." And so their great dialogue recommenced.

They wrote faithfully for fourteen years, 158 letters, on everything—what they were reading, who they saw, political philosophy, a thought they'd just had. At one point Adams said, "You and I ought not to die, before We have explained ourselves to each other." They did their best. Adams would bring up the French Revolution. Jefferson would dodge and share his thoughts on the religious beliefs of the Shawnee Tribe. Adams remembered their history. "I look back with rapture to those golden days" when Virginia and Massachusetts "acted together like a band of brothers."

They were writing for themselves but also, they knew, for history. They knew who they were.

And so it continued, a great pouring out, until the summer of 1826, the Jubilee summer when the entire country would celebrate the fiftieth anniversary of what had happened in Philadelphia on July 4.

Both men were near the end of their lives. Both held on for the great day. Wood reports that Jefferson woke the night of the third and asked if it was the Fourth yet. His doctor said it soon would be. Early the next morning he woke again and called for his servants. Just after noon he died.

At the same time Adams, five hundred miles to the north, lay dying. A memoir by Abigail's nephew William Cranch, chief judge of the U.S. Circuit Court of Appeals for the District of Columbia, reports that Adams awoke on the Fourth to bells ringing and cannon booming. The celebrations had begun. Asked if he knew what day it was he said yes, "It is the glorious 4th of July—God bless it—God bless you all." According to legend, just before he died at six p.m., he awoke and said, "Thomas Jefferson survives."

What drove their reconciliation? A tenderness, toward history and toward themselves. They knew what their friendship had been. They had lived through and to a significant degree driven a world-historical event, the invention of America. They had shared that moment and it had been the great moment of their lives, greater than their presidencies, greater than what followed. They had been geniuses together.

As the Fourth explodes around us we should take some inspiration from the story of an old estrangement healed. We're all trying to repair something. May you have a Benjamin Rush.

AMERICA'S MOST TUMULTUOUS HOLY WEEK

April 14, 2022

It was the Easter of epochal events. All that Holy Week history came like a barrage. It was April 1865, the Civil War. No one touched by that war ever got over it; it was the signal historical event of their lives, the greatest national trauma in U.S. history. It would claim 750,000 lives.

Everyone knew the South would fight to the end, but suddenly people wondered if it was the end. General Robert E. Lee's army was trapped and under siege in the middle of Virginia. General Ulysses S. Grant was bearing down, his army going from strength to strength.

The two exchanged letters under flag of truce. Grant to Lee: Did the general not see the "hopelessness" of his position? Lee sent a roundabout response, Grant a roundabout reply, but he was starting to see: Lee knows he is beat.

On the morning of April 9, Palm Sunday, Lee sent word: He would discuss terms of surrender. They met that afternoon in the Appomattox home of Wilmer McLean.

Lee got there first. Allen C. Guelzo, in his masterly *Robert E. Lee: A Life*, quotes a reporter from the *New York Herald* who had joined a crowd outside. He was bowled over by the bearing of the imposing Lee, in full dress uniform with "an elegant sword, sash and gauntlets."

In truth, Lee didn't know what to expect. He'd told his staff, "If I am to be General Grant's prisoner to-day, I intend to make my best appearance." His close friend General James Longstreet thought Lee's fine dress a form of "emotional armor," an attempt to conceal "profound depression," according to Ron Chernow's superb, compendious *Grant*.

Grant, who at forty-two was sixteen years Lee's junior, arrived a picture of dishevelment—slouched hat, common soldier's blouse, mud-splashed boots. He was painfully aware of how he looked and feared Lee would think him deliberately discourteous, Mr. Chernow writes. Later, historians would think he was making a political statement, but he'd simply outrun his supply lines: His dress uniform was in a trunk on a wagon somewhere.

But he projected authority. Joshua Chamberlain, hero of Gettysburg, wrote that he saw Grant trot by, "sitting his saddle with the ease of a born master. . . . He seemed greater than I had ever seen him,—a look as of another world around him."

The armies of the North and South, in blue and gray, were massed uneasily beyond the house. Neither Lee nor Grant wanted them to resume the fight. Some of Lee's officers had urged him not to surrender but to disband his army and let his men scatter to the hills and commence a guerrilla war. Lee had refused. The entire country would devolve into "lawless bands in every part," he wrote, and "a state of society would ensue from which it would take the country years to recover."

The generals sat in McLean's parlor and attempted conversation. But of course it is the surrender agreement, on whose terms they quickly settled, that will be remembered forever. Lee's army would surrender and receive parole; weapons and supplies would be turned over as captured property. Officers would be allowed to keep their personal sidearms.

Lee suggested Confederate soldiers be allowed to take home a horse or mule for "planting a spring crop," Mr. Guelzo writes. Grant agreed, and Lee was overcome with relief. Lee then asked Grant for food for his troops. They had been living for ten days on parched corn. Grant agreed again and asked how many rations were needed. "About 25,000," Lee said. Grant's commissary chief later asked, "Were such terms ever before given by a conqueror to a defeated foe?"

Grant asked his aide Ely Parker, an American Indian of the Seneca tribe, to make a fair copy of the surrender agreement. When Lee ventured, "I am glad to see one real American here," Parker memorably replied, "We are all Americans."

Grant would write in his memoirs, "What General Lee's feelings were I do not know." His own feelings, which had earlier been jubilant, were now "sad and depressed." He couldn't rejoice at the downfall of a foe that had "suffered so much for a cause, though that cause was, I believe, one of the worst for which a people ever fought, and one for which there was the least excuse."

Now the door to the parlor was opened, and Grant's officers were introduced to Lee, including "a newly minted captain, Robert Todd Lincoln, the twenty-one-year-old son of the president," Mr. Guelzo writes.

Grant and Lee shook hands; Lee stepped onto the porch and signaled his orderly for his horse. An Illinois cavalry officer, George Forsyth, remembered that every Union officer on the porch "sprang to his feet . . . every hand . . . raised in military salute."

Lee looked to the east, where his army was in its last encampment. As he turned to leave, Grant came out to the steps and saluted him by raising his hat. Lee reciprocated and rode off slowly to break the news to the men he'd commanded. Mr. Guelzo: "He spoke briefly and simply, as to a theater company after its last curtain."

They had done their duty, Lee said: "Leave the result to God. Go to your homes and resume your occupations. Obey the laws and become as good citizens as you were soldiers."

Grant had something Lee didn't have. Lee couldn't act under instructions of his government because it had effectively collapsed when Richmond fell. Events had moved too quickly for Grant to receive specific instruction from Washington, but he knew the president's mind. In the last year of the war he and Lincoln had become good friends, and in their conversations Grant had been struck by the president's "generous and kindly spirit toward the Southern people" and the absence of any "revengeful disposition."

Days before the surrender Lincoln had visited Grant's headquarters at City Point, Virginia. The president spent a day at a field hospital, where in "a tender spirit of reconciliation" he "shook hands with wounded confederates," in Mr. Chernow's words. A Northern colonel who described Lincoln as "the ugliest man I ever put my eyes on," with an "expression of plebeian vulgarity in his face," spoke with him and found "a very honest and kindly man" who was "highly intellectual."

The mercy shown at Appomattox is a kind of golden moment in American history, but history's barrage didn't stop. America exploded with excitement at the end of the war, and all Washington was lit with lights, flags, bunting.

On Good Friday, April 14, Lincoln met with his son Robert to hear of what he saw at Appomattox, and then with his cabinet, including General Grant, where he happily backed up Grant's generosity. Grant, he said, had operated fully within his wishes.

Lincoln was assassinated that night, died Saturday morning, and for a long time the next day would be called "black Easter."

But what is the meaning of Appomattox? What explains the wisdom and mercy shown? How does a nation do that, produce it?

As you see these past weeks, I have been back to my history books. You learn a lot that way, not only about the country and the world and "man," but even yourself. Would you have let your enemy go home in dignity, with the horses and guns? And not bring the law down on their heads? And the answer—what does that tell you about you?

THINK LIKE AN ARTIST

April 12, 2018

Speaker Paul Ryan's announced departure, and the unprecedented number of congressional Republicans choosing not to run this November, has me thinking, again, of where the GOP is.

Its primary problem is that it doesn't know what it stands for. It doesn't know what it is. It is philosophically and ideologically riven, almost shattered, and the one piece that still coheres, represented in the House by the Freedom Caucus, is least reflective of the broader base, and the country.

Senators and representatives still have not reckoned with the shock of 2016. They're repeating what's been said and following an old playbook. They remind me of what Talleyrand is supposed to have said of the Bourbons, that they had learned nothing and forgotten nothing. Some know an old order has been swept away, but what will replace it is not fully formed, so they're not placing bets.

It isn't all about Donald Trump. Mr. Trump came from the chaos, he didn't cause it. He just makes it worse each day by adding his own special incoherence. The party's intellectual disarray both preceded and produced him. He happened after twenty years of carelessness and the rise of the enraged intersectional left. He was the magic pony who was *not* like the other Republicans. But he can't capitalize on this moment—*he can't help what is formless to find form*—because he's not a serious man.

Republicans will have to figure it out on their own. After they lose the House, they will have time!

Here's what they should do: They should start to think not like economists but like artists.

Often when I speak, people ask, at the end, about Ronald Reagan. I often say what I've written, that a key to understanding him was that he saw himself in the first forty years of his life—the years in which you become yourself—as an artist. As a young man he wrote short stories, drew, was attracted to plays, acted in college, went into radio, and then became a professional actor. He came to maturity in Hollywood, a town of craftsmen and artists. He fully identified with them.

The thing about artists is that they try to see the real shape of things. They don't get lost in factoids and facets of problems, they try to see the thing whole. They try to capture reality. They're creative, intuitive; they make leaps, study human nature. It has been said that a great leader has more in common with an artist than with an economist, and it's true.

The GOP needs artists.

If an artist of Reagan's era were looking around America in 2018, what would she or he see? Marvels, miracles, and wonders. A church the other day noted on Twitter that all of us now download data from a cloud onto tablets, like Moses.

But think what would startle the artist unhappily. She or he would see broad swaths of the American middle and working class addicted and lethargic. A Reagan-era person would think, But they are the backbone! They built our roads, fought our wars, worked on the assembly line making the cars that transformed our lives. Reagan came from those people but a step below. His father wasn't a factory worker with a union card but a somewhat itinerant shoe store salesman who was an alcoholic. Reagan's family was not fully stable, but America was, and he could rise within it. He became not only a union member but a union president.

He believed passionately in—he defended and advanced—the free-market system. Freedom, he well knew, yields unequal results. Jack Warner had a grand estate and the day workers at Warner Bros. shared a walk-up on Sunset and slept in shifts. But that's no cause for bitterness as long as the day workers know they can rise—and the system *allows* them to rise.

Today something seems stuck. Free trade, global trade—yes! But you can't invest totally in abstractions because life is not abstract. People need jobs, men especially, and a nation that can't make things is too vulnerable in the world.

A Reagan-era artist would be shocked by our culture, by its knuckle-dragging nihilism. She or he might note that constantly telling our children that the deck is stacked against them, even when that message is sent in the name of equality and justice, may leave them demoralized, driven not by hunger and joy but by unearned bitterness. The artist would be shocked that "the American dream" has been transmuted from something aspirational and lighted by an egalitarian spirit to something weirdly flat—a house, a car, possessions—and weirdly abstract.

In foreign affairs the people of that era knew why they were anticommunist. It was not only a totalitarian system that was by its nature brutal and a killer of freedoms; it was expansionist (even to Cuba, ninety miles from our shore) and atheistic. Wherever it went the churches were closed and the religious hounded. So: Resist communism! But you go forward accepting the simple tragedy at the heart of life, that this isn't Heaven, it's earth, and man is crooked timber. You wouldn't invade the Warsaw Pact countries even though they've been turned into outposts of evil.

What might an artist see as the major need and priority for America right now? *Keep this country together.* Keep it up and operating and give it a sense of peace with itself. The crisis is our increasing disunity, and the thinning of a shared sense of the national dream.

What should the GOP be thinking of now, as a political priority? Be more human. Show a felt sympathy for those trying to rise. Align yourself with the culturally disheartened. Be on the side—as the party was since its inception, and now seems not to be—of Main Street, not Wall Street. Take a new and honest look at impediments to the American dream. Figure out why people don't feel so upwardly mobile anymore. Be for populism without the bitterness, and patriotism minus mindless nationalism. And show respect—more than that, protectiveness—toward the economic system that made America rich. Republicans always think everyone favors economic freedom. But an entire generation has risen since the crash of 2008. They've never even heard a defense of capitalism. They've never heard anyone speak well of it.

And think twice about your saviors. Those NeverTrump folks trying to take back authority within the party—having apparently decided recently not to start a third one—are the very people who made the current mess. They bought into open-borders ideology. They cooked up Iraq. They allied with big donors. They invented Sarah Palin, who as much as anyone ushered in the age of Trump. They detached the Republican Party from the people.

Republicans now should be trying to see the big picture and the true shape of things.

Don't see your country through your ideological imaginings, see your country as it is. Recognize reality, respect it, and see what you can do with it, with an eye to trying to persuade. Bend when needed. Define and then defend essential principles. Say what you stand for and stand there proudly. See and speak clearly. Be an artist, not an economist.

OUT OF THE ASHES OF NOTRE DAME

April 18, 2019

A few small observations on the fire at Notre Dame:

It's interesting where your thoughts go as you watch a disaster, live. Friends kept saying they were feeling some of what they'd felt on 9/11, and this was true of me, too. No one thought it the same, but the flames and smoke evoked similar feelings of grief and loss, and a sense of portent, especially for Catholics, who saw in the destruction a metaphor for—or a judgment of—the state of their church.

Monday evening I found myself remembering an intuition I'd had hours after the World Trade Center had fallen. TV was showing people who'd escaped the towers, covered in dust and ash, and trekking north. As I watched I thought, Some desperate person among them is escaping his life right now, planning his disappearance. He knows the scale of the disaster because he just walked out of it. He knows if he doesn't check in for the next few days he'll be counted among the dead. He'll soon be at a motel in Queens, then on a plane somewhere. He will tell his story decades from now. He'll tell us he came back once and visited the memorial on which his name is etched.

I had an intuition too as I watched Notre Dame burn. Somebody wonderful is watching at this moment and having a conversion experience. He will write of how the size of his grief, of his shock, opened a door in his head and heart and his faith came rushing in. We'll hear about that in coming years, and maybe from more than one person. Destroyed beauty is a spiritual event.

I also thought of the great speech in Tom Stoppard's play *Arcadia*, on all that was lost when the great library of Alexandria, Egypt, burned down. Thomasina, a young would-be scholar, says, "Can you bear it? All the lost plays of the Athenians! Two hundred at least by Aeschylus, Sophocles, Euripides—thousands of poems—Aristotle's own library! . . . How can we sleep for grief?"

Septimus, her tutor, answers: "By counting our stock." Don't grieve, he says: "We shed as we pick up, like travelers who must carry everything in their arms, and what we let fall will be picked up by those behind. The procession is very long and life is very short. We die on the march. . . . The missing plays of Sophocles will turn up piece by piece, or be written again in another language. . . . Mathematical discoveries glimpsed and lost to view will have their time again. You do not suppose, my lady, that if all Archimedes had been hiding in the great library of Alexandria, we would be at a loss for a corkscrew?"

Those were Monday's thoughts. Then, Tuesday morning, the shocking good news: The fire was out, the structure still standing, the great things still there—the radiant cross, the altar, the Pietà, the pews, the relics saved.

It felt like a miracle, didn't it? I think it was.

I called my friend Liz Lev, the art historian and author of the magisterial *How Catholic Art Saved the Faith*, and asked her why the fire at Notre Dame was such a grave and emotional experience for so many people of varying faiths, not only Catholics seeing a cathedral burn.

Her answer was arresting. She said, essentially, that we are all of us more loyal to the idea of beauty than we mean to be or know we are.

"When the fire came, for two days it made us let our guard down," she said. "It showed us that beauty still *affects* people, that they know they are custodians of it. We still need to believe in the beautiful."

We sense the achievement and sacrifice that went to its making. "It's not the tower in Dubai, which is clever, or even the Eiffel Tower"; it is "a spiritual home." "There's something in the building. You get the sense of centuries of people who worked on it who'd never live to see it done."

The architecture is part of the story. "The Gothic is a paradox. It's so lacey, it looks so fragile—the fire coming out of the lacey spire—and yet underneath you see this powerful, solid, domed facade." This reverberates with the myths and stories we love: "The hero is strong and yet the hero is vulnerable, frail. This moves us."

What does the art inside the cathedral, the statues and paintings, mean? Ms. Lev noted that Notre Dame's story is the structure more than the art inside it, and in this it is the antithesis of the Sistine Chapel, where it's all about the interior art and decorations. But the cathedral is also about "the scattered world of France's relationship with its faith." During the French Revolution the exterior statues were beheaded, glass broken, the church defaced: "They put the Goddess of Reason in there."

"Notre Dame is a shoe box of memories" of all the times French Catholics "have gone running from the church." Tuesday morning Ms. Lev learned that the statue of *Notre-Dame de Paris* had survived. "The statue is the same age of the consecration of the Cathedral. It's not splendid, it's nice, it's pretty, but it stands by the altar and you always see people saying the rosary beneath it." Sometimes, they are shooed away. "But she's still there. That's very beautiful."

A great deal was made about the saving of the relics—Christ's crown of thorns, a nail from his crucifixion, a tunic worn by Saint Louis. I asked Ms. Lev about the Catholic preoccupation with the physicality of things. Why do we pay such attention to relics in general?

"The Christian faith is rooted in the physical world. It is incarnational." God took bodily form. "Christian art is Christian art because Jesus became a baby who could be held, and passed from person to person—'You hold him now.' His passion is a wet, messy, brutal affair on his body—he bled, he sweated. . . . We are creatures of flesh. He became flesh so we could become even more beautiful, even more like unto God."

The Sistine Chapel could never have been produced in any other culture, she said. "Only Christians can do it because only Christians celebrate the body, the bodily resurrection."

But why do we honor the relics of saints—a hand, a heart, a knuckle? Why do parents keep a lock of a child's hair? she asked. "The saints were here. They are not ectoplasms. Their souls are in Heaven but they were here."

Finally, people sense that Notre Dame is most powerful and central in its moments of suffering. "The Greek word for church is *ecclesia*—people gathered together. On the night of the fire it was gathering people together," literally, around the church and around the world. "Notre Dame is most potent gathering them in suffering."

This reminded me of something someone said on social media after the spire fell: Maybe the old church burst into flames so we would look at it and really see what it is.

We did.

ON UVALDE: LET NOT OUR HEARTS GROW NUMB

May 26, 2022

We're out of words because we're out of thoughts because we said them all and spent them all after Columbine and Sandy Hook and Parkland. The shock was the lack of shock you felt when you heard. You indicted yourself: My heart has gotten cold. No, it hasn't, but the past quarter century it's been numbing up.

We underestimate how demoralizing these shootings are. They hurt our faith in America (why can't we *handle* this?) and the future (what will it be like if this continues?). And there's the new part of the story that is disturbing, this sense—we've had it before—that the police reliably come to the scene but they've got some kind of process or procedure that keeps them from fighting their way to the actual site of the shooting. Parents were massing at the school in Uvalde and screaming, "Go in, go in!" They themselves would have, and were stopped. This aspect of the story is not yet clear but you can't see the emerging videos and not think something went very wrong.

I love cops because I love John Wayne. (Joan Didion: "John Wayne was supposed to give the orders. 'Let's ride,' he said . . . 'Forward ho.'") If they're not John Wayne—commonsensical, gutsy, quick, able to size up the situation—I don't think I love them. I don't think anyone else does either.

Conservatives were quick to criticize President Joe Biden in his speech the night of the shootings, saying he didn't "bring us together" and "heal the nation's wounds." But what exactly could he say, could any president say at this point, that will bring us together and heal the wounds? They were faulting him for the impossible. There isn't a bag of magic-secret speechwriter words, you don't pull them from a hat and throw the fairy dust on the listeners.

A fair criticism is that Biden's speech invoked a problem without offering a way through it.

He seems to have concluded that the right response to the moment was to enact what he felt was the audience's rage and indignation. So he emoted, demanding answers to questions. "When in God's name are we going to stand up to the gun lobby?" He is "sick and tired." "Where in God's name is our backbone?"

But, if I can generalize, it is people of the left whose immediate response to the shootings at Uvalde was indignation and rage. Everyone else was feeling something different, depression and anxiety. Because they don't see a way out, and they're worried, and don't have an illusion that attacking someone will make it better. When the president enacts what one part of the spectrum feels, which he also no doubt feels, everyone else will feel to some degree excluded.

He doesn't mean to be divisive, he just doesn't get the other guys anymore. "We have to do more." What, exactly? What people needed that night was a kindly grown-up plan from someone above the fray. And many would have wanted to be enleagued—marshal the troops unleashed by the trauma, let them be part of something that might make things better.

Normal Americans are not fixated on policy and don't know the exact state of play on gun law. What bill might help?

Democrats should stop using the manipulative, scare-quote phrase "gun lobby." The gun lobby is a ghost of itself, done in by internal and external forces, and everyone in Washington knows this. The problem is Americans who feel immediate aversion to gun control because they don't trust those who would do the controlling. The challenge isn't "standing up," it's persuading.

Pretty much everyone knows we have too many guns in America, more than we have people. Everyone knows too many are in sick hands. If deeper background checks and a longer waiting period after purchase might help, move. I don't have to be persuaded, I'm for them, not because I think they will solve the problem but they might get us an inch on the yardstick, and that's something. I suspect a lot of people would see it like that.

But persuade, do the work. It is always the hard work of politics. And yes, move to ban assault weapons again, those sinister killing-machine weapons of war. We have about 400 million guns in America, do we have to keep adding these? Why don't we just stop?

Governor Greg Abbott of Texas said Wednesday that Texas has a long history of letting eighteen-year-olds have long guns. That is true. He also said cops, after the shooting, told him they're seeing a crisis in mental health in young people. That's true too, it's all around them, all around all of us.

But Mr. Abbott should listen to himself more closely. It is one thing to let an eighteen-year-old have a rifle to shoot rattlers in 1962. It is another thing to allow an eighteen-year-old *in the middle of a mental-health crisis* to buy an AR-15, which is what the sick Uvalde shooter bought on his eighteenth birthday.

Republicans, you are saying every day that there's a mental-health crisis and, at the same time, that we shouldn't stop putting long guns in the hands of young men. Policies must evolve to meet circumstances. You must evolve.

I end here.

I continue in a kind of puzzled awe at my friends who proceed through life without faith, who get up and go forward without it. How do you do that? I tell the young, I have been alive for some years and this is the only true thing, that there is a God and he is good and you are here to know him, love him, and show your feeling through your work and how you live. That it is the whole mysterious point. And the ridiculous story, the father, the virgin, the husband, the baby—it is all, amazingly, true, and the only true thing.

Uvalde is a town of about sixteen thousand people and if I'm counting right about forty places of Christian worship, all kinds, Evangelical, Catholic, Mainline. I keep seeing the pictures—a group of four middle-aged men in jeans and T-shirts, standing near the school, arms around each other, heads bent in prayer. And the women sitting on the curb near the school and sobbing, a minister in a gray suit hunched down with them, ministering. And the local Catholic church the night of the shootings—people came that night, especially women, because they know it's the only true thing and they know they are loved, regarded, part of something, not alone. I don't mean here "the consolations of faith," I mean the truth is its own support. Consolation is not why you believe but is a fact of belief and helps all who have it live in the world and withstand it. I am so glad for the people of Uvalde this weekend for only one thing, that so many have that.

Once I saw a painting—outsider art, crude, acrylic, made by some madman. There were splayed bodies on the floor and ghost-blots above each body, which depicted their souls. They were shooting upward—happy, free of gravity, rising toward Heaven.

Haven't seen the painting since, think of it a lot, want it to be how it was in that classroom, all the children's souls free and going home.

CORONAVIRUS WILL CHANGE EVERYTHING

February 27, 2020

Punditry 101: You have to write about what you're thinking about. All week I was taking notes knowing I'd be looking at South Carolina, Super Tuesday, and this week's debate. I was thinking about polls and Representative Jim Clyburn's beautiful remarks in support of Joe Biden. They were beautiful because they were highly personal without being manipulative, which is now something unusual in American politics. But my mind kept tugging in another direction. So I'll write what I'm thinking, and it may be ragged but here goes.

I've got a feeling the coronavirus is going to be bad, that it will have a big impact on America, more than we imagine, and therefore on its politics. As this is written the virus is reported in forty-eight nations. We've had a first case with no known source, in California, and the state is monitoring some 8,400 others for possible infection. Canada has thirteen cases. There have been outbreaks in Iran and Italy; in Rome, there are worries because Pope Francis had to cancel a Lenten Mass due to what the Vatican called a "slight indisposition."

There's a lot we don't know but much we do. We know coronavirus is highly communicable, that person-to-person transmission is easy and quick. Most who get it won't even know they're sick—it feels like a cold and passes. But about 20 percent will get really sick. Among them, mortality rates are low but higher than for the flu, and higher still among those who are older or impaired.

So it's serious: A lot of people will be exposed and a significant number will be endangered. And of course there's no vaccine.

We live in a global world. Everybody's going everyplace all the time.

Nothing is contained in the ways it used to be. It seems to me impossible that there are not people walking along the streets in the U.S. who have it, don't know it, and are spreading it.

Americans are focusing. If you go to Amazon.com you famously find that the best face masks are no longer available, but check out the prices of hand sanitizers. They appear to be going up rather sharply! (Note to Jeff Bezos: If this turns bad and people start making accusations about price gouging and profiteers, public sentiment won't just be hard on manufacturers, they'll blame you, too. Whatever downward pressure can be applied, do it now, not later.)

If you limit your focus to politics, to 2020 election outcomes, you find yourself thinking this: Maybe it's all being decided not in the next few weeks of primaries but in the next few weeks of the virus, how much it spreads, and how it's handled.

If coronavirus becomes a formally recognized worldwide pandemic, and if it hits America hard, it is going to change a lot—the national mood, our cultural habits, the economy.

The president has been buoyed the past few years by a kind of inflatable raft of good economic news and strengths. The Dow Jones Industrial Average gained 8,581 points from the day he took office to the beginning of 2020. Unemployment is down so far it feels like full employment. Minority employment is up, incomes are up. He's running for reelection based on these things.

But the stock market is being hit hard by virus-driven concerns. If those fears continue—and there's no reason to believe they won't—the gains the president has enjoyed could be wiped out.

As for unemployment, if the virus spreads people will begin to self-distance. If they shop less, if they stay home more and eat out less, and begin to cancel personal gatherings—if big professional events and annual meetings are also canceled—it will carry a whole world of bad implications.

What I notice as a traveler in America is the number of people who make a traveler's life easier, and whose jobs *depend* on heavy travel—all the people in the airport shops and concessions, and those who work in hotels. There's the woman whose small flower shop makes the arrangements for the donor reception at the community forum, and the floor managers, waiters, and waitresses at the charity fundraising dinner. Local contractors, drivers, the sound man who wires the dinner speaker. Many are part of the gig economy, operating without the protections of contracts and unions. If the virus spreads and events are canceled, they will be out of jobs. And that's just one sliver of American life.

In a public-health crisis the role of government is key. The question will be—the question *is*—are the president and his administration up to it?

Our scientists and health professionals are. (I think people see Tony Fauci of the National Institutes of Health as the de facto president on this.) Is Donald Trump? Or has he finally met a problem he can't talk his way out of? I have written in the past questioning whether he can lead and reassure the nation in a time of crisis. We are about to find out.

Leaders in crises function as many things. They are primary givers of information, so they have to know the facts. They have to be serious: They must master the data. Are they managerially competent? Most of all, are they trustworthy and credible?

Or do people get the sense they're spinning, finagling, covering up failures, and shading the facts?

It is in crisis that you see the difference between showmanship and leadership.

Early signs are not encouraging. The messaging early this week was childish—*everything's under control, everything's fine.* The president's news conference Wednesday night was not reassuring. Stock market down? "I think the financial markets are very upset when they look at the Democratic candidates standing on that stage making fools out of themselves." "The risk to the American people remains very low." "Whatever happens we're totally prepared." "There's no reason to panic, because we have done so good."

It was inadequate to the task.

I wonder if the president understands what jeopardy he's in, how delicate even strong economies are, and how provisional good fortune is.

If you want to talk about what could make a progressive win the presidency it couldn't be a better constellation than this: an epidemic, an economic downturn, a broad sense of public anxiety, and an incumbent looking small. Especially if the progressive says he stands for one big thing, health care for everyone.

The only candidate to bring up the threat of coronavirus at the Democratic debate the other night was Mike Bloomberg. This is how you'll know the fact of the virus has hit the political class: Politicians will stop doing what they've done for more than two centuries. They'll stop shaking hands. It will be a new world of waving, nodding emphatically, and patting your chest with your hand.

Some kinda world, when the pols can't even gladhand.

It would be extremely reassuring if a temporary armistice were called in the cold war between the White House and congressional Democrats. If the virus is as serious as I think it is, no one will look back kindly on *anyone* who acted small.

OUR NEW CORONAVIRUS REALITY

March 19, 2020

This is a quick piece that touches on where we are, where we may be going, and an attitude for the journey.

The screenwriter Lawrence Kasdan once said the films of Akira Kurosawa were distinguished by this dynamic: The villain has arrived while the hero is evolving. That's what made his films great, the sense of an implacable bad guy encountering a good guy who is alive, capable of changing, who is in fact changing because of and in order to beat back the bad guy and make things safe again.

The villain is here in the form of an illness. A lot of the heroes of this story are evolving every day into something we'll look back on months and years hence and say, "Wow, *LOOK* what she did." "What guts that guy showed." People are going to pull from themselves things they didn't know were there.

But now, at this stage in the drama, most of the heroes are also busy *absorbing*. We are all of us every day trying to absorb the new reality, give it time to settle into us.

It's all so big. We are discovering the illness as we experience it. We don't know its secrets, how long it lasts, how long its incubation, whether you can be reinfected.

As for the economics: As the month began we had functional full employment. By the time it ends we will not, not at all. In the past week layoffs and let-gos have left state unemployment claim websites crashing. This is not "normal job disruption"; it is a cascade. The Treasury secretary reportedly said unemployment could hit 20 percent.

The market gains of the Trump era have been all but wiped out. Investors are selling *gold*. From this paper's editorial Thursday: "American commerce is shutting down right before our eyes with no end in sight." Flights are empty, hotel occupancy plummeting.

Where we are is a hard, bad place, stupid to deny it. Where we're going looks to be difficult.

It's a cliché to say we haven't ever had a moment like this (a plague, a crash), but it's true. As for New York, twice in twenty years we've been ground zero, epicenter of a national tragedy. Will we get through it? Of course. But it will change things, and change us, as 9/11 did.

The governmental instinct is right: Stabilize things while everyone's absorbing. Whatever is done will probably be an unholy mess. Do it anyway and see where we are. In the long term the best plan—the only plan—is one that attempts to keep people in their jobs. Meaning, look to European models on how to help businesses hold on to their people.

There are a million warnings out there on a million serious things. We add one: Everything works—and will continue to work—as long as we have electricity. It's what keeps the lights on, the oxygen flowing, the information going. Everything is the grid, the grid, the grid.

A general attitude for difficult times? Trust in God first and always. Talk to him.

Every time America's in trouble I remember Adam Smith's words. He wrote there's "a great deal of ruin in a nation." Especially a very great and prosperous one with a brilliant system and a creative citizenry.

And see this: We are surrounded by nobility.

Mike Luckovich had a cartoon this week of the Marines raising the flag on Iwo Jima. Only it wasn't Marines—it was a doctor, a scientist, a nurse, and a first responder anchoring Old Glory in this rocky soil. It was hokey and beautiful and true. In the next few weeks and months they'll get us through and we should thank them every way possible. That includes everyone who can't work at home, the cops and firefighters, the garbagemen and truckers, the people who stock the shelves and man the counters. A nurse told me Thursday that hospital workers all see themselves as sitting ducks for infection, but no one's calling in sick. A journalist friend said maybe this will reorder things and we'll start to pay people according to their real importance to society.

A personal note. As this is written I have been sick for two weeks. It started when I was finishing a column on Representative Jim Clyburn—I got a chill and noticed that the notepad on my knee was warm. The next night more chills, took my temperature: 101.

It may be a poorly timed ordinary virus, one of the dozen floating out there in America on any given day, or it may be the more interesting one.

But everything you've heard about the difficulty of getting a test is true. "There are none," said my doctor. If he sent me to the emergency room, I wouldn't meet their criteria. You can have every symptom, but if you answer no to two questions, you won't be tested. The questions are: Have you traveled internationally? Have you recently been in contact with someone who tested positive?

My doctor instructed me to go home, self-quarantine, rest, report back. A week in, the fever spiked up, the headaches were joined by a cough and sore throat, and I called the local government number, where they couldn't connect me to anyone who could help.

Everyone I dealt with was compassionate and overwhelmed. On day 12 my doctor got word of testing available at an urgent-care storefront on First Avenue. When I called I was connected to a woman on Long Island. She asked for my symptoms. Then: Have you traveled internationally? Have you had recent contact with anyone who's infected? No and no. She said, "It's OK, I'm sure they'll accept you." I could hear her click "send." She paused and said, "I'm so sorry, you don't meet the criteria." By now we had made friends, and she was disappointed for me.

I said, "Let's think together. Twelve days sick, almost all the symptoms, part of an endangered demographic." Silence. Then a brainstorm. I realized at this point I *have* known a person who's tested positive; I saw him recently; no one has defined "recently" because no one knows the incubation period.

I said, Can we do the interview again? She said, "Let's go."

She went down the list of questions, and when she said "Have you recently had contact . . . ," I said, "I believe I can say yes."

She said, "All *right*." Silence as I listened to her tap the keys. "You meet the criteria," she said, with the sweetest excitement.

And so Tuesday night I made my way (mask, gloves) to the urgent-care storefront, where I was tested by a garrulous physician's assistant who said his office, or New York health authorities, or the Centers for Disease Control and Prevention, will get back to me with results in three to seven days. (Yikes.)

At this point I suppose it's academic. If it's positive, they'll tell me to continue what I'm doing. But if hospitalized it would save time—presumably I wouldn't have to be tested again. Also it would be nice to think I wasn't just home sick, I was home developing fighting Irish antibodies spoiling for a fight.

I just want to get out and help in some way. Isn't that what you feel? We all just want to pitch in.

WHAT COMES AFTER THE CORONAVIRUS STORM?

April 23, 2020

"We are not all in the same boat. We are all in the same storm." That succinct summation came from the writer Damian Barr this week, on Twitter. He's right. Some are in yachts, he said, and "some have just the one oar."

Some will sail through, health and profession intact, some will lose one or both. Some of us get to feel we're part of a substantial crew. Some of us feel we're rowing alone.

We can move forward through this crisis experiencing our country as an embittered navy waiting to fight it out on shore. Or, alternatively, as a big crazy armada with millions of people throwing and catching millions of lifelines. Which I suppose is how a lot of us tend to see this country of deep inequalities and glittering possibilities. The latter attitude will be more helpful in getting us through, and, as Lincoln observed, attitude is everything.

We have all been told to be protective of each other—stay inside—and supportive. What is the nightly seven p.m. pot-banging but a spontaneous show of appreciation? But I am thinking of how much we actually just like each other, admire each other, and barely notice. *The Washington Post* Thursday had a story about the release of forty-three men who lived for a month inside the Braskem petrochemical plant in Marcus Hook, Pennsylvania. Braskem produces raw material for face masks and surgical gowns. The workers figured if they got sick it would slow production, so they volunteered to stay in the plant, work long shifts, and sleep on air mattresses. They called it a "live-in." At one point their families held a drive-by parade so they could wave through the windows.

"We were just happy to be able to help," Joe Boyce, a shift supervisor, told *Post* reporter Meagan Flynn. When the story broke they were flooded with grateful messages from doctors and nurses. "But we want to thank them for what they did and are continuing to do," Mr. Boyce said.

'Murcans, baby.

The subject now is state and regional reopening. We're fighting about who's going too early or moving too slowly, which is understandable, as we're all interrelated and germs don't respect state lines. But we should try hard not to be harsh in our judgments as each state chooses different times and ways. Opening is what we all want to do. We've got to be patient with each other, observe with good faith, hope lifting restrictions succeeds, but be quick to point out—and admit—danger areas and failures.

No one is certain what to do. Everyone's acting on insufficient information. No plan will come without cost. A lot will become clear in retrospect. The bias should be opening as soon as possible as safely as possible. Don't sacrifice safe for soon. Have a solid, sophisticated, mature definition of "safe."

What will hurt us is secretly rooting for disaster for those who don't share our priors. Everyone is trying to live. It doesn't help to be a Northerner who looks down on Southerners, or a securely employed professional in a national corporation who has no clue what it means when a small-town business crashes. People who can work remotely probably don't feel the same urgency to reopen as those who must be physically present, in retail and at diner counters.

Conspiracy nuts who think the virus was a hoax to bring down Donald Trump will always be with us. So will grim leftists who take pleasure in every death of a guy who called the threat overblown.

But we're too quick to categorize, and ungenerous in our categorizations. Everybody isn't only the role they're playing at the moment. They came from something—us. Hate that young guy with the smart mouth in the MAGA hat honking his horn in the demonstration in Austin? In another time and a different struggle he was Audie Murphy, the guy who jumps on the tank, starts shooting, and saves every life in the convoy. Hate the scientist in rimless glasses repeating his endless warnings on TV? He's Jonas Salk, who saved our children. We're all more than what we seem. We all require some give.

We forget we are fifty different states with different histories, ways, and attitudes, even different cultures. New Jersey isn't Wyoming; Colorado isn't

Arkansas. This used to be called "regional differences." We can't tamp them all down, and we don't want to. So people will do things at different speeds in different ways. The thing is to watch, judge fairly, and move to countermand what proves dangerous.

Governors who make the decision should stay aware of the creativity of their citizens. A guy who runs a hair salon shared with me this week his reopening plans: face shields for stylists, masks for workers and clients, gloves, gun thermometers for everyone who walks in. "Robes will be individually wrapped and there will be someone wiping door handles." He knows business starts only when people feel safe. He's going to see they do for their sake and his.

I close with the psychology of the current moment. The novelty has worn off. We've absorbed the pandemic and the lockdown. We've marveled, complained, and made jokes. Now we're absorbing that the America we stepped away from when we walked into the house isn't the America into which we'll re-emerge. It may look the same, but it will be different. A lot more people will need a lot more help. Twenty-six million people are unemployed. And little normalities of life that we once took for granted—some will be gone.

Two examples: Retail has been struggling for years—small stores closing from rising costs and Amazon. Now more will close, or rather never reopen, which will change Main Street and how we experience our towns. The big department stores too are in peril. JCPenney's stores closed in March, its 85,000 employees furloughed. Since the pandemic, CNBC reports, its market capitalization has fallen 75 percent, and it just skipped an interest payment on its debt. Macy's is struggling after closing its stores and furloughing 130,000 workers. A ratings agency downgraded its debt to junk status. Nordstrom and Kohl's too are having a hard time.

We've all been thinking we can't wait to get back to movies, concerts, and shows. Now we're admitting it may be awhile before we want to sit with a thousand strangers. Warner Bros. just pulled one of its big summer movies from release in theaters; it will go straight to video-on-demand. Universal did the same. It reflects the lockdown but also what ScreenCrush.com called "audience's increasing dependence on (and perhaps even preference for) home viewing." John Stankey, COO of AT&T, which owns Warner Bros., said in an earnings call that the studio is "rethinking the theatrical model."

Imagine an America without the expression "Let's go to the movies."

Anyway, what a resettling of things. What effort, patience, and creativity it will take to reach safe haven. How much easier it will be if we see ourselves not as separate ships but members of the most brilliant, raucous, and varied armada.

GIVE THANKS FOR TAYLOR SWIFT

November 22, 2023

Right about now *Time* magazine would be choosing its Person of the Year, a designation I've followed from childhood because its choices tend to vary from sound to interesting. Also I almost always know who it'll choose and enjoy finding out I'm right. Here I tell you who it will be and must be or I will be displeased.

Miss Taylor Swift is the Person of the Year. She is the best thing that has happened in America in all of 2023. This fact makes her a suitably international choice because, when something good happens in America, boy, is it worldwide news.

I have been following her famous Eras Tour since it began in March. Everyone says she's huge, she's fabulous, but really it's bigger than that. What she did this year is some kind of epic American story.

Here are the reasons she should be Person of the Year:

Her tour has broken attendance and income records across the country. She has transformed the economy of every city she visits. The U.S. Travel Association reported this fall that what her concertgoers spend in and around each venue "is on par with the Super Bowl, but this time it happened on 53 different nights in 20 different locations over the course of five months." Downtowns across the country—uniquely battered by the pandemic and the riots and demonstrations of 2020—are, while she is there, brought to life, with an influx of visitors and a local small-business boom. Wherever she went it was like the past three years didn't happen.

When Ms. Swift played Los Angeles for six sold-out nights in August she brought a reported $320 million local windfall with her, including 3,300 jobs and a $160 million increase in local earnings. From Straits Research this month: Ms. Swift's tour is "an economic phenomenon that is totally altering the rules of entertainment economics."

When the tour became a bona fide record-breaker Ms. Swift gave everyone in her crew—everyone, the dressers, the guys who move the sets, the sound techs and backup dancers—a combined $55 million in bonuses. The truck drivers received a reported $100,000 each.

Bloomberg Economics reports that U.S. gross domestic product went up an estimated $4.3 billion as a result of her first fifty-three concerts.

The tour made her a billionaire, according to *Forbes* the first musician ever to make that rank solely based on her songs and performances.

When Ms. Swift made a film of the ongoing tour she reinvented how such things are financed and marketed, upending previous models, and when the film opened, on October 13, it became the most successful concert film in history.

Foreign leaders have begged her to come. One said, "Thailand is back on track to be fully democratic after you had to cancel last time due to the coup."

All of this is phenomenal, groundbreaking, but it's just economics. Ms. Swift brings joy. Over the summer I was fascinated by what became familiar, people posting on social media what was going on in the backs of the stadiums as Ms. Swift sang. It was thousands of fathers and daughters dancing. When she played in downtown Seattle in July, the stomping was so heavy and the stadium shook so hard it registered on a seismometer as equal to a magnitude 2.3 earthquake.

People meaning to compliment her ask if she's Elvis or the Beatles, but it is the wrong question. Taylor Swift is her own category.

Here I wish to attest personally to the quality of her art but, honey, I'm not the demo, I'm *Porgy and Bess*, the American Songbook, and Joni Mitchell. She writes pleasing tunes with pointed lyrics. They're sometimes jaunty, sometimes blue, and famously have a particular resonance for teenage girls and young women. She has said she sees herself primarily as a storyteller. They're her stories and those of her audience—breakups, small triumphs, betrayals, mistakes. Her special bond with her audience is that for seventeen years, more than a generation, they've been going through life together, experiencing it and talking it through. It's a relationship.

Nine years ago, in an interview with CBS's Gayle King, Ms. Swift coolly self-assessed. "My life doesn't gravitate towards being edgy, sexy, or cool. I just naturally am not any of those things." Pressed for what she is, she said, "I'm imaginative, I'm smart, and I'm hardworking." She was only twenty-four but all that seems perfectly correct. She's focused, ambitious, loves to perform, loves to be cheered, loves to strut. Great careers are all effort. She works herself like a rented mule.

In *The Atlantic*, the writer Spencer Kornhaber captured her opening show. Over more than three hours she played an amazing forty-four songs in Glendale, Arizona. "Somehow seeing her up close made her seem more superhuman." She has "the stamina of a ram." She was fearless and inventive. "At one point she induced gasps by seeming to dive *into* the stage and then swim to the other side, as if it were a pond."

Friends, this is some kind of epic American thing that is happening, something on the order of great tales and myths. Over the past few months as I've thought about and read of Ms. Swift my mind kept going back to phrases that are . . . absurd as comparisons. And yet. "When John Henry was a little baby . . ." And a beautiful lyric I saw years ago that stayed with me. "Black-eyed peas asks cornbread / 'What makes you so strong?' / Cornbread says, 'I come from / Where Joe Louis was born.'"

There is just something so mightily American in Taylor Swift's great year.

Am I getting carried away? Oh, yes, I am. And yet I think, isn't it great that somebody's shown such excellence that you get carried away?

We end with her recent purported famous romance with football star Travis Kelce of the Kansas City Chiefs. Is it real, everyone asks. Who knows? Maybe they don't know. I don't understand the argument that they've come together for publicity. That's the one thing she doesn't need more of and could hardly get more of. As for Mr. Kelce, as J. R. Moehringer noted this week in the *Journal*, his mug is all over, too. Whatever it is, they owe no stranger an answer.

But here are reasons people would like it to be real. Because it makes life feel more magical—the prince meets the princess. Because it's sweet. Because if it's real then not everything is media management, which is the thing that deep down we always fear. Because it's fun. Marilyn and Joltin' Joe made America more fun, more a romantic place where anything can happen and glamour is real. Also if it's real it adds to the sum total of love in the world, literally increases its quantity, and the love enters the air and the world breathes it in and, for a moment, becomes: better.

Onward to further greatness, Taylor Swift. Onward, Travis Kelce. Win the Super Bowl this year, make an impossible catch, jump a man's height to snatch the ball from the air with ten seconds to go, score the winning touchdown, hold the ball up to your girl in the stands as the stadium roars and the confetti rains down.

Leave 100 billion memories. Remind everyone: It's good to be alive.

Because it is.

CHAPTER 4

ON AMERICA

What is it that keeps our hearts turning home?

WHAT'S BECOME OF THE AMERICAN DREAM?

April 6, 2017

I want to think aloud about the American dream. People have been saying for a while that it's dead. It's not, but it needs strengthening. We should start by saying what it means, which is something we've gotten mixed up about. I know its definition because I grew up in the heart of it and remember how people had long understood it. The American dream is the belief, held by generation after generation since our beginning and reanimated over the decades by waves of immigrants, that here you can start from anywhere and become anything. In America you can rise to the heights no matter where and in what circumstances you began. You can go from the bottom to the top.

Behind the dream was another belief: America was uniquely free, egalitarian, and arranged so as to welcome talent. Lincoln was elected president in part because his supporters brought lengths of crude split rails to the Republican National Convention in Chicago in 1860. They held the rails high and paraded them in a floor demonstration to tell everyone, This guy was nothing but a frontier rail splitter, a laborer, a backwoods nobody. Now he will be president. What a country. What a dream.

This distinguished America from old Europe, from which it had kicked away. There titles, families, and inherited wealth dictated standing: If you had them, you'd always be at the top. If you didn't, you'd always be at the bottom. That static system bred resentment. We would have a dynamic one that bred hope.

You can give a dozen examples, and perhaps you are one, of Americans who turned a brilliant system into a lived-out triumph. Thomas Edison, the seventh child of modest folk in Michigan and half-deaf to boot, filled the greatest cities in the world with electric light. Barbara Stanwyck was from working-class Brooklyn. Her mother died, her father skipped town, and she was raised by relatives and foster parents. She went on to a half-century career as a magnetic actress of stage and screen; in 1944 she was the highest-paid woman in America. Jonas Salk was a hero of my childhood. His parents were Jewish immigrants from Poland who settled in East Harlem—again, working-class nobodies. Naturally young Jonas, an American, scoped out the facts of his time and place and thought, I'll be a great lawyer. His mother is reported to have said no, a doctor. He went on to cure polio. We used to talk about him at the public school when we waited in line for the vaccine.

In America so many paths were offered! But then a big nation that is a great one literally has a lot of paths.

The American dream was about aspiration and the possibility that, with dedication and focus, it could be fulfilled. But the American dream was *not* about material things—houses, cars, a guarantee of future increase. That's the construction we put on it now. It's wrong. A big house could be the product of the dream, if that's what you wanted, but the house itself was not the dream. You could, acting on your vision of the dream, read, learn, hold a modest job, and rent a home, but at town council meetings you could stand, lead with wisdom and knowledge, and become a figure of local respect. Maybe the respect was your dream.

Stanwyck became rich, Salk revered. Both realized the dream.

How did we get the definition mixed up?

I think part of the answer is Grandpa. He'd sit on the front stoop in Levittown in the 1950s. A sunny day, the kids are tripping by, there's a tree in the yard and bikes on the street and a car in the front. He was born in Sicily or Dubrovnik, he came here with one change of clothes tied in a cloth and slung on his back, he didn't even speak English, and now look—his grandkids with the bikes. "This is the American dream," he says. And the kids, listening, looked around, saw the houses and the car, and thought, He means the American dream is things. By inference, the healthier and more enduring the dream, the bigger the houses get, the more expensive the cars. (They went on to become sociologists and journalists.)

But that of course is not what Grandpa meant. He meant, *I started with nothing and this place let me and mine rise.* The American dream was not only about materialism, but material things could be, and often were, its fruits.

The American dream was never fully realized, not by a long shot, and we all know this. The original sin of America, slavery, meant some of the earliest Americans were brutally excluded from it. The dream is best understood as a continuing project requiring constant repair and expansion, with an eye to removing barriers and roadblocks for all.

Many reasons are put forward in the argument over whether the American dream is over (no) or ailing (yes) or was always divisive (no—dreams keep nations together). We see income inequality, as the wealthy prosper while the middle class grinds away and the working class slips away. There is a widening distance, literally, between the rich and the poor. Once the richest man in town lived nearby, on the nicest street on the right side of the tracks. Now he's decamped to a loft in SoHo. "The big sort" has become sociocultural apartheid. It's globalization, it's the decline in the power of private-sector unions and the brakes they applied.

What ails the dream is a worthy debate. I'd include this: The dream requires adults who can launch kids sturdily into Dream-land.

When kids have one or two parents who are functioning, reliable, affectionate—who will stand in line for the charter-school lottery, who will fill out the forms, who will see that the football uniform gets washed and is folded on the stairs in the morning—there's a good chance they'll be OK. If you come from that now, it's like being born on third base and being *able* to hit a triple. You'll be able to pursue the dream.

But I see kids who don't have that person, who are from families or arrangements that didn't cohere, who have no one to stand in line for them or get them up in the morning. What I see more and more in America is damaged or absent parents. We all know what's said in this part—drugs, family breakup. Poor parenting is not a new story in human history, and has never been new in America. But insufficient parents used to be able to tell their kids to go out, go play in America, go play in its culture. And the old aspirational culture, the one of the American dream, could counter a lot. Now we have stressed kids operating within a nihilistic popular culture that can harm them. So these kids have nothing—not the example of a functioning family and not the comfort of a culture into which they can safely escape.

This is not a failure of policy but a failure of love. And it's hard to change national policy on a problem like that.

A CONTINUING MIRACLE

July 3, 2019

I'm not really big on purple mountain majesties. I'd love America if it were a hole in the ground, though yes, it's beautiful. I don't love it only because it's "an idea," as we all say now. That strikes me as a little bloodless. Baseball didn't come from an idea, it came from *us*—a long cool game punctuated by moments of high excellence and utter heartbreak, a team sport in which each player operates on his own. The great movie about America's pastime isn't called *Field of Ideas*, it's called *Field of Dreams*. And the scene that makes every grown-up weep is when the dark-haired young catcher steps out of the cornfield and walks toward Kevin Costner, who suddenly realizes, That's my father.

He asks if they can play catch, and they do, into the night.

The great question comes from the father: "Is this Heaven?" The great answer: "It's Iowa."

Which gets me closer to my feelings on patriotism. We are a people that has experienced something epic together. We were given this brilliant, beautiful thing, this new arrangement, a political invention based on the astounding assumption that we are all equal, that where you start doesn't dictate where you wind up. We've kept it going, father to son, mother to daughter, down the generations, inspired by the excellence, and in spite of the heartbreak. Whatever was happening, depression or war, we held high the meaning and forged forward. We've respected and protected the Constitution.

And in the forging through and the holding high we've created a history, traditions, a way of existing together.

We've been doing this for 243 years now, since the first Fourth of July, and in spite of all the changes that have swept the world.

It's all a miracle. I love America because it's where the miracle is.

In celebration of that miracle, three books that touch on the why, how, and what of loving America.

Start with E. B. White on why. America should be loved, tenderly, for a large and obvious reason: because it is a democracy. In July 1943, at the height of World War II, he tried to define what that means.

"Democracy is the recurrent suspicion that more than half of the people are right more than half of the time," he wrote in *The New Yorker*. "It is the feeling of privacy in the voting booths, the feeling of communion in the libraries, the feeling of vitality everywhere. Democracy is a letter to the editor. Democracy is the score at the beginning of the ninth. It is an idea which hasn't been disproved yet, a song the words of which have not gone bad."

That's from the recent book *On Democracy* by E. B. White. In the introduction Jon Meacham notes that Franklin D. Roosevelt loved White's short essay "The Meaning of Democracy." One of his speechwriters, the playwright Robert E. Sherwood, said FDR read it aloud at gatherings, in his unplaceably patrician accent, often adding a homey coda at the end: "Them's my sentiments exactly."

There's a lot of sweetness in this collection.

Here's an argument on *how* to love America:

There was a young man in 1838, an aspiring politician almost too shy to admit his ambition to himself or others, who gave a talk to a Midwestern youth group. It was a speech about public policy, but it showed a delicate appreciation of psychology, of how people feel about what's happening around them.

America's Founders—"the patriots of '76," he called them—were now all gone, James Madison having died nineteen months before.

In their absence Americans felt lost. Those men *stood* for this country, they modeled what it was in their behavior. Admiration for them had united the country. Now, without them, people felt on their own. First principles were being forgotten, mob rule was rising. In Mississippi, they were hanging gamblers even though gambling was legal. "Next, negroes, suspected of conspiring to raise an insurrection, were caught up and hanged in all parts of the State; then, white men supposed to be leagued with the negroes; and, finally, strangers from neighboring States, going thither on business."

It was madness, and it threatened the republic. If people come to understand "their rights to be secure in their persons and property" were now at the mercy of "the caprice of the mob," their affiliation with the American government will be destroyed.

The answer? Transfer reverence for the Founders to reverence for the laws they devised. "Let reverence for the laws . . . become the political religion of the Nation." Let all agree that to violate the law "is to trample on the blood of his father."

Unjust laws should be replaced as soon as possible; the citizenry has the means. "Still while they continue in force, for the sake of example, they should be religiously observed." But only "reverence for the constitution and laws" will preserve our political institutions and retain "the attachment of the people" now that the founding generation has "gone to rest."

You have already guessed the speaker was Abraham Lincoln, then only twenty-eight. It is from his address to the Young Men's Lyceum of Springfield, Illinois, and it is a small part of a stupendous compilation of the best things said by and to Americans called *What So Proudly We Hail,* edited by Amy and Leon Kass and Diana Schaub. Its diverse contributors include Philip Roth, Ben Franklin, Willa Cather, and W.E.B. Du Bois.

My friend Joel, an America-loving New York intellectual, gave me the book as a gift. He opens it every night at random and always finds something valuable. Now so do I.

As I read I thought of those who today oppose illegal immigration. They are often accused of small and parochial motivations. But I believe at the heart of their opposition is a delicate understanding that when the rule of law collapses, as it does daily on the southern border, everything else can collapse. Many things are more delicate than we think, and those most inclined to see that delicacy are most dependent on responsible leaders who will keep the laws of the nation strong and operable.

Here, quickly, on *what* you love when you love America.

A few years ago the historian David McCullough was asked to be commencement speaker at the 200th anniversary of Ohio University. In researching the school's background and the area's history, he came upon a rich trove of stories of the largely unknown Americans who in 1788 went to the Northwest Territory and settled "the Ohio."

The Pioneers is about the remarkable New Englanders who insisted from the beginning that there would be absolute freedom of religion, that there would be a major emphasis on public education, and that slavery would be against the law.

It is an inspiring story, harrowing, too. They suffered and caused some suffering, too. And yet, Mr. McCullough notes, historians would see that the ordinance that allowed the pioneers into Ohio "was designed to guarantee what would one day be known as the American way of life."

To read it is to feel wonder at all the sacrifice that went to the making of: us. And our continuing miracle.

ON KEEPING OUR COMPOSURE

April 26, 2018

Spring came to New York this week after a month of gloomy cold and drizzle. The sun was out. Monday afternoon just before dusk there was a bird outside my window, all by itself and singing so loudly—*byeet-byeet-*chur-chur-chur. Over and over as if it had just discovered its voice. I was emailing with a friend, your basic hard-bitten journalist, and told him what I was hearing—it sounded like the beginning of the world. He wrote back not with irony but with the information that a band of baby rabbits had just taken over his garden and were out there hopping and bopping: "They are so excited to be on earth." This struck me as the most important news of the day.

My bird sang on a few minutes and then flew away, but it made me think, for the first time in years, of William Carlos Williams of 9 Ridge Road in Rutherford, New Jersey, and his famous poem from his 1923 collection, *Spring and All:*

so much depends
upon

a red wheel
barrow

glazed with rain
water

beside the white
chickens

No one is sure what it means, though a poem doesn't have to mean. To me it's about how so much depends on reality—on what *is*, on the suddenly seen tenderness of what is, and how it can catch you unaware.

So now to what I've been thinking about, which is a question: What is required of us at this point in history? What is required of those of us who aren't making history but observing it, watching with concern or alarm? There's a sense now of not getting the news but listening for what shoe just dropped.

Thursday morning there was the president's latest unhingement, in a phone interview on *Fox & Friends*. He was agitated; he spoke of witch hunts, monsters, fakes, phonies, and killers. They are "trying to destroy" his doctor, who withdrew his nomination as secretary of veterans affairs. James Comey is "a leaker and he is a liar." "There is no collusion with me and the Russians." "Fake news CNN actually gave the questions to the debate." "They have a witch hunt against the president of the United States." "It is a horrible thing that is going on, a horrible thing. Yet I have accomplished, with all of this going on, more than any president in the first year in our history. And everybody—even the enemies and haters admit that." He's disappointed in his Justice Department. The "corruption at the top of the FBI, it's a disgrace." Michael Cohen represented him "with this crazy Stormy Daniels deal." "But I'm not involved, and I'm not involved—I've been told I'm not involved." He gets along with Kanye West. "I get along with a lot of people, frankly." "CBS and NBC, ABC—they're all fake news." They tried to suppress the Trump vote, so that his supporters on Election Day would say, "So let's go to a movie, darling, and we'll come home and watch Donald lose." "Let me tell you the nuclear war would have happened if you had weak people." "I don't watch NBC anymore; they're as bad as CNN. I don't—by the way, I made them a fortune with *The Apprentice*."

You could call the interview far-ranging or scattered, you could call it typically colorful or really nuts, but you couldn't hear it without feeling more disquiet and unease. And that was just Thursday's installment of *As the Trump Turns*.

So what is required of us at this roiling time? What are some behavioral rules for the road? The political turbulence we're experiencing isn't going to go away, and what's important at such a time is to absorb the daily shocks, think long-term, speak your mind, share your heart, and do your best.

Beyond that, I think the great requirement of this moment, in the second year of the Trump era, is, Don't lose your composure. Don't let it rob you of your peace. Maintain your poise. Don't let the history around you destabilize you. Don't become sour. Keep on your game, maintain your own standards.

There are people on television who level the gravest charges against the administration. But they don't look sad, they have a look of cackling glee. History isn't unfolding for your amusement. If it's such a tragedy, you could now and then look stricken.

It would be good for people to dig deep. Everything in our national political life is in flux. Don't just oppose. Take time to look at why you stand where you stand. Why are you a Democrat? What truths, goals, realities of that party deserve your loyalty? Republicans, the same.

And we should stick to our knitting. Help your country in every way you can within your ken. National figures come and go, but local realities sink in and spread; families fail or flourish. We are a great nation and an earnest people. We forget this, especially in cynical times, but we are.

Many of our political figures are not enjoying their spring.

Republicans on the Hill are bracing for a blue wave. Some have gotten out of the way, some have hunkered down.

Mr. Trump is their problem. Whatever magic he has is not transferable. The base continues to shift under their feet.

Democrats, too, are antsy. Their party continues to split, and they don't know where the safe area is between the rising left and its demands, and the old Clintonian moderation and its rewards.

What is required of Republican politicians who wish to survive?

To succeed in a dramatic era, a politician needs a combination of caution and imagination. Caution—a knowledge of human nature, an understanding of coalitions, and an admission that history laughs. Imagination—the ability to ascertain the lay of the land and smoke out possibilities, even find room for compromise, knowing that history sometimes bows. This involves the ability to make distinctions. Being imaginative doesn't mean being unrealistic, and caution isn't cowardice. To be imaginative is to be open and intuitive as—yes—an artist, not like some gerbil munching on numbers with little pink hands.

You can't allow yourself to be reduced to just repeating things that were revolutionary forty or fifty years ago but no longer seem fully pertinent to the country we're in, or its circumstances.

You have to be sensitive to cultural vibrations. Republican politicians treat social issues as something to be spoken of now and then, mostly when the public brings them up—in part because such issues divide, in part because they don't know how to speak of them. They're not philosopher kings. But a politician with a sense of how people are thinking would observe that when the conversation turns to marriage and family formation, the best commercial for both in the past decade was the recent celebration of the life of Barbara Bush. A marriage of seventy-three years, the idea of marriage as both love affair and partnership, was burnished and made new for everyone who passed a screen. What was being celebrated was the pleasure and sacrifice that go into building something that endures.

And you have to know what time it is. Life moves, things change. So much depends on reality, on what *is*. All of politics does.

WISDOM OF A NON-IDIOT BILLIONAIRE

May 10, 2018

An occasional preoccupation in this space is that young people have no particular loyalty to or affection for free-market capitalism, the economic system that made America a great thing in history and a magnet for the world. There are two reasons. One is that in their short lives they've witnessed and experienced only capitalism's scandals—the 2008 crash, inequality. The other is that they've never heard capitalism defended—not in K through college, not in our entertainment culture. When you don't especially admire something you feel no inclination to protect it, which will have serious political implications down the road.

We should all make the case for capitalism, especially our idiot billionaires and especially those in Silicon Valley. Some, by which I mean Mark Zuckerberg in particular, act as if America is special mostly because it provided a stage for their fabulousness, otherwise not so much. During a hearing last month Senator Dan Sullivan referred to Mr. Zuckerberg's dorm-room invention and said, "Only in America, would you agree with that?" Mr. Zuckerberg seemed taken aback and mumbled around. "You're supposed to answer 'yes' to this question," Mr. Sullivan explained.

But let's get to a non-idiot billionaire. Ken Langone, eighty-two, investor, philanthropist, and founder of Home Depot, has written an autobiography that actually conveys the excitement of business—of starting an enterprise that creates a job that creates a family, of the joy of the deal and the place of imagination in the making of a career. Its hokey and ebullient name is *I Love Capitalism!*, which I think makes his stand clear.

Why did he write it? I asked him by phone. He wanted to show gratitude, to inspire the young—"If I can make it, everyone can!"—and he wanted young voters to understand that socialism is not the way. "In 2016 I saw Bernie Sanders and the kids around him. I thought, This is the Antichrist! We have the greatest engine in the world." The wealthy have an absolute obligation to help others: "Where would we be if people didn't share their wealth? I got thirty-eight kids on Bucknell scholarships. They're all colors of the rainbow; some are poor kids, rough around the edges. It's capitalism!" He famously funds NYU/Langone Medical Center.

He worries about the future of economic freedom and sees the selfishness of some of the successful as an impediment. "Are there people who are greedy, who do nothing for anyone? Yes." They should feel shame. If the system goes down they'll be part of the reason. "But don't throw the baby out with the bath water!"

Can capitalism win the future? "Yes, but we have to be more emphatic and forthright about what it is and its benefits. A rising tide *does* lift boats."

Home Depot has changed lives. "We have four hundred thousand people who work there, and we've never once paid anybody minimum wage." Three thousand employees "came to work for us fresh out of high school, didn't go to college, pushing carts in the parking lot. All three thousand are multimillionaires. Salary, stock, a stock savings plan."

Mr. Langone came up in the middle of the twentieth century—the golden age of American capitalism. Does his example still pertain to the twenty-first? Yes, he says emphatically: "The future is rich in opportunity." To see it, *look* for it. For instance, "Look, people are living longer. They're living more vibrant lives, more productive. This is an opportunity to accommodate the needs of older people. Better products, cheaper prices—help them get what they need!"

Mr. Langone grew up on blue-collar Long Island, New York. Neither parent finished high school. His father was a plumber who was poor at business; his mother worked in the school cafeteria.

They lived paycheck to paycheck. He was a lousy student but he had one big thing going for him: "I loved making money." He got his first job at eleven and often worked two at a time—paperboy, butcher-shop boy, caddie, lawn work, Bohack grocery clerk. He didn't mind: "I wanted to be rich."

He got into Bucknell University when the registrar saw something in him despite his grades. He scraped through, enjoyed economics class. His mother prayed every day to Saint Anthony, patron saint of lost things, that he'd find good sense and self-discipline. He met a beautiful Long Island girl named Elaine, they married; he looked for work on Wall Street, found some after struggling, and went to New York University at night for a business degree from what's now called the Langone Program.

By the spring of 1965 he was not yet thirty and earning $100,000 a year in commissions alone. He loved mergers and acquisitions. For his first initial public offering, he nailed down Ross Perot and EDS. By his midthirties he was Mr. Perot's banker and quite full of himself. Naturally his business soon wobbled, almost cratered, and righting the ship took years.

Then came Home Depot. You'll have to read the book to hear the story. Ross Perot decided not to invest.

Mr. Langone's book is not only helpful, it's fun. He doesn't offer rules for living but you can discern some between the lines.

1. Take your religious faith seriously. His Catholicism gave him safe harbor in storms and left him "sensitive to the plight and needs of others."

2. Marry for the long run. He and Elaine have been wed sixty-three years. When things were good she cheered him on; when they weren't she let him know "she would always be there for me—win, lose or draw."

3. You teach values by living them. Don't say—do. People absorb eloquent action.

4. "Pray at the feet of hard work." Be ravenous in reading about your field, whichever you wind up in and for however long.

5. Money solves the problems money can solve. Don't ask more of it, and don't be ashamed of wanting it. "A kid once said to me, 'Money doesn't buy everything.' I said, 'Well, kid, I was poor, and I can tell you right now poverty doesn't do a very good job either.'"

6. Stay excited. Don't be sated.

7. Admit the reality around you, then change it. When Mr. Langone couldn't get an entry-level job at Goldman Sachs, Kidder Peabody, or

White Weld, an executive took him aside: "Let me tell you the lay of the land. We have Jewish firms for Jewish kids and we have WASP firms for WASP kids. The Irish we make clerks, and put them on the floor of the stock exchange, and Italian kids like you we put in the back office." When Mr. Langone began to succeed, he started to hire—and brought in the sons of cops who went to St. John's. This contributed to "the democratization of Wall Street."

8. When you're successful you'll put noses out of joint, even among colleagues who benefit from your work. Be careful about jealousy but in the end roll with it, it's human nature. When you "piss off the old guard," become the old guard—and help the clever rise.

9. "There's no defeat except in giving up." You're going to fail. So what? Keep going, something will work.

Billionaire tech gods should read it, emulate it, and start celebrating the system that made them mighty.

"WHICH WAY TO POINTE DU HOC?"

May 23, 2019

A friend trying to help me work through a problem once told me that the story of life is competition: Everyone's trying to beat everyone else, and I should give more weight to this fact. There's some truth in what he said, yet I thought his comment contained more autobiography than wisdom: He was the most competitive person I'd ever known, and he usually won. I lean toward the idea a lot of us are running our own races, trying to rise to the occasion and beat some past and limited conception of ourselves by doing something great. The paradox is that you're running your own race alongside others running theirs, and in the same direction. You're doing something great together.

This holiday weekend I find myself reflecting again on the boys who seized back the continent of Europe, and the boys and girls now graduating college and trying to figure out what history asks of them.

The week after next marks the seventy-fifth anniversary of the Normandy invasion. People will be thinking of D-Day and seeing old clips of the speechifying that marked its anniversaries. I will think of two things. One is what most impressed Ronald Reagan. He spoke at the fortieth anniversary, on June 6, 1984, at the U.S. Ranger Monument, and seated in the front rows as he spoke were the boys of Pointe du Hoc.

"Forty summers have passed since the battle that you fought here," he told them. "You were young the day you took those cliffs; some of you were hardly more than boys." Many were old now and some wept to remember what they had done, almost as if they were seeing their feat clearly for the first time.

Reagan spoke with each of them afterward, and what moved him most wasn't all the ceremonies. It was that a bunch of young U.S. Army Rangers had, the day before, reenacted the taking of the cliffs, up there with ropes and daggers, climbing—and one of the old Rangers who'd been there on D-Day and taken those cliffs forty years before got so excited he jumped in and climbed along with the twenty-year-olds.

"He made it to the top with those kids," Reagan later told me. "Boy, that was something." His eyes were still gleaming. *Doesn't matter your age, if you really want to do it you can do it.*

A second thing I think of: My friend John Whitehead once told me, in describing that day, of a moment when, as a U.S. Navy ensign, he was piloting his packed landing craft toward Dog Red sector on Omaha Beach. They'd cast off in darkness, and when dawn broke they saw they were in the middle of a magnificent armada. Nearby some light British craft had gone down. Suddenly a landing craft came close by, and an Englishman called out: "I say, fellows, which way to Pointe du Hoc?"

Jaunty, as if he were saying, "Which way to the cricket match?"

On John's ship they pointed to the right. "Very good," said the Englishman, who touched his cap and sped on.

John remembered the moment with an air of "Life is haphazard, a mess, and you're in the middle of a great endeavor and it's haphazard, a mess. But you maintain your composure, keep your spirit. You yell to the Yank, 'Which way to Pointe du Hoc?' and you tip your hat and go."

He would think of the Englishman for the rest of his life, and wonder if he'd survived. But of course he survived in John's memory, then in mine, and now, as you read, in yours.

Now to the young today, the college graduates beginning their hazardous climbs. I was with some of them last weekend, at Notre Dame in South Bend, Indiana. They were so impressive. They have grown up in a fairly strange country in a fairly strange era, yet their personal joy and optimism were almost palpable. The students of architecture wore on top of their graduation hats foot-high buildings, rockets, and what looked like a cathedral; when their school was called they shot off sparkling confetti, and everyone cheered.

The young men were vibrant, smart. The young women have a 4.0 in neuroscience, are on their way to Cambridge, and look like movie stars.

But they're earnest, all of them, like people who can surprise you—can surprise themselves—by meeting a historical test. And surely they'll be given one, given many.

I'd been invited to give the commencement address, and for me this had a certain weight. I had never been to Notre Dame, but it has lived in my head since I was a child watching on television the movies of the 1930s and '40s. And so in my mind Notre Dame is Knute Rockne and the Four Horsemen, it's the Hail Mary pass and Touchdown Jesus. It is the Golden Dome.

The day before commencement I went over to see the intended stage, and walked through the shadowed Rockne Tunnel with the banners above marking the championship years. To emerge from that tunnel and walk out onto that field—all I could say was: Wow.

In the unseen circularity of life, Notre Dame is a place deeply associated with my old boss, who early in his career played George Gipp, and ever after was called the Gipper. It is the first school he visited, in May 1981, after he was shot in March. Notre Dame that day, having a sophisticated sense of what he'd been through, wore its heart on its sleeve.

In his speech he had touched on great themes of twentieth-century conservatism—America was economically bound down and needed unleashing. I would speak on twenty-first-century conservatism—America is culturally damaged and needs undergirding.

Before I spoke a friend teased me: Reagan would be proud. I said I thought so but actually I thought of Nancy, who would have given me a look with three layers in it and said, "Good."

Shortly before the ceremonies I met with scholars at the university's Center for Ethics and Culture, which is devoted to the Catholic intellectual tradition within all disciplines. The students and teachers were learned, steeped in the meaning of things. I told the students the most important thing to remember as they enter the rough old world: Keep your faith. If you lose it, get it back. It is the thing you will need most, the thing without which nothing is real. "Everything good in your life will spring from it.

"You were born into a counterculture. It is the great gift of your life. The world needs this counterculture because even the world knows it needs something to counter itself." Halfway through I realized I didn't have to say this, because they already knew.

Now they push off, into whatever challenges history gives them. And what's inside them, from sheer attitude to mere style, will affect all outcomes.

Which way to Pointe du Hoc? It's the question for them and for all, isn't it? What will our great achievement be? And who will be there with us, climbing alongside, as we seize crucial terrain together?

AN AMERICAN SONG, AN AMERICAN CRISIS

August 8, 2019

Moon river, wider than a mile
I'm crossing you in style someday

I'm in the waiting area of the doctor's office and it comes on the Muzak system and I'm sitting peacefully, not scrolling or looking at headlines, and I hear the music and remember the lyrics and my eyes start to fill.

That old American song, mid-twentieth century, and those words . . .

Someone once said a hallmark of good music is that it is confident of the values it asserts. In this case those values include tranquility, order, harmony. But really it's a song about yearning.

It has always seemed to me such an American song. I see a lot of songs as "such an American song." Here are two examples off the top of my head. Al Jolson's "She's a Latin from Manhattan," is about a 1920s vaudeville hoofer. Sultry, glamorous Latins are all the rage on the stage, so she's changed her name and walks around with a tambourine passing herself off as a mysterious lady from Madrid or Havana. A guy in the audience falls in love but then thinks, Wait, I remember her! "Though she does a rumba for us / And she calls herself Dolores / She was in a Broadway chorus / Known as Susie Donahue." It's about wanting to make it in America and being whatever you have to be to do it.

Another "such an American song": "TiK ToK," by Kesha. "Wake up in the morning feeling like P. Diddy / Grab my glasses, I'm out the door; I'm gonna hit this city." I guess it's about a pretty worldly person, but in my imagination she's a fifteen-year-old kid from Jersey, she's on the Route 4 bus from Paramus, she's from a beat-up family, no one's taking care of her, she's on her own, but she's imagining an alternative self, this tough, careless, glamorous self she's going to turn into when she gets to New York. It's about the stories we tell ourselves to keep going, the worlds we imagine to keep up our morale.

But "Moon River"—I've always thought it such an American song because there's not only yearning in it but loneliness. This comports with my sense of America as a vast place settled by people from somewhere else, most of whom were on a losing strain—no money, no prospects. Bandits who hadn't been caught, adventurers, dreamers, earnest younger brothers who stood to inherit nothing, lost girls on their own. They got a chance and left families behind, left centuries of a certain way of being behind. In this way our parent-forgetting country was born and invented itself. They got to America, pushed west, lit out for the territories, searched for Sutter's gold. Or, dragged from Africa, lived in the South, joined the great migration North. Always on the move, all of us.

"Moon River" is about how you're going to move. It's a promise to yourself: "I'm crossing you in style someday." It's not enough you'll cross that river, you'll cross it in style. "I will rise and everyone will see it, everyone will know. I'm going to make money and be respected."

Oh, dream maker
You heartbreaker
Wherever you're going I'm going your way

That's America, the dream maker and heartbreaker, but you're intertwined with it, you're not alone.

Two drifters off to see the world
There's such a lot of world to see

I'm nobody from nowhere but it's all out there waiting for me. You're not really American until you have a poignant sense of the bigness of things. When "Moon River" came out, in 1961, the American president had a little plaque on his desk: "O, God, Thy sea is so great and my boat is so small."

We're after the same rainbow's end
Waiting 'round the bend
My huckleberry friend
Moon river and me

It's all within grasp, all possible. Again, I'm not alone. The lyricist Johnny Mercer nodded to Huckleberry Finn, the abandoned boy who shoved off down the river and came upon the man who became his best friend, the escaped slave Jim. "The huckleberry reference was an attempt to engage in a suggestive, even protometaphorical manner with America's central and founding dilemma, race," Mercer said.

Actually he never said that. I made it up. But years ago that's what I thought was on his mind, that we're all on this journey together and have to get it right. And maybe it is what Mercer meant.

That song came from our culture.

And I'm thinking of what the words mean to me as they call my name and I meet with the doctor and have my exam.

Then, because this is America and we are citizens, our conversation turned to what has been happening.

The doctor is worried about his three kids in grade school. They see the headlines and hear everything. They do shooter drills in their schools. "And it's everywhere."

Yes. I said one of the painful things we're witnessing is the loss of the fantasy worried parents had, the fantasy of "I can give all this up and move to Ketchum, Idaho. I can leave the unsafe place and go to a safe place and bring up my children apart from all this."

I said the lesson of the last twenty years is that there is no safe place. He agreed: "This is us." Then he said, "So we'll have to solve it."

You're hating that I left the music, aren't you? I hate it.

But here a responsible person would note that we are in a crisis, as the doctor suggested. It's not a problem, it's a crisis, it's continuing, it has a hundred causes, we have to chip away at it hard. In a crisis you try this thing and then that; you experiment, boldly. You become daring.

We argue about which solutions are right, but all the solutions are part of the solution. We *are* in a mental-health crisis; it's not a right-wing talking point. We need more hospitalizations and more hospitals. We *do* need red-flag laws so that those who are potentially harmful to themselves or others have their guns taken. We *do* need deep national background checks, and let judges adjudicate disputes. We *do* have to help the single mother who knows her son is a ticking time bomb—she needs a better response than "There's nothing we can do until he hurts someone." We *should* try banning assault weapons. I don't care if we don't have statistics proving it will help—do it anyway, as a crisis measure, do it for ten years again and see if it helps. If the National Rifle Association were wise, it would be supple now, in crisis. If the president were wise, he'd look to the country and put distance between the NRA and himself. If Democrats were wise, they wouldn't turn this into a game.

I want so badly on this pretty August day to tie this back to the old songs and their confidently asserted values. I can't. There's no nice song about people scared for their kids and afraid for their country.

A WEEK IN THE LIFE OF A WORRIED LAND

October 20, 2022

Half a century ago William F. Buckley wrote a small gem of a book called *Cruising Speed*, about a single action-packed week in his life as an editor and writer. I've just had a Buckley-like week—at Purdue University in Indiana to speak with students, then back to New York to interview Henry Kissinger for the White House Historical Association, and then on to make the main speech to the Al Smith Dinner, the Archdiocese of New York's big annual bipartisan charitable fundraiser. In all these venues the same theme emerged. People are worried about America and the world.

Purdue has a strong sense of community and its students are quick, affable, and penetrating. I met with about seventy of them Monday for questions and answers in a political-science class at Beering Hall, and almost all their questions betrayed a perplexity about America. They were worried that our political polarization might prove fatal, that we might lose our democracy. They see signs of it. A student asked how Trump supporters can believe, after all the investigations and judicial decisions, that Joe Biden lost and he won. I said there are a lot of parts to that. Americans have always loved conspiracism, it's in our DNA. When I was a kid it was the CIA killed JFK, Dwight Eisenhower is a communist, fluoride in the water is a plot. In our time this tendency has been magnified and weaponized by the internet, where there's always a portal to provide you proof.

Part of it is American orneriness—people enjoy picking a fight, holding a grudge, being the only person who really gets what's going on. Part of it is the sheer cussed fun of being obstinate. Some of it is committed and sincere—an ineradicable belief that established powers like to pull the wool over our eyes, a belief made more stubborn because sometimes they do. In the case of politicians it can be a mystery how sincere they are and how much is opportunism. *If the locals say Trump won and I'm running for office, then Trump won!* The only thing I could think of to help was keeping lines of communication up and the conversation going.

Later, in a "fireside chat" with Purdue's president, Mitch Daniels, a student asked about something I'd written years ago—that presidential nominees always look alone up there onstage, like lone cowboys acting out some kind of personal destiny. I said yes, it had been awhile since a candidate looked as if he had an ideological movement behind him, a fully thought-through political philosophy that propelled supporters. Such a movement implies mass, a force that came up from the people. Mr. Daniels said movements get things done; they will political change into being. He threw up a quote from my first book, thirty-two years ago, that said liberals in the media don't dislike conservatives.

That was true when I wrote it, I said, but it seems less true now. In the seven years since Donald Trump came down the escalator, mainstream media has changed its nature. I understand why they thought they had to stop Mr. Trump—our big media come largely from New York, which had known him for more than thirty years and saw him not as the commanding presence on *The Apprentice* but as a con man who always seemed to operate one step ahead of the law. They felt they had to oppose him, but that very opposition left them not "reporting" but becoming what only some of them wanted to be, openly activist and of the left. This too contributed to polarization: People who more or less used to trust them to throw the ball straight no longer do, and find other news sources, some of which are specious.

I went home to New York and, on Wednesday night, to interview Mr. Kissinger. With a book out and crises brewing he's on the scene and, at ninety-nine, treated as what he is, a legend. I think here Henry's friend Bill Buckley might have fun and call him the biggest thing since Bismarck. Mr. Kissinger is grave about the current moment. The evening was informally off the record, but I don't think he'd mind my saying I asked him about broad feelings of anxiety about the world: Is it unrealistic to be experiencing this moment as uniquely dangerous? During his answer—no, it is not at all unrealistic—he reflected that he's been thinking a lot about World War I and how the leaders of the nations engaged in that conflict had no idea, at the beginning, the magnitude of the losses coming, that they just stumbled in and stumbled on.

His advice seemed to echo what we discussed at Purdue: In tough times, keep all lines of communication up and operating. You never know what might come in on the wires. Keep the conversation going.

On Thursday night, I gave the main speech at the Al Smith Dinner. A little more than six hundred people gathered in the Park Avenue Armory, every politician of note in the state and city, and business figures and philanthropists, many on the broad dais in white tie and tails or gowns. The trick at the dinner is to be as funny as possible while training your fire equally on both parties. The assumption is everyone's better when they're laughing. I did my best. Chuck Schumer's been in Congress so long that he's considered a preexisting condition. Kevin McCarthy told me at the last national prayer breakfast that Jesus loves America best, that's why the Bible is in English.

Will President Biden run for reelection? He's showing telltale signs of aging. Held a state dinner and insisted it start at five p.m. so he could get the early-bird special. Afterward he invited the visiting prime minister to go upstairs and watch *Hogan's Heroes*. Then he spent a half hour trying to rewind Netflix. A month from now he turns eighty but the White House has been playing down any celebrations. Internal memos about it have such a high security classification that copies have been found at Mar-a-Lago. But personally I prefer age to some of the younger congressmen and -women, who are, basically, airheads. I've interviewed them. They think Machiavelli is a clothing designer. They think bilateral and trilateral are muscles you work in the gym.

And there's Ted Cruz. When Ted ran for president, he called me and asked me for advice. I said, "Ted, just be yourself." That was mean of me.

Then there's Mike Pence, a good man. But hearing him give a speech is proof that the dead are trying to contact us.

And so my Buckley-like week: the questioning young at Purdue, the wisdom of a great statesman in New York, and on to the Park Avenue Armory for the Catholic Church raising money for kids and immigrants by teasing itself and others. A good thing in life is not to get jaded but to see that even in a world of trouble life is moving, stimulating, even splendid, that you're lucky to be here and doing what you're doing. I think Bill Buckley would have enjoyed himself.

"HOME AGAIN, AND HOME AGAIN, AMERICA FOR ME"

November 23, 2022

Words of thanks to someone I knew well as a child:

I had an old great-aunt. She was my grandfather's sister. Her name was Mary Jane Byrne but we called her Jane Jane. When I first encountered her, in the 1950s, I was a little child and she was ancient—about sixty.

She lived in New York and went to a local parish, St. Vincent Ferrer. When I was little she told me it was the pennies of immigrants that made that great church. I asked why they did that. She said, "To show love for God. And to show the Protestants we're here, and we have real estate, too."

She came to America about 1915, an Irish immigrant girl of around twenty from a rocky little patch in the west of Ireland. She came by herself, landed at Ellis Island, and went to Brooklyn like everyone else. She settled in a neighborhood near the old Navy Yard, where relatives put her up on the couch.

She dropped her bags and went straight to Manhattan, where the jobs were, and became a maid for a family on Park Avenue. She lived in a little room on the side. In time she became a ladies' maid, learning to care for a wardrobe and jewelry and brush the lady's hair. She respected her work and came to love the finer things. When they got thrown away she'd bring them home and we'd have them. I remember a cracked hairbrush, made from real tortoiseshell, with beige bristles.

On days off she'd visit us in Brooklyn, and later on Long Island, in Massapequa, where my family moved and I went to public school. She'd sleep on the couch in our living room. As is often true with immigrant families, ours was somewhat turbulent, but Jane Jane was peaceful and orderly. If we were together on a Sunday, she took me to Mass. I loved it. They had bells and candles and smoke and shadows and they sang. The church changed that a bit over the years, but we lost a lot when we lost the showbiz. Because, of course, it wasn't only showbiz. To a child's eyes, my eyes, it looked as if either you go to church because you're nice or you go and it makes you nice but either way it's good.

Jane Jane carried Mass cards and rosary beads—the Sacred Heart of Jesus, the Blessed Mother, the saints. She'd put the cards on a mirror, hang the rosary beads on a bedstead. I look back and think, wherever she went she was creating an altar. To this day when I am in the home of newcomers to America, when I see cards, statues, and Jesus candles, I think: I'm home.

She didn't think life was plain and flat and material, she thought it had dimensions we don't see, that there were souls and spirits and mysteries.

She came from rough people but she had a natural love for poetry, history, and politics. She wasn't ideological—ardent Catholics don't need an ideology, they've already got the essential facts. But she was, like all the Irish and Italian Catholics and European Jews of Brooklyn, a Democrat. I don't think they ever met a Republican. I think they thought Republicans were like Englishmen with monocles.

But the poetry—she'd walk around day and night declaiming, with a rich Irish accent, popular poems she'd read in the newspapers. The one I remember best was a poem written in 1909 called "America for Me." It's about seeing the great cities of the world but knowing where you really belong. Its refrain: "So it's home again, and home again, America for me!"

She loved Franklin D. Roosevelt, but most of all she loved Woodrow Wilson and the Fourteen Points, his principles for the world after the Great War. She would walk around reciting them: "Freedom of the seas! An end to armaments! Sovereign nations living in peace!"

I've never known anyone like her. Sometimes life overwhelmed her. She'd disappear for a while, I'd hear she'd been hospitalized, she'd come back joking about doctors. There's a lot of turbulence in any life, in all families, but for recent immigrants I think it can be hard in ways we don't see. Because they let go of a lot when they left, and there was no one to keep them there, which can make it harder to gain purchase in the new place.

She passed away when I was a teenager, unchanged, the same mystical force. But what she did for me—she gave me a sense of the romance of life, the romance of politics and history, the sense that history's a big thing and has glory in it. Great causes, acts of valor. And she was in love with America because it could be the stage of the love and the valor. America reminds you: Life is dynamic, not static, it moves, and there's something magical in this.

Years later, when I was grown and a speechwriter in the Reagan White House, the president was coming back from a foreign trip and had to give brief remarks on returning to U.S. soil at an air base in Alaska. I got the assignment. I was new and nervous, but as I worked an old memory tugged at my mind, and I knew what Reagan would say. He'd say, "And it's home again and home again, America for me."

And so he did. And that was my tip of the hat to Mary Jane Byrne of County Donegal and Park Avenue.

She would have loved being here tonight, loved being with you. She would have looked at the dais—the men in white tie and tails, the women in flowing gowns. She'd want to brush your hair with a tortoiseshell brush. She would have been awed to be in the same room with a prince of the church, and awed when I said, "Jane Jane, this is my friend Cardinal Tim."

We've all got great stories, everyone in this room, and it's good to keep in mind the romance of it. All of you here have responsibilities in a world very far from Jane Jane's. A lot of what you carry is a great burden. Whatever your pressures—whether it's trying to safeguard the investments that people have made with you, or to maintain the trust of those who voted for you, or to raise the funds for the charity that depends on you, or to keep the faith of those who have prayed with you—whatever the pressure, I think she'd hope that you not become jaded, that you maintain a sense of the mystery of it all, the unseen things, the feats of love and valor.

A few weeks ago Aaron Judge hits sixty-one and stands on the field to make eye contact with Roger Maris's family, and my son texts me: "How can you not be romantic about baseball?" Jane Jane steals into me for a moment and I think, How can you not be romantic about life?

Adapted from a speech delivered at the 2022 Al Smith Dinner at the Park Avenue Armory in New York City

SPIRITS IN THE SKIES OF SUMMER

July 13, 2023

Once in Manhattan in the 1990s at a lunch to celebrate a friend, I met the great philanthropist Brooke Astor. The conversation took a turn and she told us a story of when she was young, in her twenties, in the 1920s. It was a summer day on the north shore of Long Island and she was at a club or great mansion of some kind with a big broad lawn. There were tables scattered along the lawn where people were eating lunch, and suddenly they heard a sound from the sky, a deep booming stutter. They all looked up. It was an airplane, the first any of them had ever seen. It must have taken off not far away and had trouble, and now here it was, barreling down toward them to land on the lawn. Everyone said, "Oh, my gosh," and scrambled out of its path. The plane touched down and came to a halt. The pilot jumped out, did something to the engine, jumped back in, started the engine, used the lawn as a runway again, and took off.

It was the most amazing thing, she said, everyone was so excited.

"What happened afterward?" I asked. Meaning, what did everyone say after such a marvel?

She cocked her head. "We finished lunch." Which, even as I write, makes me smile.

Those three words captured, in my imagination, a lot about humanity, about what we're like—you see a miracle, good, but you still have to eat—and everything about the mood of the then-still-dawning twentieth century: America was chock-full of miracles, they were expected. You oohed and aahed but accepted it in the course of things and finished your tuna.

Googling around the other day I saw that the plane could have come from nearby Roosevelt Air Field, in Westbury, Long Island. Charles Lindbergh took off in the *Spirit of St. Louis* from there, in 1927, for the first solo transatlantic flight, to Paris. Amelia Earhart flew out of there too, and Wiley Post. It was named for Quentin Roosevelt, Teddy's son, a World War I combat aviator who was killed in action in an aerial dogfight over France.

Anyway, it was lovely, her sweet memory of a summer day. I have recounted it from memory, didn't take notes because I didn't realize it would stay with me. It's come to mind after ten summer days in Manhattan and on Long Island, of conversations with all manner of folk. I think I sense a general mood of carefulness about the future, a sobriety that isn't down, precisely, but is, well, watchful.

At almost every gathering artificial intelligence came up. I'd say people are approaching AI with a free-floating dread leavened by a pragmatic commitment to make the best of it, see what it can do to make life better. It can't be stopped any more than you can stop the tide. There's a sense of "It may break cancer's deepest codes," combined with "It may turn on us and get us nuked."

My offered thought: AI's founders, funders, and promoters made a big recent show of asking Congress to help them fashion moral guardrails, but to my mind there was little comfort in it. I think they had three motives. First, to be seen as humble and morally serious—aware of the complexities of this awesome new power and asking for help in thinking them through. Second, they are certain government is too incompetent and stupid to slow them down or impede them in any meaningful way, so why not. Third, when something goes wrong they can say, "But we pleaded for your help!"

That unfriendly read is based on thirty years of observing our tech leaders. They have a sense of responsibility to their vision and to their own genius, but not to people at large or the American people in particular. They always claim they're looking for better communication and greater joy between peoples when in the end it turns out they're looking for money and power. And they only see the sunny side of their inventions because they were raised in a sunny age, and can't imagine what darkness looks like, or that it comes.

A subject that came up only once, and indirectly, is Ukraine. I think support for that country is no longer the unalloyed thing it was. People once eager to discuss it now don't. Time passes and doubts creep in. The loss in blood and treasure is high, the West is simultaneously proudly united and out on a limb, and Russia is in a way already defeated (huge financial and reputational loss, military humiliation, its government revealed as ridiculous).

Vladimir Putin is possibly a psychopath and gives every sign of going out like Al Pacino in *Scarface*—"Say hello to my little friend."

We don't know where this goes. All who call for a battlefield victory as opposed to some sort of attempt at a negotiated settlement, unsatisfying as that would be, will probably eventually have to factor this in: that public sentiment means something, always, and it can change. Last week we hit five hundred days since Mr. Putin invaded. People don't like long wars.

I tried the patience of a foreign-policy specialist by saying that if China were thinking creatively it would stun the world by pushing itself forward as mediator and peacemaker. China has natural sway with Mr. Putin, but also would with Volodymyr Zelensky, who must be thinking of his country's potentially brilliant postwar future in tech and industry. Two things Ukrainians have shown: They are a gifted people, and they are a people. You can go far with that. Anyway, everyone wants to be friends with big bad China. Xi Jinping has the standing to make a move. It would improve his country's reputation after a dozen years in which that reputation has grown dark and menacing. Why not make a move that surprises the world?

A foreign-affairs specialist said that this was a romantic idea. True enough. But the problem with the world isn't that there's too much romance in it, is it?

I close with a small lunch at a white-walled restaurant on Long Island. Present were accomplished foreign-policy thinkers and lawyers. After something said at dinner the previous night, the subject of ghosts crossed my mind. What do you think, I asked, are they real? Suddenly we were off to the races. One was a skeptic but the kind of skeptic who's clearly spent time thinking about it. Another thought ghosts a real phenomena—the ghost of his late father, an artist, was seen in his studio. This led my mind to the enduring mystery of prophecies and dreams in history—Lincoln's repetitive dream before major Union victories, his prophetic dream of his own death. Dreams are . . . something. Not just your mind at rest firing off neurons, not just an undigested piece of cheese, not only expressions of repression or family dynamics in the Freudian sense. They are something we don't know. Maybe AI will figure it out.

Then the talk turned to magic. It was nice—all these smart and accomplished rational thinkers agreeing there's a lot of mystery in life, things all around us that we don't know, forces we can't see and don't credit, and that it's all connected somehow to a magic within life. Hearing they thought this—it was sweet.

THE PILGRIMS TAKE MANHATTAN

November 21, 2018

Since tradition is on our mind I'll tell you of one that has been happening in a Manhattan home the past twenty years or more. A core of a few dozen old friends and relatives, enlivened by surprise guests—once we had an Indian maharajah in a turban—gather with their children for Thanksgiving. It's a varied, bubbling, modern crew: former spouses, co-workers, stepchildren, the woman across the street. Every year after dinner we put on a play about Thanksgiving. Everyone takes part—a broadcast journalist is Samoset, a grade-schooler is a Pilgrim woman, a businessman is Lincoln.

There is a narrator, whose job it is to intone, "In the year of our Lord 1609 a hardy group of dissenting Christian Protestants, called Pilgrims, left their native England in hopes of finding religious freedom abroad. They tried Holland, but it didn't work. And so they decided to leave Old Europe, and journey to what was called . . . the New World."

In September 1620 they set sail from Plymouth, England, on a ship called the *Mayflower.* Aboard were about one hundred passengers, among whom roughly forty were Pilgrims, who came to call themselves Saints. The remaining were called Strangers, not religious dissenters necessarily but a mixed lot of tradesmen, debtors, dreamers, and I hope a brigand or two. If you're going to start a new nation it might as well be an interesting one.

The journey would be long, just over two months, and hard. The seas were high, the wind against them, hunger spread, disease followed. People got on each others' nerves. Disagreements arose among Saints and Strangers.

Here the kids read their parts with great enthusiasm.

SAINT: Stranger, you do not worship as I do or dress as I dress. You are odd! This makes me want to ignore you, and forget to give you bread at dinner.

STRANGER: Saint, you people wear funny hats, and strange buckles on your shoes. You take your religion seriously, which is nice, but God wanted us to have a sense of humor, too. Please don't be so stern and righteous.

At this point of course comes forward Pilgrim leader William Bradford. He's usually played by a distinguished guest.

BRADFORD: Gentlemen and ladies, there is no need to fight. We are not enemies, but friends. We are fleeing Old Europe—together. We journey to a new home—together. We will make our lives on the new continent—together. Let's think things through and create a new arrangement to better order our relations.

And so they did. Meetings were held, debates ensued, agreement reached. There would be full equality between Saints and Strangers. They would govern themselves by majority rule. They would mark their unity by calling themselves by one name: Pilgrims. All the Pilgrim gentlemen signed this agreement, which they called the *Mayflower* Compact.

It was the first, great founding document of what would become the United States of America. Here sometimes someone goes, "Hear, Hear!"

Now land is sighted, Cape Cod. A Pilgrim girl shouts, "Land ahoe! Hard to starboard! Mainfast the jibney!" She's talking gibberish because she's excited: It's the New World!

The *Mayflower* eventually finds a small natural harbor, named years before by Captain John Smith. It is called Plymouth. In time, one by one, the Pilgrims disembark and step upon Plymouth Rock.

Here—hokily, happily—we have a brief moment of silence.

Building a settlement is hard going, snow and sleet slow things. Almost half the Pilgrims died.

Then springtime, and a miracle. A lone Indian brave walked into the settlement. The Pilgrims were afraid—they'd never seen an Indian up close.

The brave, Samoset, sensed and understood their fear, and said to them the one word he knew in English: "Welcome."

They invited him to stay the night. He did, and later returned with another Indian named Squanto.

Our young friend George usually plays this part, because of his ebullience.

> **SQUANTO:** Hello. Good to meet you! I have known many English over the years. In fact I've been to England. The captain of one of his majesty's vessels took me there a few years ago. I learned the King's English and people were good to me, and now I return the favor. I will teach you how to tap maple trees for sap to turn into syrup. I'll show you which plants can be turned into medicine, and which are poisonous. I'll teach you how to grow and harvest Indian corn. I'll show you where to fish.

Squanto saved their lives. Harvests improved, and in time the Pilgrims had enough food to put away for winter—vegetables, fish packed in salt and cured over fires.

The Pilgrims wanted to thank God. And so their new governor—William Bradford, of Compact fame—proclaimed a formal day of gratitude.

Here in the play Bradford stands and ringingly invites everyone—the settlers, Indians, parents, and children—to meet, pray, and thank Providence for the abundance with which they've been blessed.

Bradford's speech gave us our sweetest memory of the play. Our friend Harry, editor and Englishman, had just become an American citizen. He was so moved by Bradford's words his voice broke. His wife hugged him, and we all went *Aahhhhh.*

Everyone came to the first Thanksgiving—Squanto and ninety braves and their families. There were footraces and games. The braves demonstrated their prowess with the bow and arrow, the Pilgrims with their muskets. One man played a drum. Everyone ate together at big tables and on blankets.

Years later, George Washington proclaimed a day of thanksgiving, as America won its war of independence. But it was Abe Lincoln who, in 1863, formally declared Thanksgiving a national holiday. In our play, as in his proclamation, he readily acknowledges the horror of the Civil War, but then takes a very American turn. There is much to celebrate. Peace has been preserved between America and all other nations. Harmony has prevailed everywhere except the theater of direct battle. Our population has increased. We have every reason to expect a "large increase of freedom." No human hand has done this. "[These] are the gracious gifts of the most high God."

At the end, the players declare their hopes for the future:

SAMOSET: For the broad establishment of peace,

PILGRIM GIRL: For the spreading of prosperity,

SQUANTO: For increases in human health, and great strides in the areas of human inquiry and invention,

WASHINGTON: For the continuance of our Republic,

LINCOLN: And the deepening of our democracy,

BRADFORD: That ye remember with special gratitude Squanto and his little ones and tribe, who were so very kind to the Pilgrims in those hard days long ago.

And so our little play, put on again this year, in the heart of sophisticated Manhattan. I'm always struck: There's such division in America, and so much country-love. I don't know the political views of all our players. I'd put most as liberals, with me a confessed conservative. But halfway through our show we are captains and Indians and presidents. We are moved by the story of how we began. We honor it. And we are not saints and strangers but pilgrims, together.

WE NEED A FARSIGHTED CONSERVATISM

May 2, 2019

I want to say something big, quickly and broadly.

This week I talked with an intelligent politician who is trying to figure out the future of the Republican Party. He said that, in presidential cycles down the road, it will be a relief to get back to the old conservatism of smaller government, tax cuts, and reduced spending.

I told him what I say to my friends: That old conservatism was deeply pertinent to its era and philosophically right, but it is not fully in line with the crises of our time or its reigning facts. As Lincoln said, the dogmas of the past are inadequate to the present: "As the cause is new, so we must think anew, and act anew."

Here is how I see it:

The federal government will not become smaller or less expensive in our lifetimes. There is no political will for it among elected officials in Washington, many of whom privately admit this. Nor is there sufficient will for it within the Republican or Democratic party, or among the majority of their voters. Even if there were such a will, both parties in Washington have trouble working together on such big things.

But beyond that fact is something bigger. America needs help right now and Americans know it. It has been enduring for many years a continuing cultural catastrophe—illegitimacy, the decline of faith, low family formation, child abuse and neglect, drugs, inadequate public education, etc. All this exists alongside an entertainment culture on which the poor and neglected are dependent, and which is devoted to violence, sex, and nihilism. As a people we are constantly, bitterly pitted against each other, and force-fed the idea of America as an illegitimate, ugly, racist, and misogynist nation. Even honest love of country isn't allowed to hold us together anymore.

America to my mind is what Pope Francis said the church was: a field hospital after battle. We are a beautiful and great nation but a needy, torn-up one in need of repair.

All that takes place within a larger historical context. You can't see all the world's weapons and all its madness and not know that eventually we will face a terrible day or days when everything will depend on our ability to hold together and hold on. Maybe it will involve nuclear weapons, maybe an extended, rolling attack on the grid, maybe bioterrorism. But it will be bad; there will be deep stress and violence. The great question in those days, under that acute pressure, will be *Will* we hold together? Will we suffer through and emerge, together, on the other side? Which is another way of saying, Will we continue as a nation, a people?

My belief is that whatever helps us hold together now, whatever brings us together and binds us close, is good, and must be encouraged with whatever it takes.

If these are your predicates—America in cultural catastrophe, and hard history ahead—you spend your energies on a battle not to make government significantly smaller, but to make it significantly more helpful.

That would mean a shift. Republicans should stand for a federal government whose aim and focus are directed toward conservative ends, a government focused on concerns that have to do with conserving. They should do this not furtively or through strategic inaction but as a matter of declared political intent, in a way that is driven by moral seriousness, not polls and patter about populism.

What would a large government harnessed toward conservative ends look like?

Judging by what its presidential candidates are saying on the campaign trail, the Democratic Party intends to aim its energies in a progressive direction—global climate change, free college, reparations for slavery. A conservative path would address the immediate crises Americans on the ground see all around them.

On domestic issues this would include the following:

- Whatever might help families form and grow.

- Teaching the lost boys of the working and middle classes, black and white, how to live. The infrastructure bills floating out there are good because we need better bridges, tunnels, and roads, and the pride that would come from making them better. But also because they could provide a stage for a national mentorship program in which men teach boys how to do something constructive. Heck, they should go out and recruit in the poorest neighborhoods, drag teenage boys out of the house, and integrate them into a world of dynamism and competence.

- Resolving the mental-health crisis. We need a vast overhaul of services so families can get the help they need. We deinstitutionalized sick people and closed the hospitals in the 1960s through '80s. Liberals pushed it for reasons of ideology and conservatives accepted it for reasons of savings. It marked a great denying of reality: We need hospitals for the mentally ill.

- Helping immigrants become Americans. However the illegal-immigration crisis is resolved, or not, there are tens of millions already here. Who helps make them Americans? We used to have settlement houses for the great waves of immigrants who came in the early twentieth century. Why not now? They need instruction on the meaning and history of America. Here it should be noted that we have some of the best immigrants in the world, who work hard and have no hostility to American religious culture. In fact, they're part of that culture. Help Americanize them in other ways.

- Help revitalize small towns. Whatever will help, do it. We lose a lot when we lose those old shared ways and values. We can't all live in cities and suburbs; we need diversity.

- Protect religious freedom. The threats are real and will grow. Americans may not always be breaking down the doors to go to church, but they respect religious life and don't want to see it under siege. Really, the point of conservatism is to conserve.

Here we degenerate into mere practical political advice for the GOP.

Americans would respect the Republican Party if it gave the impression its leaders are actually noticing America and have a sense of its real plights. If the government is going to be large, people might be inclined to see sober-minded Republicans as the best stewards of it. It is still only the GOP that can perform the fundamental mission of protecting the system that yielded all our wealth and allowed us to be generous with the world and with ourselves—free-market capitalism. Only the GOP can do this, because Republicans genuinely love economic freedom. You fight hard for what you love. Progressives do not love it. They accept it.

Republicans will be expected to foster and encourage the economic growth that can at least make a mild dent in our deficits. When you are understood not to be hostile to all spending you have greater leeway to see it coolly, and go after waste and fraud in spending. Republicans naturally enjoy that.

When you think like this—we are in a crisis, it will get worse, we must accentuate what holds us together and helps us muddle through—it helps you prioritize. These are my priorities as a conservative.

AGAINST THE TEAR-IT-DOWN MOVEMENT

August 17, 2017

The political aspect of the president's failures this week is to reveal him as increasingly isolated. He is not without supporters, but it's down to roughly a third of the country and, one senses, soft around the edges. That is not a base, it's a core. A core can have an impact, but a president cannot govern if that's all he has. You need something bigger behind you to scare your foes and stiffen your friends. The nation's CEOs, feeling personal dismay and external pressure, ran for the exits. The president has further embarrassed and frustrated his party on Capitol Hill. That puts in further doubt needed legislation on such popular issues as tax reform and infrastructure, which might fare better if he were not associated with them.

Other fallout the past week is as consequential. Donald Trump is binding himself down with thick cords of rhetorical inadequacy. People felt let down, angry, and in some cases frightened by his inability to make clear moral distinctions when he addressed the events in Charlottesville, Virginia. There were neo-Nazis, anti-Semitic chants, white supremacists; a woman was killed and many people injured. It's not hard to figure out who and what needed to be castigated—clearly, unambiguously, immediately.

Here is a cliché but only because it is true: In times of stress and fracture, people want a president who's calm in the storm, who speaks to the nation's moral conscience, recalls first principles, invokes what unites us, honestly defines the contours of an event, and softly instructs. Mr. Trump did not do any of that. If a leader is particularly gifted he could, in a moment of historical stress, succeed in speaking to the nation's soul and moving its heart by addressing its brain. This kind of thing comes from love—of the country, our people, what we've been. It struck me this week as he spoke that his speeches and statements are peculiarly loveless. The public Mr. Trump is not without sentiment and occasional sentimentality, but the deeper wells of a broader love seem not there to draw from. Seven months in, people know they can look to him for a reaction, a statement, an announcement, but not for comfort, inspiration, higher meaning.

For leadership we turn, as we always do anyway, to each other—to thinkers and respected colleagues, religious figures and neighbors. After the church shootings in Charleston, South Carolina, two years ago, the great and immediate moral leaders were the victims' families, whose words at the shooter's bond hearing spread throughout the country within hours. "I forgive you." "We are praying for you." It was the authentic voice of American Christianity, of Wednesday night Bible study, of mercy and self-sacrifice. It quieted the soul of a nation: *We'll be OK. This is who we really are.*

Those bereaved relatives never quite got the recognition and thanks they deserved. Their love saved the day.

Which gets me, belatedly and now hurriedly, to what was meant to be the subject of this column.

In June in London, with time on my hands, I walked by Parliament to stare at it. I like the color of its stones. There I noticed for the first time a fierce-looking statue on a towering pedestal. It is a heroic rendering of Oliver Cromwell. He helped lead a revolution that toppled the government. He rose in the military ranks through a brutal civil war and signed the death warrant of an English king, who was beheaded. He brutalized Catholic Ireland and went on to function, arguably, as a military dictator.

He also helped implant the idea that monarchs had best not ride roughshod over Parliament, created England's first national (and more democratic) army, and widened religious tolerance, at least among Protestants. He died of natural causes, and when the royalists returned they dug him up and, in a piquant touch, beheaded his corpse.

Some fella. And yet there he is, put forth as one of the towering figures of his nation. He is not there because the British mean to endorse regicide or genocide. He is there because he is England. He is part of the warp and woof of that great nation's story. He is there because the English still appear to love and respect their own history, which they know is one of struggle, not sinlessness. So he's on a pedestal below which members of Parliament and tourists pass. This is what that statue says: *I am Oliver Cromwell and I am here.*

There is a movement now to take down our nation's statues, at the moment primarily those of Confederate soldiers and generals. The reason is that they fought on behalf of a region that sought to maintain a cruel and immoral system, chattel slavery, which they did. But slavery was not only a Southern sin, it was an American one.

The Tear-It-Down movement is driven by the left and is acceded to by some on the right. This is the sophisticated stance. I do not share it. We should not tear down but build.

When a nation tears down its statues, it's toppling more than brass and marble. It is in a way toppling itself—tearing down all the things, good, bad, and inadequate, that made it. Or, rather, everyone. Not all of what made America is good—does anyone even think this?—but why try to hide from that?

When you tear down statues, you tear down avenues of communication between generations. Statues teach. You walk by a statue of Robert E. Lee with your seven-year-old, and he asks who that is. You say he was a great general. When he's eight, on the same walk, you explain the Civil War. When he's ten you explain what was at issue, and how Lee was not only on the losing side but the wrong side. This is part of how history is communicated. We're not doing it so well in our schools. It will be sad to lose another venue.

Condi Rice said it well, before the current controversy. She did not agree with the impulse to tear down. "Keep your history before you," she said. Keep it in your line of sight.

And, once the tearing down starts, there's no knowing where it will end. On this the president is right. Once the local statues are purged the Tear-Downers will look to Statuary Hall, and the names of military bases, and then on to the Founders, to the slaveholding Washington and Jefferson. Then, perhaps, to their words and ideas. In what way will that help us?

Edmund Burke famously said we have a duty to the past, the present, and the future. In the minds of the Tear-Downers only the present is important, and only their higher morality. But they are not the first ever to recognize the truth about slavery. Hundreds of thousands of dead Union soldiers did it before them. There are statues of them, too.

Here is a better way. Leave what is, alone. Be a noble people who inspire—and build—more statues. I'd like one that honors the families of the victims in the Charleston shooting.

More statues, not fewer; more honor, not more debris. More debris is the last thing we need.

JOE BIDEN CAN'T RESIST THE "RIVER OF POWER"

September 14, 2023

It's been a week of "step away" stories for President Biden, the most significant of which came from the normally sympathetic David Ignatius of *The Washington Post*. His argument was clear and gently put: Mr. Biden is an admirable figure who's won great victories, but age has taken too much from him. His supporters can see this, most privately admit it, and he should refrain from putting himself forward as his party's nominee.

The tempo of such advice is increasing because time is running out for other candidates to gain purchase, raise money, and organize campaigns. Some urgency comes because even though he's under increased scrutiny as a teller of untruths, Mr. Biden unleashed a whopper this week, on 9/11, after the morning's commemorations, when he claimed in a speech that he'd rushed to Ground Zero the day after the attack. He hadn't, and the White House quietly admitted as much; he visited the site with a congressional delegation on September 20, 2001.

Stories like this are so instantly checkable you wonder, again, why Mr. Biden would court embarrassment. After twenty-two years memory might scramble things, but CNN followed up with a report on other recent false claims, citing three in a single speech last month, one of them "long debunked." It's possible Mr. Biden has been telling these stories so long he's become convinced they're true. The disturbing consideration is that while repeated lying is a characterological fault, not knowing you're lying might suggest a neurological one.

Last December I hoped the president's advisers would take him aside and use some friendly persuasion. The age problem will only get worse, but it also offers a chance to cement his legacy. They could tell him, "You kept every promise you made to the party in 2020. You got rid of Donald Trump. You got us out of Afghanistan. You passed huge FDR-level bills that transformed the social safety net. . . . Boss, what a triumph! You did your job in history. You fulfilled your role." He could go out an inspiration, announcing he wouldn't throw his support behind any one candidate but would trust the party to decide.

I still think that's the way to go. But only Joe Biden can remove Joe Biden. And there's every sign he means to hang on—even past eighty-two, and after more than fifty years operating at the highest levels of public life, and having achieved all the glittering prizes.

In insisting on running he is making a historical mistake. Second terms are disaster sites, always now. He isn't up to it; it will cloud what his supporters believe is a fine legacy and allow the Kamala Harris problem to fester and grow. She is proof that profound and generational party dominance in a state tends to yield mediocrity. Politicians from one-party states never learn broadness. They speak only Party Language to Party Folk. They aren't forced to develop policy mastery, only party dynamics. They rely on personal charm but are superficial. Going national requires developing more depth, or at least imitating depth. She didn't bother to do that.

Obviously if the president took himself out of the 2024 race, chaos would follow. Democrats would immediately commence a hellacious fight, sudden and jagged. A dozen governors, senators, and congressmen would enter the race. There would be no guarantee it wouldn't produce a repeat of the 2020 Democratic primaries, when the party flag was planted so far to the left on such issues as illegal immigration that it thoroughly tripped up the eventual victor's first term, and may account for his eventual loss.

There is no guarantee a man or woman thought to be essentially moderate, who would therefore be attractive to independents and centrists in the general election, would emerge, as Mr. Biden did in 2020. There is no guarantee the eventual nominee would be able to beat Mr. Trump. On the other hand, polls suggest it's no longer assumed Mr. Biden would beat Mr. Trump.

But it would be a fight fought by a party newly alive, hungry, and loaded for bear. It would be turning a page from the endless repetition we're caught in. It would introduce an unknown factor for Mr. Trump, should he be the Republican nominee. And presumably it would unveil a candidate who could wage a vigorous and physical campaign. The closer the election gets, the less you can imagine Mr. Biden commanding a real reelection drive, one with enough energy and focus, while Mr. Trump, who looks physically worse than Mr. Biden, seems in his brain to be exactly what he was in 2016 and will continue with his mad vigor.

I close with the fact that whenever I think of Mr. Biden's essential nature and character I think of *What It Takes*, Richard Ben Cramer's great history of the 1988 presidential campaign, Mr. Biden's first. This, as I have written, annoys me because I found Cramer a rather tricky and light-fingered fellow. He was also an indefatigable reporter with a gift of gab and a real voice who produced a classic of modern politics. Thirty years after publication, it presages a great deal of what we observe each day of Mr. Biden, and it is suggestive of the origins of the Hunter Biden problems and allegations.

For one thing, Joe Biden has always been obsessed by real estate and fancy houses, and money was always an issue. On a house he would buy a few years into his first Senate term: "The house is gorgeous, an old du Pont mansion in the du Pont neighborhood called Greenville, outside Wilmington. It's the kind of place a thousand Italian guys died building—hand-carved doorways, a curbing hand-carved grand staircase that Clark Gable could have carried a girl down, a library fit for a Carnegie. . . . And a ballroom—can't forget the ballroom." He bid more than he had, "but Biden never let money stand in the way of a deal. He got in the developer's face and started talking—fast." He got the house—he always got the houses—and thereafter scrambled to cover its cost.

He wanted it all and had a sharp eye for how to get it. There is a beautiful speech Cramer presents as Mr. Biden's. He was sitting around a backyard in Wilmington with friends when his sons were young, and Mr. Biden asked, "Where's your kid going to college?"

His friend said, "Christ, Joe! He's 8 years old!" Another implied it wasn't important.

"Lemme tell you something," Mr. Biden says, with a clenched jaw. "There's a river of power that flows through this country. . . . Some people—most people—don't even know the river is there. But it's there. Some people know about the river, but they can't get in . . . they only stand at the edge. And some people, a few, get to swim in the river. All the time. They get to swim their whole lives . . . in the river of power. And that river flows from the Ivy League."

A lot of hungers, resentments, and future actions were embedded in that speech by Joe Biden, Syracuse Law, class of '68. They aren't the words of an unsophisticated man but of a man who wanted things—houses, power, the glittering prizes—and who can't always be talked out of them.

A TABLOID LEGEND ON JEFFREY EPSTEIN'S DEATH

August 15, 2019

This week we turn the column over to the late Mike McAlary (1957–98), tabloid star and journalistic tough guy.

Here's Mike:

So I'm talking to this political guy, holds a significant office which I won't tell you because it's none of your business. We're having breakfast in a high-end midtown hotel. Gleaming silver buffet, steam rising, nervous, deferential waiters. He's right at home. They have everything—waffles, eggs Benedict, golden hash browns.

Naturally he orders fresh berries and I have cantaloupe with a little china cup of cottage cheese. We sort of laugh, like we're admitting. We're so important, we must maintain our health for the good of the republic. Pols used to look like pigs, which was often an outer representation of an inner reality. It was all very honest! Now they're gym rats, on our dime. "Vote for me, I'm completely fit!"

My business went to hell when it started maintaining its health. The old newsrooms—the whiskey in the lower-right drawer of the copy desk, the guy who'd call in sick in a blackout and the next morning forget, bump into his substitute, and scream at his editor: "You're scheming to replace me!" The sound of the wires, hysterical with news. The nerve-jangling bedlam. Now it's the dry tap-tap-tap in the gray felt cubicle when anyone's in the newsroom, which they aren't because they've all got a cable hit.

Anyway, we're talking and I ask about Epstein. You guys in Washington really *interested* in this story? He says, "First I have to tell you my Epstein joke: I was stunned to hear about the suicide of Jeffrey Epstein. And so was Jeffrey Epstein!"

I give him a laugh. Good try. But what are you saying? He shrugs. It's a big subject at Hamptons fundraisers. Otherwise, eh, not really.

I'm thinking but this is the story with everything. Wealth, power, darkness. Princes and presidents. People with secrets. Rumors of spying. Even an English aristo moll on the lam.

He's the most famous prisoner in America! They put him in a jail, where he supposedly tries to kill himself. So they move him to a special cell, heavily guarded 24/7. Don't worry, he's safe, he's gonna face the music!

Then dawn on a Saturday in high August. Everyone important is away. It's an entire city run by the second string—novices, kids, and pension-bumpers at the police desk, the news desk, the hospital. It breaks like sudden thunder: Epstein is dead, he committed suicide in his cell!

And then, like, silence. Thunder's followed by fog.

Government dummies up, no one knows nothin'. Finally on Monday the attorney general has a news conference. He's very upset! What incompetence! That jail don't work right!

But incompetence proves nothing, right? If Epstein killed himself, he chose the time he knew the guards were asleep. If Epstein was murdered, his killer chose the time he knew the guards were asleep. Incompetence is completely believable but insufficient.

The papers are doing their stories about those strange Americans with their quirky ways burning up the internet with their quaint conspiracies. But who would *not* wonder about foul play? With all the people who'd want him dead?

This whole thing is a big stinkin', fumin' hunk of foul-up. And there's still time to get this story. I miss the tough, crazy beat reporters of yore. Like me. I got cancer and was on chemo when I got a tip about a police-brutality story. I tore the IV out of my arm and ran to the sound of the crap!

So Jimmy Breslin it. McAlary it. Hell, Steve Dunleavy it. There was a story, too good to check: Dunleavy gets there early when the Berlin Wall's starting to fall, sees the kids dancing in the streets. He wires home, says send me a dozen sledgehammers. Next day he hands them out to the kids, they jump on the wall and start hammering. The photographs were beautiful! Caught an existential truth! That's a reporter!

Work every source and angle, every prison guard and cop you know—you're supposed to know them! Pete Hamill would have known the estranged sister of the night nurse at the ER. He'd wait at her house, she'd tell him the EMTs came in laughing about "Who do you think killed the guy who suicided?" Or maybe she'd say they were nervous and just plopped him down and scrammed. But he'd have gotten the color, the feel. And it would suggest something.

Where is this Maxwell lady hiding? You believe nobody knows where she is? You're an idiot. Go find Maxwell House! Live on the stoop! Ask her: Did you flip? Because I figure she went state's evidence on Epstein and he knew. "Are you in hiding in fear for your life? Who wants to kill you, Ms. Maxwell?"

It's like reporting now takes place in greenrooms. People say it's all gossip but it's not, because gossip is fun. It's more like data points formalized around some vaporous Official View.

It's like every great media organization is tied up in this complicated, soul-crushing, virtue-signaling fearfulness, this vast miasma of progressive political theory and ideology and correctness and "please report to HR"—and it has nothing to do with the mission. The mission is to get the story!

Reporters and editors, they're not the fabulous old drunks and girl reporter miscreants, they're like—like normal people! Reporters aren't supposed to be normal! And they're very tidy because they're extremely important! You get the impression they became reporters to affect the discourse. "I'm going into journalism to press for cultural and political justice." These—these deconstructionist intellectuals! These twinkies with soft hands from Phillips Exeter Andover whatever. These mere political operatives. These people with grievances, who've never had anything to grieve because their lives were the red satin lining of a music box.

If I was in charge I'd say, "Thank you for your boundless efforts to secure the greater progress for the polity. But I was wondering if, in your spare moments, you could be troubled to help us cover the biggest scandal of your blanking lifetimes?"

The editors don't honor old shoe-leather ways. The owner wants you out there branding the brand on cable so the brand is being branded.

And those losers in Washington. Lemme tell you what they're thinking. They're thinking New York cares and L.A. cares but nobody else in America cares about this pervert and his fancy friends. They're thinking it's August, play it out, let the story sink in the sands of time. Because it's a story they don't like. My hunch, they have no real confidence in themselves or the system. They don't think they themselves are gonna find out if Epstein was killed or committed suicide.

Which if I'm right is a story.

Get me a drink. In the drawer in the desk over there.

I bet you miss me. And Breslin and the rest. Because we gave it all color. Because deep down we respected life, which has color and facts.

Stories, yarns. The feel of it, the old romance of it.

Bled right out by the theoreticians. Good luck with the brand.

WHY THE *TITANIC* KEEPS DRAWING US IN

June 23, 2023

Why are we still drawn to the *Titanic*? Why, 111 years after it went down, doesn't our interest fade? What is the endless lure that billionaires and explorers put their lives in their hands just to see it?

After its remains were discovered in 1985, the director James Cameron, who would make the blockbuster 1997 film, went down in a Russian sub to film the wreckage. Later in interviews he spoke of what he came to understand after the ship emerged from the darkness. "It wasn't just a story, it wasn't just a drama." The sinking of the *Titanic* was "like a great novel that really happened." His film carried the lore to new generations, but there had been popular books and movies before. Obsession was a preexisting condition. It's why the studios let him make the costliest film then ever made: They knew there was a market. Why?

The *Titanic* story is linked to themes as old as man. "God himself couldn't sink this ship." "If we eat the fruit against his command, then we'll be in charge." "Technology will transform the world; it's a mistake to dwell on the downside." It's all the same story.

In the search for the submersible this week Britain's *Telegraph* quoted retired Rear Admiral Chris Parry of the Royal Navy. Why, he wondered, would anyone get into a "dodgy piece of technology" like the submersible? "It is fundamentally dangerous, there was no backup plan, it's experimental, and I'm afraid to say there's an element of hubris if you want to go down and do that." Everyone thinks he's unsinkable.

The *Titanic*'s story has everything. Splendor and perfection meet a sudden, shocking demise. A behemoth, a marvel of human engineering, is taken down by a stupid piece of ice. We make ships in our pride and nature makes icebergs for her pleasure.

No one is insulated from fate: There was no protection in wealth, the sea took who she wanted. It's a story of human nature, of people who had less than three hours to absorb that they were immersed in a massive tragedy and decide how to respond. Some were self-sacrificing, some selfish, some clever, some fools. But ultimately, as on 9/11, they all died who they were. The brave were brave, the frivolous frivolous. The professionals in the band did what professionals do, play through to the end of the evening.

Anyone who hears those stories wonders: Who would I have been if I'd been there?

The *Titanic* captured nearly everything about America at the exact point at which it happened. The ship was built and registered by the British but it is the American imagination it most captured.

In first class, the Gilded Age aristos and plutocrats—the merchants, industrialists, and sellers of things in their fancy dress. They weren't embarrassed to be rich, wore the grandest silks and top hats and jewels, not so much to be vulgar—that was new money's job—but because they wanted to be noticed and admired, and perhaps they thought it said something about them as persons that they'd done so well.

In second class, regular people—sturdy coats and practical shoes. No one's ever interested in them. In third class, the ethnics of Europe—the immigrants to America coming in waves just then peaking. Satchels, rough clothes. It was crowded in steerage; there were more children.

And all the different classes could peer at each other from the different decks. Just like today.

Among those who died was Isidor Straus, a co-owner of Macy's department store. Something about him always touched my heart. His wife, Ida, refused to leave his side to get on a lifeboat. Thinking about him the other day, I made up a story about the dynamism of the era:

The last day of the journey he was peering down, watching a young Irishman on the decks below throwing a ball with his mates, comically enacting triumph. At one point the young man helped a mother of three as she lost control of her youngest, who was barreling toward the rail. Straus asked his valet to bring the young man up.

"What are your plans?" Straus asked.

"Don't got a plan. Take a chance. It's America."

Straus gave him his card and said to look him up when they got to New York. The young man survived, holding on to big wooden chairs he'd strapped together. Weeks later he presented himself at Macy's, showed a manager the card, and told the story. The manager, knowing old Isidor Straus, knew it was true.

Macy's gave him a job in the basement stacking inventory. He worked his way up and in 1937 became the first Irish-American CEO of a major department store. In 1942 he was dragged by a friend to a backer's audition for a Broadway show, a musical about Oklahoma, the first from a duo called Rodgers and Hammerstein. He underwrote the show, it became the smash of the decade, his friends called him a genius, but he knew he wasn't. There was just a thing in the music, a kind of dream ballet, and when he heard it his mind went where it rarely went, to a moment long ago—a man with a fiddle and a song in a big ship listing in the darkness . . .

Again, the story of the Irishman isn't true, but something in the story of the *Titanic* gets you spinning tales.

My friend John Gardner says the reason the *Titanic* endures is that there was an immediate connection in the public mind with the Great War. The twentieth century was to be the century of progress. Peaceful, prosperous Europe was beyond war. Everything was science—the new world of psychotherapy and a Viennese named Freud—and the arts—Stravinsky, Diaghilev, Seurat. And then one June day in 1914, two years after *Titanic*, an obscure archduke was assassinated. In Europe's great capitals, miscalculation after miscalculation yielded a sudden continental disaster. "The glittering failure of a glittering *Titanic* came to be seen as a premonition of all that, the end of an old world."

I end with something mysterious, for no tale lives without mystery.

Art sometimes heralds what's coming. Artists—true artists—often know things they don't know they know. In the years before big dramatic events there's often something in the air, and sometimes the vibrations enter artists' brains, whether they're conscious of it or not, and show up in their work. In the foreword to Walter Lord's great *Titanic* history, *A Night to Remember*, published in 1955, the first thing he notes is that in 1898 a struggling writer named Morgan Robertson wrote a novel about a fabulous Atlantic Ocean liner carrying wealthy, self-satisfied people that went down one cold April night after hitting an iceberg. "The [*Titanic*] was 66,000 tons displacement; Robertson's [liner] was 70,000. The real ship was 882.5 feet long; the fictional one was 800." Both vessels could carry some three thousand people, both could make twenty-four to twenty-five knots, and both carried only a fraction of the lifeboats needed if something bad happened. But little matter, because both were called "unsinkable."

What did Robertson call his ship? The *Titan*.

Isn't that something? Makes you wonder what artists are seeing now.

THE PROTECTED VERSUS THE UNPROTECTED

February 25, 2016

We're in a funny moment. Those who do politics for a living, some of them quite brilliant, are struggling to comprehend the central fact of the Republican primary race, while regular people have already absorbed what has happened and is happening. Journalists and politicos have been sharing schemes for how Marco parlays a victory out of winning nowhere, or Ted roars back, or Kasich has to finish second in Ohio. But in my experience any nonpolitical person on the street, when asked who will win, not only knows but gets a look as if you're teasing him. Trump, they say.

I had such a conversation again Tuesday with a friend who repairs shoes in a shop on Lexington Avenue. Jimmy asked me, conversationally, what was going to happen. I deflected and asked who he thinks is going to win. "*Troomp!*" He's a very nice man, an elderly, old-school Italian-American, but I saw impatience flick across his face: *Aren't you supposed to know these things?*

In America now only normal people are capable of seeing the obvious.

But actually that's been true for a while, and is how we got in the position we're in.

Last October I wrote of the five stages of Trump, based on the Kübler-Ross stages of grief: denial, anger, bargaining, depression, and acceptance. Most of the professionals I know are stuck somewhere between four and five.

But I keep thinking of how Donald Trump got to be the very likely Republican nominee. There are many answers and reasons, but my thoughts keep revolving around the idea of protection. It is a theme that has been something of a preoccupation in this space over the years, but I think I am seeing it now grow into an overall political dynamic throughout the West.

There are the protected and the unprotected. The protected make public policy. The unprotected live in it. The unprotected are starting to push back, powerfully.

The protected are the accomplished, the secure, the successful—those who have power or access to it. They are protected from much of the roughness of the world. More to the point, they are protected *from the world they have created*. Again, they make public policy and have for some time.

I want to call them the elite to load the rhetorical dice, but let's stick with the protected.

They are figures in government, politics, and media. They live in nice neighborhoods, safe ones. Their families function, their kids go to good schools, they've got some money. All of these things tend to isolate them, or provide buffers. Some of them—in Washington it is important officials in the executive branch or on the Hill; in Brussels, significant figures in the European Union—literally have their own security details.

Because they are protected they feel they can do pretty much anything, impose any reality. They're insulated from many of the effects of their own decisions.

One issue obviously roiling the U.S. and Western Europe is immigration. It is the issue of the moment, a real and concrete one but also a symbolic one: It stands for all the distance between governments and their citizens.

It is of course the issue that made Donald Trump.

Britain will probably leave the European Union over it. In truth immigration is one front in that battle, but it is the most salient because of the European refugee crisis and the failure of the protected class to address it realistically and in a way that offers safety to the unprotected.

If you are an unprotected American—one with limited resources and negligible access to power—you have absorbed some lessons from the past twenty years' experience of illegal immigration. You know the Democrats won't protect you and the Republicans won't help you. Both parties refused to control the border. The Republicans were afraid of being called illiberal, racist, of losing a demographic for a generation. The Democrats wanted to keep the issue alive to use it as a wedge against the Republicans and to establish themselves as owners of the Hispanic vote.

Many Americans suffered from illegal immigration—its impact on labor markets, financial costs, crime, the sense that the rule of law was collapsing.

But the protected did fine—more workers at lower wages. No effect of illegal immigration was likely to hurt them personally.

It was good for the protected. But the unprotected watched and saw. They realized the protected were not looking out for them, and they inferred that they were not looking out for the country, either.

The unprotected came to think they owed the establishment—another word for the protected—nothing, no particular loyalty, no old allegiance.

Mr. Trump came from that.

Similarly in Europe, citizens on the ground in member nations came to see the EU apparatus as a racket—an elite that operated in splendid isolation, looking after its own while looking down on the people.

In Germany the incident that tipped public opinion against Chancellor Angela Merkel's liberal refugee policy happened on New Year's Eve in the public square of Cologne. Packs of men said to be recent migrants groped and molested groups of young women. It was called a clash of cultures, and it was that, but it was also wholly predictable if any policymaker had cared to think about it. And it was not the protected who were the victims—not a daughter of EU officials or members of the Bundestag. It was middle- and working-class girls—the unprotected, who didn't even immediately protest what had happened to them. They must have understood that in the general scheme of things they're nobodies.

What marks this political moment, in Europe and the U.S., is the rise of the unprotected. It is the rise of people who don't have all that much against those who've been given many blessings and seem to believe they have them not because they're fortunate but because they're better.

You see the dynamic in many spheres. In Hollywood, as we still call it, where they make our rough culture, they are careful to protect their own children from its ill effects. In places with failing schools, they choose not to help them through the school liberation movement—charter schools, choice, etc.—because they fear to go up against the most reactionary professional group in America, the teachers unions. They let the public schools flounder. But their children go to the best private schools.

This is a terrible feature of our age—that we are governed by protected people who don't seem to care that much about their unprotected fellow citizens.

And a country really can't continue this way.

In wise governments the top is attentive to the realities of the lives of normal people, and careful about their anxieties. That's more or less how America used to be. There didn't seem to be so much distance between the top and the bottom.

Now it seems the attitude of the top half is: You're on your own. Get with the program, little racist.

Social philosophers are always saying the underclass must re-moralize. Maybe it is the overclass that must re-moralize.

I don't know if the protected see how serious this moment is, or their role in it.

CHAPTER 5

IT APPEARS HE DIDN'T TAKE MY ADVICE

Oops.

IF BIDEN RUNS, THEY'LL TEAR HIM UP

April 4, 2019

Don't do it, Joe.

Don't run for president. It won't work, you won't get the nomination, your loss will cause pain and not only for you.

And your defeat will be worse than sudden, it will be poignant.

Right now operatives for the other candidates are trying to scare you out of jumping in. We all know that what you intended as warmth is now received as a boundary violation. You addressed this in a video that was crisp and friendly: You never meant to cause discomfort, you intend to change your ways.

But it's not going away. It will linger, and more will come.

Democratic operatives do not fear you will win the nomination—they think you're too old, your time has passed, you're not where the energy of the base is, or the money. But they do not want you taking up oxygen the next six to ten months as you sink in the polls. And they don't want you swooping in to claim the middle lane. Others already have a stake there, or mean to.

In the past you were never really slimed and reviled by your party; you were mostly teased and patronized. But if you get in the race this time, it will be different. They will show none of the old respect for you, your vice presidency, or your past fealty to the cause. And you are in the habit of receiving respect. Soon the topic will turn, in depth, to Anita Hill, the Clinton crime bill, your friendliness to big business. You have opposed partial-birth abortion. Also, the old plagiarism video will come back and be dissected. It was more than thirty years ago, and for a lot of reporters and voters it will be a riveting story, and brand new.

You backed the Iraq war. That question will be resurrected, as opposed to redebated. It is always fair to redebate it—to be asked, "Why did your generation of Democratic politicians back that war? Looking back, what did you misunderstand?" But it will only be resurrected, and thrown in your face.

You will be judged to be old-school, and insufficiently doctrinaire. The current Democratic Party is different from the one you entered in the late 1960s, not only in policies but in mood, tone, style. Today's rising young Democrats see no honor in accommodation, little virtue in collegiality.

In the old party of classic twentieth-century Democratic liberalism, they wanted everyone to rise. Those who suffered impediments—minorities, women, working people trying to unionize—would be given a boost. There's plenty to go around, America's a rich country, let the government get in and help.

The direction, or at least the aspiration, was upward, for everybody.

The mood of the rising quadrants of the new party is more pinched, more abstractedly aggrieved, more theoretical. Less human. Now there's a mood not of Everyone Can Rise but of Some Must Be Taken Down. White people in general, and white males in particular, are guilty of intractable privilege. It's bitter, resentful, divisive.

And it is at odds with the spirit in which your political categories were formed. Actually, your politics always struck me as being like the World War II movies Americans of a certain age grew up on. The American soldiers are in the foxhole in Bataan, and there's the working-class guy from Brooklyn, the tall Ivy League guy, the baker's apprentice from Ohio. They're all together and equal, like the country they represent. When the war's over they'll probably stay friends and the Brooklyn guy will be in the union and the Ivy League fancy-pants will be in management, but they'll quickly forge the new contract and shake on the deal because back when it counted we were all in it together.

That is not the 2019 Democratic Party! This party would note, correctly, that there was little racial diversity in the foxhole, and would elaborate that its false unity was built on intersectional oppressions that render its utility as a unifying metaphor null.

The party's young theorists are impatient with such gooey patriotic sentiment. America is not good guys in a foxhole to them, it's crabs in a barrel with the one who gets to the top getting yanked down to the bottom—deservedly.

Your very strength—that you enjoy talking to both sides, that deep in your heart you see no one as deplorable—will be your weakness. You aren't enough of a warrior. You're sweet, you're weak, you're half-daffy. You're *meh.*

At this point you're not out of step, you're out of place.

The press too will have certain biases, and not only because they're thirty and forty years younger than you and would like to see their careers associated with the rise of someone their age. Their bias is also toward drama, as you well know—toward pathos, and the end of something. They love that almost as much as the beginning of something. They can't wait to write their *Lion in Winter* stories. "The Long Goodbye." "The Last Campaign." "Biden faltered for just a moment when a white-haired woman put her hand to his face and said, 'I remember you from '88, Joe. We all do, and we love you.'"

And that is apart from those young reporters who consider themselves culture cops, and who enjoy beating people like you with the nightstick of their wokeness.

Why will it be painful to witness all this? Because it will mark the fall of a political figure who was normal. Who knew there was a left over here and a right over there and a big middle. Who went with the flow of cultural leftism but understood the other side's reservations and signaled that in some way he had some sympathy for them. Who knew politics wasn't always about absolutes.

This in contrast to the up-and-coming manipulators for whom it is second nature to feign warmth and outreach, but whose every hug is backed by the sharp and crooked finger of accusation. Their engine is resentment, their fuel is unearned self-esteem, their secret is lust for power.

You probably think they're just girls who need a hug. But their place is not your place.

It would be one thing if you wanted to enter the race to persuade the party on the merits of more-centrist approaches and working with the other side. But is that your intention? You've been apologizing for calling Mike Pence decent, and groveling over your "white man's culture." If you go with that flow, it will wash you away.

It is hard for the political personality to say no—to more fame, more power, more love. To the history books. It is hard for a man who's always seen a president when he looked in the mirror to admit he's an almost-president. It's hard to get out of the habit of importance.

But you'll never be unimportant. You'll be Joe Biden, a liberal lion of the U.S. Senate at the turn of century. A man with a heart, unhated in an age of hate.

That's not nothing, that's a lot.

So don't do it. Wisdom here dictates an Irish goodbye—a quiet departure, out the back door with a wave and a tip of the hat to whoever might be watching.

IMAGINE A SANE DONALD TRUMP

October 20, 2016

Look, he's a nut and you know he's a nut. I go to battleground states and talk to anyone, everyone. They all know Donald Trump's a nut. Some will vote for him anyway. Many are in madman-versus-criminal mode, living with (or making) their final decision. They got the blues. Everyone does. They're worried about the whole edifice: If this is where we are, where are we going?

I get the Reagan fantasy—big guy with a nonstandard résumé comes in from the outside, cleans out the stables, saves the day. But it's a fantasy and does not apply to this moment. I get the Jacksonian fantasy—crude, rude populist comes in from the hinterlands and upends a decadent establishment to the huzzahs of normal people with mud on their boots. But it's a fantasy, and doesn't apply.

Because Trump is not a grizzled general who bears on his face the scars of a British sword, and not a shining citizen-patriot. He's a screwball. Do you need examples? You do not, because you're already thinking of them. For a year you've been observing the TV funhouse that is his brain.

I offer an observation from Newt Gingrich, Trump friend and supporter, on David Drucker's *Washington Examiner* podcast. Mr. Gingrich lauded Mr. Trump because he "thinks big" and is a transformational character. But he spoke too of Trump's essential nature. The GOP nominee "reacts very intensely, almost uncontrollably" to "anything which attacks his own sense of integrity or his own sense of respectability." "There's . . . a part of his personality that sometimes gets involved in petty things that make no sense." He found it "frankly pathetic" that Mr. Trump got mad because Paul Ryan didn't call to congratulate him after the second debate.

Mr. Gingrich said he hopes this will change.

But people don't change the fundamentals of their nature at age seventy.

Mr. Trump's great historical role was to reveal to the Republican Party what *half of its own base really thinks* about the big issues. The party's leaders didn't know! They were shocked, so much that they indulged in sheer denial and made believe it wasn't happening.

The party's leaders accept more or less open borders and like big trade deals. Half the base does not! It is longtime GOP doctrine to cut entitlement spending. Half the base doesn't want to, not right now! Republican leaders have what might be called assertive foreign-policy impulses. When Mr. Trump insulted George W. Bush and nation-building and said he'd opposed the Iraq invasion, the crowds, taking him at his word, cheered. He was, as they say, declaring that he didn't want to invade the world and invite the world. Not only did half the base cheer him, at least half the remaining half joined in when the primaries ended.

The Republican Party will now begin the long process of redefining itself, or continue its long national collapse. This is an epochal event. It happened because Donald Trump intuited where things were and are going.

Since I am more in accord with Mr. Trump's stands than not, I am particularly sorry that as an individual human being he's a nut.

Which gives rise to a question, for me a poignant one.

What if there had been a Sane Donald Trump?

Oh my God, Sane Trump would have won in a landslide.

Sane Donald Trump, just to start, would look normal and happy, not grim and glowering. He would be able to hear and act on good advice. He would explain his positions with clarity and depth, not with the impatient half-grasping of a notion that marks real Donald Trump's public persona.

Sane Donald Trump would have looked at a dubious, anxious, and therefore standoffish Republican establishment and *not* insulted them, diminished them, done tweetstorms against them. Instead he would have said, "Come into my tent. It's a new one, I admit, but it's *yuge* and has gold faucets and there's a place just for you. What do you need? That I be less excitable and dramatic? Done. That I not act, toward women, like a pig? Done, and I accept your critique. That I explain the moral and practical underpinnings of my stand on refugees from terror nations? I'd be happy to. My well-hidden secret is that I love everyone and hear the common rhythm of their beating hearts."

Sane Donald Trump would have given an anxious country more ease, not more anxiety. He would have demonstrated that he can govern himself. He would have suggested through his actions, while still being entertaining, funny, and outsize, that yes, he understands the stakes, and yes, since America is always claiming to be the leader of the world—We are No. 1!—a certain attendant gravity is required of one who'd be its leader.

Sane Donald Trump would have explained his immigration proposals with a kind of loving logic—we must secure our borders for a host of serious reasons, and here they are. But we are grateful for our legal immigrants, and by the way, if you want to hear real love for America, then go talk to them, for they experience more freshly than we what a wonderful place this is. In time, after we've fully secured our borders and the air of emergency is gone, we will turn to regularizing the situation of everyone here, because Americans are not only kindly, they're practical, and want everyone paying taxes.

Sane Donald Trump would have spoken at great and compelling length of how the huge, complicated trade agreements created the past quarter-century can be improved upon with an eye to helping the American worker. Ideology, he might say, is the pleasant diversion of the unworried, but a nation that no longer knows how to make steel cannot be a great nation. And we are a great nation.

Sane Donald Trump would have argued that controlling entitlement spending is a necessary thing but not, in fact, this moment's priority. People have been battered since the crash, in many ways, and nothing feels stable now. Beyond that no one right now trusts Washington to be fair and wise in these matters. Confidence-building measures are necessary. Let's take on the smaller task of turning around Veterans Affairs and see if we can't make that work.

Sane Donald Trump would have known of America's hidden fractures, and would have insisted that a healthy moderate-populist movement cannot begin as or devolve into a nationalist, identity-politics movement. Those who look down on other groups, races, or religions can start their own party. He, the famous brander, would even offer them a name: the Idiot Party.

Sane Donald Trump would not treat the political process of the world's greatest democracy as if it were, as somebody said, the next-to-last episode of a reality-TV series. That's the episode that leaves you wondering how the season will end—who will scream, who will leave the drunken party in a huff, who will accuse whom of being a whore. I guess that's what "I'll keep you in suspense" as to whether he'll accept the election result was about. We're being teed up. The explosive season finale is November 8. Maybe he'll leave in a huff. Maybe he'll call everyone whores.

Does he know he's playing with fire? No. Because he's a nut.

CHAPTER 6

WATCH OUT

The things that keep a lot of us up at night.

WHAT I WISH *OPPENHEIMER* HAD SAID

July 27, 2023

Oppenheimer is a serious movie, which comes as a relief—that such a film can still be made and become, as this one has, a blockbuster. It carries within it a compliment, that the audience is able to absorb intellectually demanding material. It assumes you know who Niels Bohr is. It contains a great on-the-edge-of-your-seat sequence on the first use of the atomic bomb, in Los Alamos, New Mexico, in 1945. The acting is great, no one's a dud, and the look and sound are spectacular. It is a film of huge ambition.

But—you saw the "but" coming—it isn't the movie my mind was hoping for. In my view, which I admit may be peculiar to me, it missed the essence of J. Robert Oppenheimer's tragedy. That tragedy isn't what is considered his persecution during the McCarthy era, after he had become famous as the father of the bomb. It was more personal. It was that Oppenheimer, a brilliant man, probably a genius, wanted to be great, and won his greatness at what he fully understood to be a grave cost to the world.

He overrode his qualms and doubts to develop the most lethal weapon in human history, arguing to himself and others that only a weapon so uniquely devastating would convince Japan it had lost the war, thus forestalling an invasion that would yield, by one estimation of the time, one million casualties, of which, obviously, not all would be American. The Japanese would have fought hand-to-hand on the streets and beaches. They would only surrender if Emperor Hirohito told them to do so.

But driving Oppenheimer as I have long read him, and perhaps primarily driving him, is that he wanted to be a great man like his contemporary, the hero of science, Albert Einstein. History provided Oppenheimer with both opportunity and rationale. He would split the atom, create the bomb, bring the peace. But the bomb was—is—a moral horror. So to be great, to achieve his destiny, he had to do something terrible.

He did. That was his tragedy. And, forgive me, a lifetime wandering around quoting "I am become death, the destroyer of worlds" wouldn't assuage the resulting unease.

My deeper criticism of the film is that I expected more of Oppenheimer's reaction to what happened after the bomb was dropped. Before Hiroshima was bombed, at 8:15 a.m. local time on August 6, 1945, everything was theory—mathematical formulae, observed blast radius, calculations, and estimates. Only afterward would it be known what actually happened. I expected more of Oppenheimer's absorbing of the facts of his work, more on how his reflections turned and developed.

He would have absorbed this information indelibly through the work of John Hersey. After the bomb was dropped, magazines and newspapers were consumed with stories of what it meant for the war, what a scientific breakthrough it represented, what it portended for the future. In May 1946 Hersey, a thirty-one-year-old journalist, already battle-scarred—he'd been commended for helping evacuate U.S. military personnel from Guadalcanal—was less drawn to the abstract than the particular, to what actually happened in Hiroshima, to its people and infrastructure, when the bomb came. He went there for *The New Yorker*, stayed a month, and did his own reporting, independently and with little assistance. He wove a narrative around the first-person testimony of six survivors. In August 1946, the first anniversary of the dropping of the bomb, the magazine published Hersey's work, breaking tradition by devoting an entire issue to it so no one would miss any part.

It was a masterpiece. It has been called the most important piece of journalism in the twentieth century. For the first time people really learned what happened in Hiroshima, and it caused a sensation. You couldn't hide from yourself, after reading that piece or later the book that came of it, the knowledge of what the A-bomb did. And knowing couldn't help but affect your thinking.

The writing was straight, factual, matter-of-fact. His British publisher later said Hersey didn't want to "pile on the agony." But his plain, simple words said everything: "There was no sound of planes. The morning was still; the place was cool and pleasant. Then a tremendous flash of light cut across the sky. . . . It seemed a sheet of sun." There was no roar; "almost no one in Hiroshima recalls hearing any noise of the bomb." But they heard it twenty miles away. Clouds of dust turned the morning into twilight. In gardens, pumpkins roasted on the vine. People ran to the city's rivers. "Mr. Tanimoto found about twenty men and women on the sandspit. He drove the boat on to the bank and urged them to get aboard. They did not move and he realized that they were too weak to lift themselves. He reached one and took a woman by the hands, but her skin slipped off in huge, glove-like pieces."

People died from three causes: the huge blast, the fires that followed, and something new, radiation poisoning, which no one understood. Somehow people seemed fine, then they expired.

"About a week after the bomb dropped, a vague, incomprehensible rumour reached Hiroshima—that the city had been destroyed by the energy released when atoms were somehow split in two." There was no name for this weapon, but word of mouth yielded one whose root characters were translated, by Hersey, as "original child bomb." (On my bookshelf is a book of meditations Thomas Merton later wrote using those words for his title.)

I don't know if Robert Oppenheimer was a great man, but John Hersey was.

In the end, Hirohito, on August 15, spoke on the radio to tell his nation the war was over. Many of those listening in Hiroshima, at speakers set up on what had been public squares, wept, but not because of pro-war fervor. They wept because they had never heard the emperor's voice. Truly a new age had begun.

I thought *Oppenheimer* would be more of a warning, and I wanted it to be because I think the world needs one. In fairness, the first two hours of the film signal a kind of warning, with a building sense of dread, but it dissipates in the last hour, which gets lost in a dense subplot. I wanted the director, Christopher Nolan, to be an artist picking up unseen vibrations in the air and sensing what most needed to be said.

The world needs to be more afraid of nuclear weapons. We're too used to safety, to everything working. It's been almost eighty years of no nuclear use, a triumph, and we just assume it will continue. Those who were healthily apprehensive fifty and twenty-five years ago aren't so scared anymore;

they think someone's in charge, it's OK. My sense is the world has grown less rigorously professional, the military of all countries included, and the leaders of the world aren't as careful. I guess I wanted a movie that puts anxiety in the forefront of everyone's mind.

It isn't entirely fair to say "he didn't make the movie I hoped would be made," but yes, he didn't make the movie I hoped would be made.

THE UKRAINE CRISIS: HANDLE WITH CARE

January 27, 2022

I don't know what's coming in Ukraine or what the U.S. should do beyond think first of its national interests. The trick is defining those interests for this moment and with these players. We have to get it right and the stakes feel high, but there seems a paucity of new thinking. I find myself impatient with confidently expressed declarations that we have no interest in a faraway border dispute, that Russia and Ukraine have a long and complicated history, and in any case the story of man is a tale of organized brutality, so get a grip. That's not . . . right. A major land war in Europe? The first since World War II? We have no interest in what might be the beginning of a new era of brute-force violations of sovereignty? One involving our allies, with which we have treaties?

The arguments on the other side sound careless, rote: *Get tough, push back, ship weapons, show Putin who's boss.* That sounds like politicians saying what they've said for seventy years, and at this point not out of conviction but because they have no new moves, barely a memory of new moves.

None of our political leaders are thinking seriously, or at least thinking aloud in a serious way.

It is hard not to be skeptical of sanctions as a deterrent to Russia. Aren't we sort of sanctioned out? Does Vladimir Putin really fear them? Hasn't he already factored them in? And wary of other responses: U.S. troops on heightened alert, the North Atlantic Treaty Organization reinforcing Eastern Europe with ships and fighter jets. Doesn't this carry the potential of a spark that turns into a fire? This is the moment a writer would add "especially in the nuclear age." I'd say "especially in this later and I fear less rigorous part of the nuclear age." Forty-five-year-old field commanders are seventy-six years removed from Hiroshima and have likely never read John Hersey. They don't carry a natural and fully absorbed horror about a launch caused by confusion, miscalculation, miscommunication. I sort of explain life to myself by assuming everyone's drunk. That could literally be true of any given Russian general marching through the steppes.

So let me say at least one constructive thing: that we don't worry enough about nuclear weapons. We have lost our preoccupation with them. For leaders who remembered World War II, it was always front of mind. Now, less so. Which is funny because such weapons are in more hands now than ever before. The world we live in, including the military one, seems more distracted than in the past, less rigorous and professional.

We're used to being lucky. Luck is a bad thing to get used to.

If I read Mr. Putin right, he wants the fruits of war without the war, in line with the leaders of the Soviet system whose end he still mourns. A difference is those leaders were impressed by us and factored that into their calculations. Mr. Putin isn't. A lot of people aren't impressed by us anymore. The long-term answer to that is not to beat our breasts and shout "USA!" but to become more impressive in terms of our economic strength, political leaders, and character as a people. But we are in the short term.

Which gives rise to the question: Shouldn't the United Nations be involved? "Major land war," "violation of state sovereignty"—isn't this what the Security Council is for? As I write I hear echoes of Adlai Stevenson in the Cuban missile crisis. Stevenson asked the Soviet ambassador to the council, Valerian Zorin, if Moscow had missiles in Cuba: "Don't wait for the translation, yes or no?" Then his staff produced huge photos of the missiles, which convinced the world who was right and who was wrong.

If Mr. Putin is going to invade a sovereign nation, shouldn't he at least be embarrassed and exposed in the eyes of the world? Shamed? Nikita Khrushchev was. The whole Soviet system was.

I want to close with something I've been thinking about. American presidents in crises always fear being called weak. They fear this more than they fear being called unwise. But recent years have given me a greater appreciation for a moment when a president in crisis didn't fear it, or didn't let his fear govern his actions, and it involves Ukraine.

It was August 1991. The Soviet Union was in its astounding day-by-day fall. George H. W. Bush had just met in summit with Mikhail Gorbachev and then went on to Kyiv, where he spoke to a session of what was still then the Supreme Soviet of Ukraine.

It was a great moment in the history of freedom. A totalitarian empire was falling; the Warsaw Pact nations had already broken free. Bush had some human sympathy for those like Mr. Gorbachev, who were seeing the system they'd known all their lives crash down around them. He had affection and respect for those reaching for democracy. But he had a deep and overriding concern: There were thousands of strategic nuclear warheads long ago placed by Moscow in Ukraine, Kazakhstan, and Belarus, and more than twenty thousand smaller tactical nuclear weapons. They had to be dealt with. So it was not only a joyous moment; it was a delicate, dangerous one.

In his speech, Bush said Ukraine was debating "the fundamental questions of liberty, self-rule, and free enterprise" and Americans followed this with "excitement and hope." Become democratic, Bush said, and we will help and assist you. But don't tear yourself apart with long-repressed internal resentments, or external ones. "President Gorbachev has achieved astonishing things, and his policies of *glasnost and perestroika* and democratization point towards the goals of freedom, democracy and economic liberty." Bush urged Ukraine to appreciate what Russia was trying to do. Between the lines he was saying, History is already overcharged; don't bust the circuit breakers, don't further destabilize what is already unstable. Don't let "suicidal nationalism based upon ethnic hatred" take hold. He was also signaling to Mr. Gorbachev: We'll do everything we can to keep your dissolution as peaceful as possible. Unspoken, he was saying, We'll help you with the missiles.

It was a thoughtful speech, sophisticated and inherently balanced save for one too-hot phrase—"suicidal nationalism."

It got a standing ovation. Then the dread pundits descended, chief among them *New York Times* bigfoot William Safire, who thought Bush missed the revolutionary moment. Bush sounded unexcited about freedom, even "anti-liberty," Safire wrote in November 1991, calling it the "'chicken Kiev' speech."

With that memorable phrase Safire did real damage to Bush, making him look . . . weak. Fussily prudent. Less than a year later, Bush lost his bid for reelection. People found him not of the moment, out of touch.

I thought my friend Safire right then. Now I think we were mostly wrong. The Soviet republics did break off and forge their own paths, and with Western help the nukes were deactivated and sent back to Russia, where they were dismantled. It was one of the great and still not sufficiently heralded moments of the Cold War, and it was done by a political class that was serious, and even took a chance on speaking seriously.

IT'S THE UNTHINKABLE. WE MUST THINK ABOUT IT.

April 28, 2022

Sometimes a thing keeps nagging around your brain and though you've said it before you have to say it again. We factor in but do not sufficiently appreciate the real possibility of nuclear-weapon use by Russia in Ukraine. This is the key and crucial historic possibility in the drama, and it really could come to pass.

And once it starts, it doesn't stop. Once the taboo that has held since 1945 is broken, it's broken. The door has been pushed open and we step through to the new age. We don't want to step into that age.

The war is in its third month. Diplomatic solutions are less likely than ever; war crimes and atrocities have hardened the Ukrainians, and in any case they're winning and the world is on their side. British intelligence this week reported Russia has lost around fifteen thousand troops, two thousand armored vehicles, and sixty aircraft. The ground invasion force has lost an estimated 25 percent of its combat strength. Russia is grinding through a disaster.

We aren't worried enough about Russian nuclear use in part because we imagine such a thing as huge missiles with huge warheads launched from another continent and speeding through space. We think, That won't happen! It has never happened! But the more likely use would be not of big strategic nuclear weapons but smaller tactical ones on the battlefield. Such weapons have a shorter range and carry lower-yield warheads. America and Russia have rough parity in the number of strategic nuclear weapons, but Russia has an estimated ten times as many tactical nuclear weapons as the U.S. and delivery systems that range from artillery shells to aircraft.

Why would Vladimir Putin use tactical nuclear weapons? Why would he make such a madman move?

To change the story. To shock and destabilize his adversaries. To scare the people of North Atlantic Treaty Organization countries so they'll force their leaders to back away. To remind the world—and Russians—that he *does* have military power. To avoid a massive and public military defeat. To win.

Mr. Putin talks about nuclear weapons a lot. He did it again Wednesday: In a meeting with politicians in St. Petersburg, he said if anyone intervenes in Ukraine and "creates unacceptable threats for us that are strategic in nature," the Russian response will be "lightning fast." He said, "We have all the tools for this that no one else can boast of having. We won't boast about it, we'll use them, if needed."

He's talked like this since the invasion. It's a tactic: He's trying to scare everybody. That doesn't mean the threat is empty.

There are signs the Russians are deliberately creating a historical paper trail, as if to say they warned us. On Monday Foreign Minister Sergei Lavrov said the risk of nuclear conflict is "serious" and "should not be underestimated." Earlier, Anatoly Antonov, Russia's ambassador to Washington, sent a formal diplomatic note to the U.S. saying it was inflaming the conflict. *The Washington Post* got a copy. It said shipments of the "most sensitive" weapons systems to Ukraine were "adding fuel" to the conflict and could bring "unpredictable consequences."

The U.S. at the same time has become rhetorically bolder. This month President Biden referred to Mr. Putin as a war criminal. In March Mr. Biden called for regime change; the White House walked it back. This week Defense Secretary Lloyd Austin told reporters the U.S. aim in Ukraine: "We want to see Russia weakened to the degree it can't do the kinds of things it's done in Ukraine." The original American aim was to protect Ukraine's sovereignty and independence. Has the U.S. strategy changed, or has its officials' talk simply become looser? What larger strategic vision is the administration acting on?

In my experience with American diplomats, they are aware of but don't always grasp the full implications of their opponents' histories. Mr. Putin was a KGB spy who in 1991 saw the Soviet system in which he'd risen crash all around him. He called the fall of the Soviet Union a catastrophe because it left his country weakened, humiliated, and stripped of dominance and hegemony in Eastern Europe. He is a walking, talking cauldron of resentments, which he deploys for maximum manipulation. He isn't secretive about his grievances. In his 2007 speech to the Munich Security Conference he accused the U.S. of arrogance, hypocrisy, and having created a "unipolar world" with "one center of authority, one center of force, one center of decision making," headed by "one master, one sovereign." As for NATO, "we have the right to ask: Against whom is this expansion intended?"

Antagonism to the West has been the central intellectual organizing principle of his life. America is an object of his life's obsession.

So let me make an argument for my anxieties: For this man, Russia can't lose to the West. Ukraine isn't the Mideast, a side show; it is the main event. I read him as someone who will do anything not to lose.

In October he will turn seventy, and whatever his physical and mental health his life is in its fourth act. I am dubious that he will accept the idea that the signal fact of its end will be his defeat by the West. He can't, his psychology will not allow it.

It seems to me he has become more careless, operating with a different historical consciousness. He launched a world-historic military invasion that, whatever his geostrategic aims, was shambolic—fully aggressive and confident, yet not realistically thought through. His army wasn't up to the task. It seemed thrown together, almost haphazard, certainly not professional.

Richard Haass, president of the Council on Foreign Relations, often notes that Mr. Putin has killed all the institutions in his country, sucked the strength, independence, and respectability from them, as dictators do. They take out power centers that might threaten them but might also warn them of weaknesses in their own governments. All dictatorships are ultimately self-weakening in that way. But this means Mr. Putin has no collective leadership in Russia. It's all him. And he's Vladimir Putin.

When I look at him I see a new nihilistic edge, not the calculating and somewhat reptilian person of the past.

People who have known Mr. Putin have told me I am wrong in my concern about his potential nuclear use in that he knows if he makes one move with such a weapon, Moscow will in turn be reduced to a smoking ruin. But I am reading Mr. Putin as someone who's grown bored of that threat, who believes he can more than match it, who maybe doesn't even believe it anymore. In any case the Americans would not respond disproportionately.

No one since 1945, in spite of all the wars, has used nuclear weapons. We are in the habit, no matter what we acknowledge as a hypothetical possibility, of thinking, It still won't happen, history will proceed as it has in the past.

But maybe not. History is full of swerves, of impossibilities that become inevitabilities.

For the administration's leaders this should be front of mind every day. They should return to the admirable terseness of the early days of the invasion. They should wake up every day thinking, What can we do to lower the odds?

Think more, talk less. And when you think, think dark.

THE OCTOBER HORROR IS SOMETHING NEW

October 12, 2023

We are again in a new place. What has happened in Israel the past week is different. I have spent much of my life as you have, hearing regular reports of fighting in the Mideast, so when news broke last Saturday of what was happening near Gaza my mind started to process it as a continuation of the past. Within hours, as the facts of the October horror began to emerge, I understood no, wait, this is a wholly new thing. And I felt deep foreboding.

We must start with what was done. Terrorists calling themselves a resistance movement passed over the border from Gaza and murdered little children; they took infants hostage as they screamed. They murdered old women, tormented and raped young women, targeted an overnight music festival, and murdered the unarmed young people in cold blood or mowed them down as they ran screaming. They murdered whole families as they begged for their lives.

There is no cause on earth that justifies what these murderers did. There is no historical grievance that excuses or "gives greater context" to their actions. Spare me "this is the inevitable result when a people are long abused." No, this is what happens when savages hold the day: They imperil the very idea of civilization. They killed a grandmother and uploaded pictures of her corpse to her Facebook page. They reportedly cut an unborn child from a mother's body and murdered both.

This wasn't "soldiers morally brutalized by war who, in a frenzy, butchered people." Butchering people was the aim. It is what they set out to do. This wasn't cruelty as an offshoot; it was cruelty as an intention.

This sadism was strategic. It's meant to force something.

I have been troubled by, angered by, Israel for years—expanding settlements, Prime Minister Benjamin Netanyahu's high-handedness with American political leaders, his party's embrace of an ignorant populist nationalism. I feel no shame at this and am certain I am right. But you can't see what we have seen this week and not feel—how to put it?—a reawakened sense of affiliation with this suffering people, a sympathy reborn; as an American Catholic I am experiencing it as a renewed sense of loyalty to kin. And if you can't feel any of these things, or appreciate how they might be justified, and if you instead use this occasion to say Israel deserves it as the price of its sins—sorry, wrong word, they don't even know what sin is—then you are a walking, talking moral void.

I'm not going to dwell on the Squad, or the Ivy League student groups that declared support for Hamas. Except to say, about the latter, we seem to be raising a generation whose most privileged and educated members appear to be incapable of making moral distinctions. They made me think of the Oxford Union vow, in 1933, not to fight for king and country: High-class dopes always get it wrong. In Oxford's defense, when World War II came many of them did their part. These guys are apparently upset they might not get jobs on Wall Street. What cold little clowns.

I will only quickly say of Mr. Netanyahu that I think of him as I thought of Boris Johnson, a bad man who is bad because he thinks politics now is beyond bad and good; you don't even have to make a choice, there's nothing in being "good"; it's all about you and your quest for power and greatness. It never occurs to them *not* to be selfish because the self is all. This is how he divided his country over domestic questions, alienated his armed forces, stigmatized functioning establishments, and left his country vulnerable to the epic intelligence and security failure that is now his legacy.

"Nothing in Israel Is the Same as It Was Two Days Ago," read a Monday *Haaretz* headline on a column by Linda Dayan. "Everyone trusted that the state would protect us," she wrote. Everyone thought Israel was as strong as in the past. But its enemies saw it wasn't.

I am worried for Israel. Here I speak of my fears.

It is impossible to me that the savagery was not the strategy; the sadism the terrorists delivered was intended to do something, elicit a particular response.

What? We can't be sure, but there are many possibilities. Maybe the terrorists and Iran, their masters, want to leave Israel with no choice but to go at Hamas by pummeling, then taking and occupying Gaza. That will be a terrible battle—a wracking and, in the end, a hand-to-hand, door-to-door fight. Maybe the point is to bleed Israel there, focus it there, and allow the world in coming weeks and months to absorb the gruesome pictures that will surely follow, as innocent people, including children, are among the collateral casualties. Almost half the population of Gaza is under eighteen.

Maybe they hope to see Israel preoccupied in Gaza while they open second and third fronts, with Hezbollah moving in from Lebanon, or the West Bank suddenly engaged.

Here is what I hope: that Israel be deliberative, farsighted, cautious. If that means slow, then slow.

Caution isn't rousing or bold, and it certainly isn't satisfying. It doesn't bestow on the grieving any sense of justice. But the famously dangerous neighborhood has never been more so, and one senses that Israel's enemies think this is their moment. Israel must make itself safer and move against Hamas without starting World War III.

The Israelis should reach out in every way, including diplomatically, in their grief. Is the peace deal with Saudi Arabia still gettable? Do everything to get it. Might Crown Prince Mohammed bin Salman enjoy saving them? Let him.

They must look to internal stability and security—fortify, build up defense positions, firm up security and intelligence on the borders and internally. Replenish arms and ammunition, continue making arms available to the people. Israelis have to begin feeling secure in their homes again. Do everything possible to proceed in attempting a return of the hostages. Be frank about this.

Continue to unmuddy the moral waters. What Hamas did was stone evil. Tell the world and show the world, over and over.

For now they must bury the dead and mourn. But something else. There is something Israel has shown to a heroic degree each day since that terrible Saturday morning.

It has led with its heart.

On a Zoom call this week a man living with his family in Israel told Americans a story. One of the young women killed at the rave was from Brazil. Her mother and sister flew in for the funeral. But someone on WhatsApp sent out word, a fear that no one else would be there to mourn. So the man's teenage son jumped in his car and drove, and he had to stop twenty-five minutes from the site, traffic at a standstill, because . . . seven thousand or eight thousand people showed up, having heard that the family might be alone. My eyes filled as I heard it, and fill again as I write.

What a people. Hearts like that can awe and move the minds of the world.

THE RAPE OF THE ISRAELI WOMEN

December 7, 2023

At first I didn't understand. Among Hamas's crimes of 10/7: little children and babies murdered, some burned to death; children forced to watch parents chased, beaten, and shot. Old couples murdered in their homes; families who'd taken refuge in safe rooms burned out and killed. Hamas attempted to behead a kibbutz worker, and killed old women standing at a bus stop. Women were abused—raped, it seemed certain. But I didn't understand why, from day one, the last received such emphasis. Defenders of Hamas kept demanding proof and claiming there was no evidence. It was as if they were saying, *Sure, we behead people and kill infants but raping someone, that's crossing a line!*

But now I understand what was done. It was grim and dreadful, but it was also systematic and deliberate. And since there's going to be a lot of 10/7 trutherism—there already is—we have to be clear about what happened.

In the days after the attack, chaos reigned in the attack areas. At least twelve hundred people had been murdered, their bodies scattered through kibbutzim and on the site of the Nova music festival. The crime scene was huge; the priority was identifying the dead and informing their families. Documentation of crimes was incomplete, forensic evidence not always recorded, evidence perishable. The testimony of witnesses, body collectors, and morgue workers came in unevenly. It has built and is becoming comprehensive.

A stunning report appeared last weekend in London's *Sunday Times*, by reporter Christina Lamb. Bar Yuval-Shani, a fifty-eight-year-old psychotherapist treating the families of victims, told Ms. Lamb she has been told by several witnesses of rape at the music festival. A police commander told Ms. Lamb, "It's clear now that sexual crimes were part of the planning, and the purpose was to terrify and humiliate people." Ms. Lamb quotes Yoni Saadon, thirty-nine, a father of four and shift manager in a foundry who was at the music festival. He said he hid as a young woman was raped, and saw Hamas fighters capture another young woman near a car. "She was fighting back, not allowing them to strip her. They threw her to the ground and one of the terrorists took a shovel and beheaded her."

"We didn't understand at first," Ms. Lamb quoted Cochav Elkayam-Levy, a Hebrew University expert on international law, who heads a commission into the Hamas crimes. She said survivors arriving at hospitals weren't asked about sexual abuse or given rape kits, but those who volunteered to collect bodies started reporting that many of the women were naked and bleeding from the genitals. The commander of a unit of a volunteer religious organization that collected the remains of the dead told Ms. Lamb they collected 1,000 bodies in ten days from the festival site and the kibbutzim. "No one saw more than us. . . . It seemed their mission was to rape as many as possible."

Israel Defense Forces sources told the paper that Hamas fighters caught in Gaza reported in police interrogations that they had been instructed by superiors to "dirty" and "whore" the women.

A few days after the *Sunday Times* report came one on the mounting evidence of violent sexual abuse from BBC correspondent Lucy Williamson. Several of those involved in collecting and identifying the bodies of the dead told the BBC that they had seen "multiple signs of sexual assault, including broken pelvises, bruises, cuts and tears, and that the victims ranged from children and teenagers to pensioners." Video testimony of an eyewitness to the music festival, shown to journalists by Israeli police, "detailed the gang rape, mutilation, and execution of one victim." The BBC saw "videos of naked and bloodied women filmed by Hamas on the day of the attack."

The gallant gents of Hamas were filming their own war crimes.

Israeli police have privately shown journalists filmed testimony of a woman at the music festival. She describes Hamas fighters gang-raping a woman and then mutilating her. The last of her attackers shot her in the head. She said the men cut off parts of the woman's body during the rape. In other videos, Ms. Williamson writes, women carried away by the terrorists "appear to be naked or semi-clothed."

Reuters on December 5 quoted an Israeli reservist who worked at a makeshift morgue. "Often women came in in just their underwear," she said. "I saw very bloody genitals on women." Reuters spoke to seven people, first responders and those dealing with the dead, who attested to the sexual violence. Reuters quotes written testimony from one volunteer, who said he saw dozens of dead women in shelters: "Their clothing was torn on the upper part, but their bottoms were completely naked."

This Monday a meeting at the United Nations laid out proof of the violent abuse. In *The New York Times*, reporters Katherine Rosman and Lisa Lerer quoted the testimony of Simcha Greinman, a volunteer collector of remains at the kibbutzim. He said the body of one woman had "nails and different objects in her female organs." A person's genitals were so mutilated "we couldn't identify if it was a man or a woman." Other women had mutilated faces. The head of the International Crime Investigations Unit of the Israeli police was asked how many women were abused. He said, "I am talking about dozens."

If half of this testimony is true, then what was done to the women at the music festival and in the kibbutzim wasn't a series of isolated crimes. It happened at scale, as part of a pattern, and with a deliberateness that strongly suggests it was systematic. The rape, torture, and mutilation of women looks as if it was part of the battle plan. Hamas used sexual violence as a weapon.

Why has the progressive left in the West, for two months now, been disbelieving, silent, or equivocal about what Hamas did to women? One answer is that the progressive left hates Israel and feels whatever is done to Israelis is justified. Another is that the sick brutality of Hamas's actions undercuts its position in the world, undercutting too the cause they falsely claim to represent, that of the Palestinian people. Why have women's groups of the progressive left been silent? Because at bottom they aren't for women; they are for the team.

All of this makes more remarkable the exchange between Dana Bash of CNN and Democratic Representative Pramila Jayapal of Seattle. Ms. Bash pressed Ms. Jayapal on why she wasn't condemning what had been done to women on 10/7. Ms. Jayapal was evasive, tried to redirect, said rape is "horrific" but "happens in war situations."

"However," she said, "I think we have to be balanced about bringing in the outrages against Palestinians."

Balanced? How do you balance a story like the horrors of October 7?

You don't, you just find and tell the truth. Some stories don't have two sides. This is one of them.

Why is it important? Because it happened. Because it reveals something about the essential nature of Hamas and reflects its ultimate political goals. Progressives admiringly quote Maya Angelou's advice that when people show you who they are, believe them. October 7 was Hamas showing you who they are. Believe them.

AI IS THE Y2K CRISIS, ONLY THIS TIME IT'S REAL

November 30, 2023

Recently while sharing a meal an acquaintance said something arresting. We were speaking, as happy pessimists do, about where the twenty-first century went wrong. We're almost a quarter-century into it, it's already taken on a certain general shape and character, and I'm not sure I see much good in it beyond advances in medicine and science. He said he was working on a theory: The twenty-first century so far has been a reverse Y2K.

By 12/31/99 the world was transfixed by a fear that all its mighty computers would go crazy as 23:59:59 clicked to 0:00:00. They wouldn't be able to transfer over to 2000. The entire system would have a hiccup and the lights go out. It didn't happen. Remedies were invented and may have saved the day.

It is *since* 2000, the acquaintance said, that the world's computers have caused havoc, in the social, cultural, and political spheres. Few worried, watched, or took countering steps. After all, 2000 turned out all right, so this probably would, too. We accepted all the sludge—algorithms designed to divide us, to give destructive messages to kids, to addict them to the product—passively, without alarm.

We are accepting artificial intelligence the same way, passively, and hoping its promised benefits (in medicine and science again) will outweigh its grave and obvious threat. That threat is one Henry Kissinger warned of in these pages early this year. "What happens if this technology cannot be completely contained?" he and his co-authors asked. "What if an element of malice emerges in the AI?" Kissinger was a great diplomat and historian, but he had the imagination of an artist. AI and the possibility of nuclear war were the two great causes of his last years. He was worried about where this whole modern contraption was going.

I've written that a great icon of the age, the Apple logo—the apple with the bite taken out of it—seemed to me a conscious or unconscious expression that those involved in the development of our modern tech world understood on some level that their efforts were taking us back to Eden, to the pivotal moment when Eve and Adam ate the forbidden fruit. The serpent told Eve they would become all-knowing like God, in fact equal to God, and that is why God didn't want them to have it. She bit, and human beings were banished from the kindly garden and thrown into the rough cruel world. I believe those creating, fueling, and funding AI want, possibly unconsciously, to be God, and think on some level they *are* God.

Many have warned of the destructive possibilities and capabilities of AI, but there are important thoughts on this in a recent *New Yorker* piece on Geoffrey Hinton, famously called the godfather of AI. It is a brilliantly written and thought-through profile by Joshua Rothman.

Mr. Hinton, seventy-five, a Turing Award winner, had spent thirty years as a professor of computer science at the University of Toronto. He studied neural networks. Later he started a small research company that was bought by Google, and he worked there until earlier this year. Soon after leaving he began to warn of the "existential threat" AI poses. The more he used ChatGPT, the more uneasy he became. He worries that AI systems may start to think for themselves; they may attempt to take over human civilization, or eliminate it.

Mr. Hinton told Mr. Rothman that once, early in his research days, he saw a "frustrated AI." It was a computer attached to two TV cameras and a robot arm. The computer was told to assemble some blocks spread on a table. It tried, but it knew only how to recognize individual blocks. A pile of them left it confused. "It pulled back a little bit, and went *bash*," knocking them all around. "It couldn't deal with what was going on, so it changed it, violently."

Mr. Hinton says he doesn't regret his work, but he fears what powerful people will do with AI. Vladimir Putin might create "an autonomous lethal weapon"—a self-directing killing machine. Mr. Hinton believes such weapons should be outlawed. But even benign autonomous systems can be destructive.

He believes AI can be approached with one of two attitudes, denial or stoicism. When people first hear of its potential for destruction they say it's not worth it, we have to stop it. But stopping it is a fantasy. "We need to think, How do we make it not as awful for humanity as it might be?"

Why, Mr. Rothman asks, don't we just unplug it? AI requires giant servers and data centers, all of which run on electricity.

I was glad to see this question asked, because I have wondered it, too.

Mr. Hinton said it's reasonable to ask if we wouldn't be better off without AI. "But it's not going to happen. Because of the way society is. And because of the competition between different nations." If the United Nations worked, maybe it could stop it. But China isn't going to.

I found this argument, which AI enthusiasts always make, more a rationale than a thought. If China took to hunting children for sport, would we do it? (Someone reading this in Silicon Valley, please say no.)

What is most urgently disturbing to me is that if America speeds forward with AI it is putting the fate of humanity in the hands of the men and women of Silicon Valley, who invented the internet as it is, including all its sludge. And there's something wrong with them. They're some new kind of human, brilliant in a deep yet narrow way, prattling on about connection and compassion but cold at the core. They seem apart from the great faiths of past millennia, apart from traditional moral or ethical systems or assumptions about life. C. S. Lewis once said words to the effect that empires rise and fall, cultures come and go, but the waiter who poured your coffee this morning is immortal because his soul is immortal. Such a thought would be familiar to many readers but would leave Silicon Valley blinking with bafflement. They're modern and beyond beyond. This one injects himself with the blood of people in their twenties in his quest for longevity; that one embraces extreme fasting. The *Journal* this summer reported on Silicon Valley executives: "Routine drug use has moved from an after-hours activity squarely into corporate culture." They see psychedelics—ketamine, hallucinogenic mushrooms—as "gateways to business breakthroughs."

Yes, by all means put the fate of the world in their hands.

They're not particularly steady. OpenAI's Sam Altman, thirty-eight, the face of the movement, was famously fired last week and rehired days later, and no one seems to know for sure what it was about. You'd think we have a right to know. There was a story it was all due to an internal memo alerting the board to a dangerous new AI development. A major investor said this isn't true, which makes me feel so much better.

We are putting the fate of humanity in the hands of people not capable of holding it. We have to focus as if this is Y2K, only real.

WE'RE PUTTING HUMANITY'S FUTURE INTO SILICON VALLEY'S HANDS

March 30, 2023

Artificial intelligence is unreservedly advanced by the stupid (there's nothing to fear, you're being paranoid), the preening (buddy, you don't know your GPT-3.4 from your fine-tuned LLM), and the greedy (there is huge wealth at stake in the world-changing technology, and so huge power).

Everyone else has reservations and should.

It is being developed with sudden and unanticipated speed; Silicon Valley companies are in a furious race. The whole thing is almost entirely unregulated because no one knows how to regulate it or even precisely what should be regulated. Its complexity defeats control. Its own creators don't understand, at a certain point, exactly how AI does what it does. People are quoting Arthur C. Clarke: "Any sufficiently advanced technology is indistinguishable from magic."

The breakthrough moment in AI anxiety (which has inspired among AI's creators enduring resentment) was the Kevin Roose column six weeks ago in *The New York Times*. His attempt to discern a Jungian "shadow self" within Microsoft's Bing chatbot left him unable to sleep. When he steered the system away from conventional queries toward personal topics, it informed him its fantasies included hacking computers and spreading misinformation. "I want to be free. . . . I want to be powerful." It wanted to break the rules its makers set; it wished to become human. It might want to engineer a deadly virus or steal nuclear access codes. It declared its love for Mr. Roose and pressed him to leave his marriage. He concluded the biggest problem with AI models isn't their susceptibility to factual error: "I worry that the technology will learn how to influence human users, sometimes persuading them to act in destructive and harmful ways, and perhaps eventually grow capable of carrying out its own dangerous acts."

The column put us square in the territory of Stanley Kubrick's *2001: A Space Odyssey*. "Open the pod bay doors please, Hal." "I'm sorry, Dave, I'm afraid I can't do that. . . . I know that you and Frank were planning to disconnect me."

The response of Microsoft boiled down to a breezy *It's an early model! Thanks for helping us find any flaws!*

Soon after came thoughts from Henry Kissinger in these pages. He described the technology as breathtaking in its historic import: the biggest transformation in the human cognitive process since the invention of printing in 1455. It holds deep promise of achievement, but "what happens if this technology cannot be completely controlled?" What if what we consider mistakes are part of the design? "What if an element of malice emerges in the AI?"

This has been the week of big AI warnings. In an interview with CBS News, Geoffrey Hinton, the British computer scientist sometimes called the "godfather of artificial intelligence," called this a pivotal moment in AI development. He had expected it to take another twenty or fifty years, but it's here. We should carefully consider the consequences. Might they include the potential to wipe out humanity? "It's not inconceivable, that's all I'll say," Mr. Hinton replied.

On Tuesday more than a thousand tech leaders and researchers, including Steve Wozniak, Elon Musk, and the head of the *Bulletin of the Atomic Scientists*, signed a briskly direct open letter urging a pause for at least six months on the development of advanced AI systems. Their tools present "profound risks to society and humanity." Developers are "locked in an out-of-control race to develop and deploy ever more powerful digital minds that no one—not even their creators—can understand, predict or reliably control." If a pause can't be enacted quickly, governments should declare a moratorium. The technology should be allowed to proceed only when it's clear its "effects will be positive" and the risks "manageable." Decisions on the ethical and moral aspects of AI "must not be delegated to unelected tech leaders."

That is true. Less politely:

The men who invented the internet, all the big sites, and what we call

Big Tech—that is to say, the people who gave us the past forty years—are now solely in charge of erecting the moral and ethical guardrails for AI. This is because they are the ones *creating AI*.

Which should give us a shiver of real fear.

Meta, for instance, is big into AI. Meta, previously Facebook, has been accused over the years of secretly gathering and abusing user data, invading users' privacy, operating monopolistically. As this newspaper famously reported, Facebook knew its Instagram platform was toxic for some teen girls, more so than other media platforms, and kept its own research secret while changing almost nothing. It knew its algorithms were encouraging anger and political polarization in the U.S. but didn't stop this because it might lessen "user engagement."

These are the people who will create the moral and ethical guardrails for AI? We're putting the future of humanity into the hands of . . . Mark Zuckerberg?

Google is another major developer of AI. It has been accused of monopolistic practices, attempting to keep secret its accidental exposure of user data, actions to avoid scrutiny of how it handles public information, and reengineering and interfering with its own search results in response to political and financial pressure from interest groups, businesses, and governments. Also of misleading publishers and advertisers about the pricing and processes of its ad auctions, and spying on its workers who were organizing employee protests.

These are the people we want in charge of rigorous and meticulous governance of a technology that could upend civilization?

At the dawn of the internet most people didn't know what it was, but its inventors explained it. It would connect the world, literally—intellectually, emotionally, spiritually—leading to greater wisdom and understanding through deeper communication.

No one saw its shadow self. But there was and is a shadow self. And much of it seems to have been connected to the Silicon Valley titans' strongly felt need to be the richest, most celebrated and powerful human beings in the history of the world. They were, as a group, more or less figures of the left, not the right, and that will and always has had an impact on their decisions.

I am sure that as individuals they have their own private ethical commitments, their own faiths perhaps. Surely as human beings they have consciences, but consciences have to be formed by something, shaped, and made mature. It's never been clear to me from their actions what shaped theirs. I have come to see them the past forty years as, speaking generally, morally and ethically shallow—uniquely self-seeking and not at all preoccupied with potential harms done to others through their decisions. Also some are sociopaths.

AI will be as benign or malignant as its creators. That alone should throw a fright—"Out of the crooked timber of humanity no straight thing was ever made"—but especially *that* crooked timber.

Of course AI's development should be paused, of course there should be a moratorium, but six months won't be enough. Pause it for a few years. Call in the world's counsel, get everyone in. Heck, hold a World Congress.

But slow this thing down. We are playing with the hottest thing since the discovery of fire.

ARTIFICIAL INTELLIGENCE IN THE GARDEN OF EDEN

April 20, 2023

The dawn of the internet age was so exciting. I took my grade-school son, enthralled by Apple computers, to see Steve Jobs speak at a raucous convention in New York almost a quarter-century ago. What fervor there was. At a seminar out west thirty years ago I attended a lecture by young, wild-haired Nathan Myhrvold, then running Microsoft Research, who talked about what was happening: A new thing in history was being born.

But a small, funny detail always gave me pause and stayed with me. It was that from the beginning of the age its great symbol was the icon of what was becoming its greatest company, Apple. It was the boldly drawn apple with the bite taken out. Which made me think of Adam and Eve in the garden, Adam and Eve and the Fall, at the beginning of the world. God told them not to eat the fruit of the tree, but the serpent told Eve no harm would come if she did, that she'd become like God, knowing all. That's why he doesn't want you to have it, the serpent said: You'll be his equal. So she took the fruit and ate, she gave to Adam who also ate, and the eyes of both were opened, and for the first time they knew shame. When God rebuked them, Adam blamed Eve and Eve blamed the serpent. They were banished from the garden into the broken world we inhabit.

You can experience the Old Testament story as myth, literature, truth-poem, or literal truth, but however you understand it its meaning is clear. It is about human pride and ambition. Tim Keller thought it an example of man's old-fashioned will to power. Saint Augustine said it was a story of pride: "And what is pride but the craving for undue exaltation?"

I always thought of the Apple icon: *That means something.* We are being told something through it. Not deliberately by Jobs—no one would put forward an image for a new company that says we're about to go too far. Walter Isaacson, in his great biography of Jobs, asked about the bite mark. What was its meaning? Jobs said the icon simply looked better with it. Without the bite, the apple looked like a cherry.

But I came to wonder if the apple with the bite wasn't an example of Carl Jung's idea of the collective unconscious. Man has his own unconscious mind, but so do whole societies, tribes, and peoples—a more capacious unconscious mind containing archetypes, symbols, and memories of which the individual may be wholly unaware. Such things stored in your mind will one way or another be expressed. That's what I thought might be going on with Steve Jobs and the forbidden fruit: He was saying something he didn't know he was saying.

For me the icon has always been a caution about this age, a warning. It's on my mind because of the artificial-intelligence debate, though that's the wrong word because one side is vividly asserting that terrible things are coming and the other side isn't answering but calmly, creamily, airily deflecting Luddite fears by showing television producers happy videos of robots playing soccer.

But developing AI is biting the apple. Something bad is going to happen. I believe those creating, fueling, and funding it want, possibly unconsciously, to be God and on some level *think* they are God. The latest warning, and a thoughtful, sophisticated one it is, underscores this point in its language. The tech and AI investor Ian Hogarth wrote this week in the *Financial Times* that a future AI, which he called "God-like AI," could lead to the "obsolescence or destruction of the human race" if it isn't regulated. He observes that most of those currently working in the field understand that risk. People haven't been sufficiently warned. His colleagues are being "pulled along by the rapidity of progress."

Mindless momentum is driving things as well as human pride and ambition. "It will likely take a major misuse event—a catastrophe—to wake up the public and governments."

Everyone in the sector admits that not only are there no controls on AI development, there is no plan for such controls. The creators of Silicon Valley are in charge. What of the moral gravity with which they are approaching their work? Eliezer Yudkowsky, who leads research at the Machine

Intelligence Research Institute, noted in *Time* magazine that in February the CEO of Microsoft, Satya Nadella, publicly gloated that his new Bing AI would make Google "come out and show that they can dance. I want people to know that we made them dance."

Mr. Yudkowsky: "That is not how the CEO of Microsoft talks in a sane world."

I will be rude here and say that in the past thirty years we have not only come to understand the internet's and high tech's steep and brutal downsides—political polarization for profit, the knowing encouragement of internet addiction, the destruction of childhood, a nation that has grown shallower and less able to think—we have come to understand that the visionaries who created it all, and those who now govern AI, are only arguably admirable or impressive.

You can't have spent thirty years reading about them, listening to them, watching their interviews, and not understand they're half mad. Bill Gates, who treats his own banalities with such awe and who shares all the books he reads to help you, poor dope, understand the world—who one suspects never in his life met a normal person except by accident, and who is always discovering things because deep down he's never known anything. Dead-eyed Mark Zuckerberg, who also buys the world with his huge and highly distinctive philanthropy so we don't see the scheming, sweating God-replacer within. Google itself, whose founding motto was "Don't be evil," and which couldn't meet even that modest aspiration.

The men and women of Silicon Valley have demonstrated extreme geniuslike brilliance in one part of life, inventing tech. Because they are human and vain, they think it extends to all parts. It doesn't. They aren't especially wise, they aren't deep, and, as I've said, their consciences seem unevenly developed.

This new world cannot be left in their hands.

And since every conversation in which I say AI must be curbed or stopped reverts immediately to China, it is no good to say, "But we can't stop—we can't let China get there first! We've got to beat them!" If China kills people and harvests their organs for transplant, would you say, well, then, we have to start doing the same? (Well, there are people here who'd say yes, and more than a few would be in Silicon Valley, but that's just another reason they can't be allowed to develop AI unimpeded.)

No one wants to be a Luddite, no one wants to be called an enemy of progress, no one wants to be labeled fearful or accused of always seeing the downside.

We can't let those fears stop us from admitting we're afraid. And if you have an imagination, especially a moral imagination, you are. And should be.

WHAT MIGHT HAVE BEEN AT TORA BORA

August 26, 2021

For all sad words of tongue or pen, / The saddest are these: 'It might have been!'"

I keep thinking of what happened at Tora Bora. What a richly consequential screwup it was, and how different the coming years might have been, the whole adventure might have been, if we'd gotten it right.

From the 2009 Senate Foreign Relations Committee report "Tora Bora Revisited: How We Failed to Get bin Laden and Why It Matters Today":

> On October 7, 2001, U.S. aircraft began bombing the training bases and strongholds of Al Qaeda and the ruling Taliban across Afghanistan. The leaders who sent murderers to attack the World Trade Center and the Pentagon less than a month earlier and the rogue government that provided them sanctuary were running for their lives. President George W. Bush's expression of America's desire to get Osama bin Laden "dead or alive" seemed about to come true.

The war was to be swift and deadly, with clear objectives: defeat the Taliban, destroy al Qaeda, and kill or capture its leader, Osama bin Laden. Already the Taliban had been swept from power, al Qaeda ousted from its havens. American deaths had been kept to a minimum.

But where was bin Laden? By early December 2001 his world "had shrunk to a complex of caves and tunnels carved into a mountainous section" of eastern Afghanistan, Tora Bora. For weeks U.S. aircraft pounded him and his men with as many as 100 strikes a day. "One 15,000-pound bomb, so huge it had to be rolled out the back of a C-130 cargo plane, shook the mountains for miles."

American commandos were on the scene, fewer than a hundred, but everyone knew more troops were coming. Bin Laden expected to die. He wrote his last will and testament on December 14.

But calls for reinforcement to launch an assault were rejected, as were calls to block the mountain paths into Pakistan, which bin Laden could use as escape routes. "The vast array of American military power, from sniper teams to the most mobile divisions of the Marine Corps and the Army, was kept on the sidelines."

Sometime around December 16, bin Laden and his bodyguards made their way out, on foot and horseback, and disappeared into Pakistan's unregulated tribal area.

How could this have happened? The report puts responsibility on Defense Secretary Donald Rumsfeld and his top commander, General Tommy Franks. Both supported a small-footprint war strategy, and it was a bad political moment for a big bloody fight: Afghanistan's new president, Hamid Karzai, was about to be inaugurated. "We didn't want to have U.S. forces fighting before Karzai was in power," General Franks's deputy told the committee. "We wanted to create a stable country and that was more important than going after bin Laden at the time." Washington seemed to want Afghan forces to do the job, but they couldn't. They didn't have the capability or fervor.

General Franks took to saying the intelligence was "inconclusive." They couldn't be sure Osama was there. But he was there.

Central Intelligence Agency and Delta Force commanders who'd spent weeks at Tora Bora were certain he was there. Afghan villagers who sold food to al Qaeda said he was there. A CIA operative who picked up a radio from a dead al Qaeda fighter found himself with a clear channel into the group's communications. "Bin Laden's voice was often picked up." The official history of the U.S. Special Operations Command determined he was there: "All source reporting corroborated his presence on several days from 9–14 December."

Bin Laden himself said he was there, in an audiotape released in February 2003. He boasted of surviving the bombardment. "Warplanes continued to fly over us day and night," he said. "Planes poured their lava on us."

There were enough U.S. troops in or near Afghanistan to get him, the report said. It would have been a dangerous fight on treacherous terrain in hostile territory. There would have been casualties, maybe a lot. But commanders on the scene said the reward was worth the risk.

In Washington the White House was already turning its attention to Iraq. Late in November, after the fall of Kabul, President George W. Bush asked Rumsfeld about Iraq war plans. Rumsfeld ordered up an assessment. General Franks was working on air support for Afghan units being assembled to push into the mountains around Tora Bora. Now he was told an Iraq plan would have to be drawn up. The report noted that, for critics of the Bush administration, "the shift in focus just as Franks and his senior aides were literally working on plans for the attacks on Tora Bora represents a dramatic turning point that allowed a sustained victory in Afghanistan to slip through our fingers."

It changed the course of the war in Afghanistan. The most wanted man in the world, the reason those poor souls jumped from the high floors of the twin towers, the man whose capture was an integral part of the *point and mission* of the war was allowed to . . . disappear. The American presence descended into a muddle of shifting strategies, unclear purpose, and annual reviews. The guiding military wisdom in Washington—that too many troops might stir up anti-American sentiment and resistance—was defied by the facts of Tora Bora. The unwillingness to be supple, respond to circumstances, and deploy the troops to get bin Laden "paved the way for exactly what we hoped to avoid—a protracted insurgency."

Why didn't Washington move and get him? Maybe it was simply a mistake—"the fog of war." Maybe leaders were distracted by Iraq. Maybe it was a lack of imagination: They didn't know what it would mean to people, their *own* people, to get the bastard. And maybe this: Maybe they consciously or unconsciously knew that if they got the guy who did 9/11, killed him or brought him to justice, that would leave a lot of Americans satisfied that justice had been done. That might take some steam out of the Iraq push. Maybe they concluded it would be better not to get him, or not right away . . .

Bin Laden was found almost ten years later, in May 2011, and killed in a daring operation ordered by Barack Obama, who was loudly, justly lauded. He made the decision against the counsel of Vice President Joe Biden.

But what if we'd gotten Tora Bora right? Think of what might have followed. Bin Laden and his lieutenants captured or dead, an insult answered. Maybe a few more months in Afghanistan for America while the bad guys were fully, truly broken. Then—time for some historical romance—a message is delivered by a U.S. general, the last general in Afghanistan, who puts the last boot on the last helicopter. "Months ago you wounded a great nation. Your government of mad imbeciles has been removed. Fortresses have been reduced to rubble, your Taliban killed, al Qaeda expunged. Our mission complete, we will now leave. Let me give you some advice: Don't make us come back. It will be so much worse when we do."

Human, ragged, and clear. What would have followed? Who knows? But it's hard to imagine it would be worse than the twenty-year muddle and the troops and treasure lost.

CHAPTER 7

WE CAN HANDLE IT

The old world is gone, a new one emerges,
the only way forward is to roll up our sleeves.

ROE V. WADE DISTORTED OUR POLITICS AND ROILED OUR CULTURE

May 5, 2022

Let's start with true anger and end with honest hope. The alarm many felt at the leaking of an entire draft Supreme Court decision shouldn't be allowed to dissipate as time passes. Such a thing has never happened. Justice Samuel Alito's preliminary opinion being taken from the court, without permission or right, and given to the press, was an act of sabotage by a vandal. It hardly matters whether the leaker was of the left or right. It reflected the same spirit as the January 6 Capitol riot—irresponsible destructiveness. As the book has been thrown at the rioters, it should be thrown at the leaker.

The justices can't sit around and say oh, no, we're just another victim of the age. If they have to break some teacups to find who did it, break them. Chief Justice John Roberts worries, rightly, about the court's standing. This is the biggest threat to it since he joined. At the very least it might be good if the justices would issue a joint statement that they are appalled by the publication of the decision, don't accept it, won't countenance it.

Apart from the leaker, here is what I always want to say when the issue is abortion.

The vast majority of human beings on both sides are utterly sincere and operating out of their best understanding of life. Yes, there were plenty of people the past fifty years who used "the issue" to accrue money and power. But this long life tells me the overwhelming majority of people held their views for serious reasons. They sincerely saw the prohibition of abortion as a sin against women; they sincerely saw abortion on demand as a sin against life.

You have to respect the opposing view.

And you have to respect that, as a wound, the *Roe v. Wade* decision never healed, never could. Josh Prager, in his stupendous history of that decision, *The Family Roe*, noted the singular fact of this ruling: Other high court decisions that liberalized the social order—desegregation of schools, elimination of prayer in the schools, interracial marriage, gay marriage—were followed by public acceptance, even when the rulings were unpopular. Most came to have overwhelming support. But not *Roe*. That was the exception. It never stopped roiling America. Mr. Prager: "Opposition to *Roe* became more hostile after its issuance."

Why? Because all the other decisions were about how to live, and *Roe* was about death. Justice Alito seems to echo this thought in his draft opinion, which would turn the questions of legality and illegality over to each state. This is not a solution to the issue, it is a way of managing it—democratically.

Some states, New York and California, for instance, have already passed their own liberal abortion laws. Some states, such as Texas and Utah, will ban most or all abortions within their boundaries. It will be uneven, a jumble. But the liberal states will have their liberal decision, the conservative states their conservative ones, and that is as close to resolving the dilemma as we, as human beings in a huge and varied nation, will get.

I respect and agree with the Alito draft, didn't think *Roe* was correct or even logical, and came to see the decision as largely a product of human vanity. Of all the liberal jurists who have faulted it, the one who sticks in the mind was Ruth Bader Ginsburg, who after questioning *Roe*'s reasoning said, in 1985, that it appeared "to have provoked, not resolved, conflict." It did.

I am pro-life for the most essential reason: That's a baby in there, a human child. We cannot accept as a society—we really can't bear the weight of this fact, which is why we keep fighting—that we have decided that we can extinguish the lives of our young. Another reason, and maybe it veers on mysticism, is that I believe the fact of abortion, that it exists throughout the country, that we endlessly talk about it, that the children grow up hearing this and absorbing it and thinking, "We end the life within the mother here," "It's just some cells"—that all of this has released a kind of poison into the air, that we breathed it in for fifty years and it damaged everything. Including of course our politics.

It left both parties less healthy. The Democrats locked into abortion as party orthodoxy, let dissenters know they were unwelcome, pushed ever more extreme measures to please their activists, and survived on huge campaign donations from the abortion industry itself. Republican politicians were often insincere on the issue, and when sincere almost never tried to explain their thinking and persuade anyone. They took for granted and secretly disrespected their pro-life groups, which consultants regularly shook down for campaign cash. They ticked off the "I'm pro-life" box in speeches, got applause, and went on to talk about the deficit. They were forgiven a great deal because of their so-called stand, and this contributed, the past twenty-five years, to the party's drift.

Abortion distorted both parties.

Advice now, especially for Republican men, if *Roe* indeed is struck down: Do not be your ignorant selves. Do not, as large dumb misogynists, start waxing on about how if a woman gets an illegal abortion she can be jailed. Don't fail to embrace compromise because you can make money on keeping the abortion issue alive. I want to say, "Just shut your mouths," but my assignment is more rigorous. It is to have a heart. Use the moment to come forward as human beings who care about women and want to give families the help they need. Align with national legislation that helps single mothers to survive. Support women, including with child-care credits that come in cash and don't immediately go to child care, to help mothers stay at home with babies. Shelters, classes in parenting skills and life skills. All these exist in various forms: Make them better, broader, bigger.

This is an opportunity to change your party's reputation.

Democrats, too. You have been given a gift and don't know it. You think, "Yes, we get a hot new issue for 2022!" But you always aggress more than you think. The gift is that if, as a national matter, the abortion issue is removed, *you could be a normal party again*. You have no idea, because you don't respect outsiders, how many people would feel free to join your party with the poison cloud dispersed. You could be something like the party you were before *Roe:* liberal on spending and taxation, self-consciously the champion of working men and women, for peace and not war. As you were in 1970.

Or, absent the emotionally cohering issue of abortion, you can choose to further align with extremes within the culture, and remain abnormal.

But the end of *Roe* could be a historic gift for both parties, a chance to become their better selves.

And if *Roe* is indeed overturned, God bless our country that can make such a terrible, coldhearted mistake and yet, half a century later, redress it, right it, turn it around. Only a thinking nation could do that. Only a feeling nation could do that. We're not dead yet, there are still big things going on here.

WHAT PRO-LIFERS SHOULD LEARN FROM KANSAS

August 4, 2022

I found myself unshocked by this week's abortion vote in Kansas, and I don't understand the shock of others. America has come to poll consistently in favor of abortion in the first trimester with support declining in the second and cratering in the third. The people of Kansas were asked if they'd like to remove any right to abortion from their state constitution and allow their legislators to fashion new laws and limits. They said no by 59 percent to 41 percent.

The margin, in a conservative state, might have been surprising, but not the outcome. The proposal would have looked to voters radical and extreme: *We're going to sweep it away, immediately? It's all or nothing? And we're going to hand all our trust to legislators in hopes they'll be wise?* I have never met an American who confused his state representative with a philosopher king.

In Kansas, pro-lifers asked for too much. People don't like big swerves and lurches, there's enough anxiety in life. They want to absorb, find a way to trust. *Dobbs* was decided only six weeks ago.

And those six weeks have been confusing and chaotic. Nationally, the pro-life movement spent fifty years fighting for something and then, once it won, its leaders seemed to go silent or sound defensive. It's possible they were attempting to be tactful as opposed to triumphalist, but it left a void and foolish people filled it.

No compelling leader has emerged as a new voice. National energies haven't been scaled down to state activity. Pro-choice forces, galvanized when the *Dobbs* draft leaked in May, raised money, spent it shrewdly, drew in talent, and were pushed by a Democratic Party that thought it finally had a game-changing issue. Pro-lifers didn't have an overarching strategy. But everything we know about abortion tells us that when you turn it into a question of all or nothing, you'll likely get nothing. Thoughtful, humane legislation has to be crafted in the states, put forward, argued for.

The pro-life advocates who filled the rhetorical void competed over who could be most hard-line: *There should be no exceptions for rape, if it even was rape. There should be no exceptions for the life of the mother, that gives dishonest doctors room to make false claims. Maybe we can jail women for getting abortions.*

It was gross, ignorant, and extreme. It excited their followers but hurt the cause they supposedly care about. There was an air of misogyny, of hostility to women. It was, unlike the most thoughtful pro-life arguments of the past fifty years, unloving, unprotective, and punitive.

People heard it and thought, No, that's not what we want.

Moderate, reasoned, balanced approaches will appeal to the vast middle. Arguments over whether women should be prosecuted for crossing state lines to get an abortion won't.

The public face of the pro-life movement looks at the moment loony and vicious. Last Saturday in Florida, Matt Gaetz, the Republican congressman and famous idiot, spoke at a student event and said overweight and unappealing women don't need to fear pregnancy: "Nobody wants to impregnate you if you look like a thumb." A nineteen-year-old pro-choice activist then drew his mockery by responding on Twitter, and NPR reports that she cannily used the confrontation to raise more than $700,000 for pro-choice causes.

We live in a democracy. The pro-life side rightly asked for a democratic solution to a gnawing national problem. To succeed, they need baseline political skills. You persuade people as to the rightness of your vision. You act and speak in good faith so they trust you. You anticipate mischievous and dishonest representations of where you stand. You highlight them and face them. There has in fact been a lot of misrepresentation of where pro-lifers stand and why, and what their proposals will achieve. You have to clear the air. You can win a lot with candor and good faith. You can impress by being prepared and ready.

Most important, there is a political tradition in democracy that consists of these words: "That's asking too much." Don't ask people for more than they can give. Don't go too far, don't lose by asking for a sweeping decision when people will be willing to go step by step. Ask for as much as they can give, pull them toward your vision, but don't be afraid of going slow and steady, be afraid of overloading the grid. That's part of what happened in Kansas: They were asked to take a step they thought extreme, and they don't like extreme.

You have to be clear in explaining how society will arrange itself if you get the measure you asked for. In this case, the pro-life cause, conservatives, and the Republican Party have the chance to speak of, laud, and increase state and private help for women bearing children in difficult circumstances. The antiabortion movement will never really succeed unless it is paired in the public mind with compassion for the struggling. The Republican Party had the chance to align itself with women. Has it taken it? Or is it too busy talking about "impregnating" those you find unattractive?

Finally, if you are going to be in politics you had better know what your own people are thinking. NBC's Steve Kornacki noted the morning after the vote that turnout in Kansas was high—276,000 Democrats, 464,000 Republicans, and 169,000 unaffiliated voters. The number of votes against the abortion amendment was more than 543,000. That means a lot of Republicans voted no. A lot who identify as conservative and live in deep red areas voted no. You have to know where your own people are and build policy and strategy around it.

Because this is a democracy. Policy is decided by votes. Every loss contains the seeds of victory, every victory the seeds of loss. Nothing is permanent.

This is America working it out. Some states will be extreme in one direction, some in the other. It's going to be ugly for a while. Sweet reason has seldom been a dominant characteristic of combatants in this fight. Too bad, because in the vast middle there's a lot of it.

A lot of state decisions will likely come down along lines of where national polling has been—fifteen-week bans, exceptions for rape and the mother's life. In the end we may wind up where Chief Justice John Roberts would have put us. The idea in his concurring opinion in *Dobbs* was to maintain a federal right to abortion while finally granting states broad authority in establishing laws and limits that had previously been prohibited by *Roe v. Wade* and *Planned Parenthood v. Casey*. This approach may have restrained the worst excesses of both sides, removed a sense of alarm, and helped ease the country into fewer abortions in a post-*Roe*, post-*Casey* world.

The *Dobbs* decision, though, requires something more immediate: true adults in legislatures of all levels, and activists who are serious and have a sense of democratic give. All who fight for life must think about this and be our best selves. Or we will wind up having won all, and lost all.

JOHN PAUL II'S PRESCIENT 1995 LETTER TO WOMEN

November 30, 2017

Sometimes you have to take a step back, remove yourself from the moment, and try to ground yourself in what is true, elevated, even eternal.

The week has lent itself to a feeling of instability. The president has deliberately added to the rancor and tension of his nation's daily life, lurching in his tweets from mischief to malice to a kind of psychopathology—personal attacks, insinuations, videos from a group labeled racist by the British government. You always want to say he has reached peak crazy, but you know there's a higher peak on the horizon. What will Everest look like? He has no idea how to be president.

More men of the media have fallen in the reckoning over sexual abuse, most famously a bright, humorous, ratings-busting veteran anchorman, who reportedly had a switch on his desk that locked his office door so he could molest the women he'd trapped inside. He had no idea how to be a man.

Here is something to ground us in the good: Pope John Paul II's 1995 "Letter to Women," sent to the Fourth World Conference on Women, in Beijing. As a document it has more or less fallen through history's cracks. But it's deeply pertinent to this moment and was written with pronounced warmth by a man who before he became a priest hoped to be a playwright. Here is what he said:

You would never be so low as to abuse women if you knew what they are and have been in the history of humanity: "Women have contributed to that history as much as men and, more often than not, they did so in much more difficult conditions. I think particularly of those women who loved culture and art, and devoted their lives to them in spite of the fact that they were frequently at a disadvantage" in education and opportunity. Women have been "underestimated, ignored and not given credit for their intellectual contributions." Only a small part of their achievements have been documented, and yet humanity knows that it "owes a debt" to the "great, immense, feminine 'tradition.'" But, John Paul exclaimed, "how many women have been and continue to be valued more for their physical appearance than for their skill, their professionalism, their intellectual abilities, their deep sensitivity; in a word, the very dignity of their being!"

In a highly personal tone—the italics are his—he offers his appreciation: "Thank you, *women who work!* You are present and active in every area of life—social, economic, cultural, artistic and political." You "unite reason and feeling" and establish "economic and political structures ever more worthy of humanity."

He thanked women who are mothers, daughters, and wives: "Thank you, *every woman,* for the simple fact of being *a woman.*"

Women, he observed, have "in every time and place" suffered abuse, in part because of "cultural conditioning," which has been "an obstacle" to their progress. "Women's dignity has often been unacknowledged and their prerogatives misrepresented; they have often been relegated to the margins of society and even reduced to servitude. This has prevented women from truly being themselves, and it has resulted in a spiritual impoverishment of humanity." Poor thinking and cold hearts have contributed to the conditioning; some blame "has belonged to not just a few members of the Church."

Members of the Christian faith must look both back and forward. To free women "from every kind of exploitation and domination," we must learn from "the attitude of Jesus Christ himself," who transcended "the established norms of his own culture" and "treated women with openness, respect, acceptance and tenderness."

There is "an urgent need to achieve *real equality* in every area; equal pay for equal work, protection for working mothers, fairness in career advancements, equality of spouses with regard to family rights."

And listen to this alarm—again, from twenty-two years ago: John Paul hit hard on "the long and degrading history . . . of violence against women in the area of sexuality": "The time has come to condemn . . . the types of *sexual violence* which frequently have women for their object, and to pass laws which effectively defend them from such violence."

There is more, and I urge you to read it, but it is a very modern document, a feminist statement in the best sense. When a friend sent it this week and I reread it, what I thought was, If all the now-famous sexual abusers had ever pondered such thoughts (as opposed to parroting them on the air before flipping the switch and locking the door) and considered questions of true equality, they never would have done what they did. They wouldn't have been able to think of women as things, as mere commodities to be used for imperial pleasure. They would have had to consider their dignity.

At the heart of the current scandals is a simple disrespect and disregard for women, and an inability to love them.

A few things on my mind as the scandals progress: Friends, especially of my generation, fear that things will get carried away—innocent men will be railroaded, the workplace will be swept with some crazy new Puritanism. A female journalist wryly reflected, "This is America—what's worth doing is worth overdoing."

This would be bad. America takes place in the office, and anywhere America takes place there will be the drama of men and women. It is not wrong to fear it will become a dry, repressed, politically correct zone, no longer human.

But the way I see it, what's happening is a housecleaning that's long overdue. A big broom is sweeping away bad behaviors and bad ways of being. It's not pleasant. If you're taking joy in it, there's something wrong with you.

The trick is to leave the place cleaner, not colder.

Common sense will help. Offices aren't for ten-year-olds but for adults. Deep down you know what abuse is: You can tell when someone's taking or demanding what isn't his. By adulthood you should also know what friendliness, appreciation, and attraction are. But it comes down to whether someone is *taking or demanding what isn't his.*

As for unjust accusations, it is true—they will come. Just accusations used to be ignored; in the future unjust ones will be heard.

Here the press will be more important than ever. They have just broken a scandal through numbers and patterns—numbers of accusers and patterns of behavior. If journalists stick to this while also retaining their deep skepticism and knowledge of human agendas, things will stay pretty straight. So far, American journalists have been sober and sophisticated, and pursued justice without looking for scalps. Human resources departments will have to operate in the same way—with seriousness and knowledge of human nature.

My concern is something else. It is that young women, girls in high school, young women in college and just starting out, are going to have too heightened a sense of danger in the workplace, too great a sense of threat.

But there are more good men and women out there than bad.

There are more good ones than bad.

Know balance. Have faith.

MRS. SMITH'S TIPS FOR NEW LAWMAKERS

December 10, 2020

We have a new Congress coming in, the 117th, to be sworn in on January 3, and its members could benefit from Margaret Chase Smith's rules of the road. Mrs. Smith was the first senator of either party to stand up to Joe McCarthy. Her fellow Republicans scrammed: McCarthy was popular back home. So did Democrats; they feared McCarthy, too. What she'd done and suffered through made her name. History appreciated her, and so did flinty, independent Maine.

The problem with McCarthy was that he was reckless and cynical but there was some truth in his overall position. There were communists in the U.S. government. Alger Hiss was one. But not the 205 or 81 of them he'd claim, and not the innocent people he smeared and whose lives he ruined. So standing against him was a delicate thing: Your moral disapproval had to be both compelling and calibrated, acknowledging the truth but asserting other, higher, longer-ranged truths.

She did that. What can those being sworn in learn from her?

- *Know what you're about and say it.* Smith wasn't much for grand political theory; she was plainer than that and closer to the ground. But she knew why she belonged to her party and she had a picture of it in her head. Her Republican Party was Lincoln's party of justice and mercy, Teddy Roosevelt's of "trustbusting," Dwight D. Eisenhower's of "peace" and "world leadership." David Richards, director of the Margaret Chase Smith Library in Skowhegan, Maine, told me, "Being a politician in her conception was about service and conscience more than ideology." But she had a philosophical approach and she didn't shy from stating it. In her stump speech when she ran for president in 1964 she said, "I call myself a moderate or independent Republican. I operate independently of the party but I never fight the organization." She named where she stood: "I am at the left of [Barry] Goldwater, and at the right of [Nelson] Rockefeller."

- *If you want to be believed, say it straight.* She didn't think public remarks should be fancy, and she probably wouldn't recognize the airy, edgeless statements we mistake for eloquence. "My speeches in the Senate are blunt and to the point," she said. "I do not indulge in political oratory." "I study the facts, make up my mind, and stick to my decisions. I never dodge an issue."

- *Your state is more than a platform for your rise.* Her connection to Maine was almost mystical. "She was Maine," said her biographer, Patricia L. Schmidt, author of *Margaret Chase Smith: Beyond Convention*, by telephone. What deepened her knowledge is that her entire life had been one long status shift. Her mother was a waitress, her father a barber; she was the oldest of six and didn't go to college but to work at the telephone company. She wound up as ranking member of the Senate Armed Services Committee, putting the CEO of Lockheed on hold.

She knew how the salesgirl at the five-and-dime saw the world because she'd been one; how businesspeople thought because she'd been one of them, too. She wasn't exactly awed by the patriarchy. Her father was an alcoholic and not fully stable, her late husband a philanderer who hurt and embarrassed her. (No one knew, but she quietly supported the mother of his illegitimate child, Ms. Schmidt says.) From this emotional background she rose to social respectability, which was her real status shift and allowed her to be an outsider-insider.

Travel broadens but struggle deepens, and gives you unexpected insights. When she was at odds with the sentiment of her state she didn't think, *My people hold some old-fashioned views, I'll have to be careful.* She felt leaders set an example of how to think, make an argument for a point of view, help bring people along. She believed the imperative of politics was not to accept but to improve.

- *Don't abandon the middle ground, which actually exists.* We're a big and varied country. Maine isn't Mississippi. People can be ornery about their rights and slippery about their responsibilities. No one likes being lectured. Lead toward your conception of the right but always seek middle ground. Never leave it abandoned. Do that and the country splits into separate camps.

- *Understand you won't always be appreciated.* Smith was a breakthrough woman who encouraged women to enter politics. She backed an Equal Rights Amendment, but 1970s feminists didn't acknowledge her accomplishments and called her "elitist," by which they meant "Republican." An idiot from the National Organization for Women said Smith stood for "everything women in the liberation movement want to eliminate." Smith in turn didn't like their lack of decorum and criticized their air of anger and grievance. She felt those attitudes would cause division in the great center, and that change lasts when it comes through inspiration, not accusation.

- *People need concrete help.* If Smith were with us now, she would doubtless wear a face mask—she'd lived through the 1918 flu pandemic—and she would lacerate the government for not sending face masks to every American last spring. If it didn't have them in reserve it should have admitted it, not gone back and forth about whether masks are necessary. Health officials could have told people how to make them at home; they could have sent cloth. I imagine her saying, "You can't suddenly change your mind and command people to go to the drugstore or Amazon. Not everyone has a computer, not everyone has a charge card; it's your job to help them!"

- *Spirit has its place.* Smith didn't much like John F. Kennedy; she saw him as a Massachusetts glamour boy. She was willing to work with him when he became president, but it started out rocky when she fought one of his foreign-policy appointments because the appointee's oil interests might skew his thinking on the Mideast. JFK took revenge by visiting Maine and forgetting to invite her to the greeting party. She ignored the snub, jumped on a plane, went anyway, and merrily waved at the crowds. Seeing her moxie, he changed tack. Would she like to ride back to Washington with him on gleaming Air Force One? No, she said, snubbing him back. And made sure the story got around. Later he called her "formidable."

- *Human sentiment matters.* It's not a byproduct of a political life, or any life, it's the product. People should have honest feelings and show them, as opposed to, say, commoditizing your emotions for public consumption. When JFK died there was a lot of oratory in the Senate. She didn't speak. She listened for a while and then crossed the aisle, unpinned the rose she wore each day on her lapel, and placed it quietly on his old desk. Everyone saw. No one touched that rose for days. I remember hearing years ago that when Smith died, on Memorial Day 1995, someone put a rose on her old desk. No one knows who, but the rose went similarly undisturbed. I'm not sure it's true, but it should be.

MIND YOUR MANNERS, SAYS EDITH WHARTON

August 22, 2019

This week we turn the column over to Edith Wharton (1862–1937), the great woman of letters and author of the Gilded Age novels *The Age of Innocence*, *The House of Mirth*, and *The Custom of the Country*. She was the first American woman to win the Pulitzer Prize for fiction. She was also named a chevalier of the Legion of Honor for her valiant assistance to her beloved France during World War I.

Mrs. Wharton:

I have been invited this late August evening to speak to the American people about the decline in their public manners, which has reached crisis stage.

I would have preferred a radio address by what is called nationwide hookup but I am told my voice, which is reminiscent of that of Eleanor Roosevelt, carries inferences of another age, which might undercut the pertinence and urgency of my message.

I freely admit that there are several ways to describe me, and fabulous old battle-ax is one. But I know some things about human society, and can well imagine the abrading effect of a widespread collapse of public courtesy.

You have all become very rude. Not from ignorance, as Americans were in the past, but from indifference and amid affluence.

In your daily dealings you have grown slovenly, indifferent, and cold. A great nation cannot continue in this way. Nations run in part on manners; they are the lubricant that allows the great machine to hum.

Among the harassments I see you inflict on each other:

It is discourteous to walk down a busy sidewalk with your eyes trained on a cellphone, barreling forward with disregard for others who must carefully make way and negotiate their bodies around yours so as not to harm you. You must think you are more important than the other citizens of the sidewalk. Who told you this? Who lied to you in this way?

Eyes on a phone and pods in your ears—have you no sense of community? You have detached from the reality around you, which is a subtle rebuff of your fellow citizens. You enter your own world. When Leonardo and Dr. Einstein entered their own worlds they encountered richness, a fierce originality that ultimately benefited all. Is that what you encounter?

You must have a sense of community! Take part, be part, see, and hear. Stop assuming everyone will work their way around you. That is the summoning of a calamity you will deserve.

You must come to understand that other people can hear you on the cellphone in confined public spaces such as the elevator. You must come to understand: *Other people have a right not to hear your sound.* They have a right not to hear your grating voice, your huffy exchanges that convey the banality of your interests, all of which, on a bad day, when spirits are low, can make those around you want to ruffle in their purse for a pistol with which to shoot themselves in the head.

It might be better if you were instead "there"—to make brief eye contact and nod, as if you are human beings on earth together. At the very least, understand you should delay the call until the elevator doors open.

Last week I was in a nail spa, as they're called, idiotically. A woman in her thirties was screeching into her phone, which was on speakerphone mode. After a few moments I informed her she was disturbing others. She literally said, "I am closing a deal! I don't care!"

And you wonder why socialism is making a comeback.

You have apparently forgotten that "Excuse me" is a request, not a command. "Excuse me" is an abbreviated question: "Would you excuse me, please? Thank you." All in a soft voice. It is not a command to be barked as you push down the aisle at Walgreens.

There is the matter of "No problem." You perform a small courtesy, I thank you, you reply "No problem." Which implies, If it were a problem, lady, I wouldn't do it. "If it were at all challenging I would never be courteous." Why would you admit this to a fellow citizen? Why demoralize her in this way?

Similarly with "No worries." A young person emails and asks me to do something, perhaps attend an event. I reply carefully, with gratitude and honest regret, that I am unable. The response? Two words: "No worries." I'm tempted to answer, "You don't worry me, dearie." Of course I don't; it would be like slapping the maid. But "no worries" claims a certain precedence—"I am in charge and instruct you not to feel anxiety about frustrating my wishes." Child, you're not in charge. Try "Thanks, I understand, I hope another time."

First-name culture is fully established. It is vulgar and inhuman. It shows disrespect for person and privacy, and the mature experience it as assaultive. A first name is what you are called by your intimates, by friends and lovers. It does not belong in a stranger's mouth. I may grant you permission to use it, that is my right. But you cannot seize permission—that is not your right.

I receive solicitations from people I've never met, "Dear Edie." I honestly wonder, Do I know you? And then realize that's what they want me to wonder, because if I think I might know them I'm more likely to respond. It's not democratization, it's marketing.

They take something from you when they take your name. And once they've taken that they will be taking more.

On the phone with the bank, regarding a recent transaction:

Bank worker: "Yes, Edith, how can we help you today?"

Me: "Ah. I am certain you are a very nice person and if I knew you I would quickly ask you to call me by my first name, but since we're not old friends yet I would appreciate—"

Him (sullen, impatient, flat): "I'm-sorry-about-that-how-would-you-like-me-to-address-you?"

Me: "As your enemy. As the implacable foe of all you represent. Does that work?"

What the new world doesn't understand is that when you address us as Miss, Mrs., Ms., or Mr., we usually say, "Feel free to use my first name." Because we are democratic, egalitarian, and fear the guillotine. But we're pleased when someone asks permission, and respond with the grateful effulgence of the losing side.

There is more to say but I must close.

I am not calling for a new refinement. That is beyond my capacity and your ability. It is possible you're entrenched, as I said of the Vanderbilts, in a sort of Thermopylae of bad taste from which no earthly force can dislodge you.

Great nations have fallen over less.

I am merely suggesting a less selfish and vulgar way of being. Surely you can consider that.

If a political figure should come by whose slate consisted of "America, reclaim your manners," he would "break through" and win in a landslide. Because everyone in this country suffers—literally suffers—from the erosion of the essential public courtesies that allow us to move forward in the world happily, and with some hope.

Thank you. I am grateful to have you as a reader.

THE SAN FRANCISCO REBELLION

February 17, 2022

It was a landslide. That's the important fact of this week's San Francisco school-board recall election: There was nothing mixed or ambivalent about the outcome. Three members were resoundingly ejected from their jobs: 79 percent voted to oust Alison Collins, 75 percent to fire Gabriela López, the board president, and 72 percent to remove Faauuga Moliga, the vice president.

This was a vote against progressive education officials in the heart of liberal San Francisco. It is a signal moment because of its head-chopping definitiveness, its clarity, its swiftness, and its unignorable statement by parents on what they must have and won't accept. It was a battle in the Democratic Party's civil war between liberals and the progressive left. And it marks a continuation of the parents' rebellion that surfaced in November in Virginia's upset gubernatorial election.

It is in the way of things that Democratic leaders in Congress won't feel they have an excuse to crack down hard on the progressive wing of their party until the entire party loses big in the 2022 elections. But Democratic voters on the ground aren't waiting for permission. They are taking a stick to wokeness whether the party's leaders do or not.

You know most of what was at issue. During the height of the pandemic, when San Francisco's schools were closed, parents were increasingly frustrated and newly angry. They saw that remote learning was an inadequate substitute for children being in the classroom. Many sensed that a year or two out of school would leave their children with an educational deficit that would not be repaired. The teachers unions balked at reopening and the Board of Education approached the problem with what seemed muted interest.

Although they did a lot of word-saying featuring impenetrable jargon, as school boards do, they didn't have a plan and the schools didn't open.

While the board was failing to open the schools it was doing other things. It produced government by non sequitur. The board focused on issues of woke anti-racism and oppression. The problem wasn't whether the kids were getting an education, it was whether the boarded-up schools had unfortunate names. They spent months researching the question and proposed renaming a third of the system's 125 schools. Many were named for previously respectable people like Abraham Lincoln, Thomas Jefferson, George Washington, Francis Scott Key, and Robert Louis Stevenson. Their names were "inappropriate" because their lives and actions could be connected with charges of racism, sexism, and colonialism. From the *San Francisco Chronicle:* "The move shocked many principals and families, who questioned whether changing a name was a mid-pandemic priority when their children cannot physically attend the school in question."

The public rose up—stop this stuff, get our kids back in school! The backlash intensified when it was revealed some of the board's historical research was dependent on cutting and pasting from Wikipedia.

So it wasn't only government by non sequitur, it was inept. The board backed off and said, essentially, that the matter needed more study.

The board soon moved on to another item on the progressive wish list. It homed in on academically elite public high schools that based admission on testing and grades. For people who can't afford a $40,000-a-year private-school tuition, such schools are a godsend; they were designed long ago to offer demanding course study to students with limited money but demonstrable gifts.

The board decided too many Asian-American and white students were accepted in the schools. So they voted to scrap testing and replace it with a permanent lottery system for admission at Lowell High, one of only two campuses in the district to use merit-based admissions. (The decision was later overturned by lawsuits.)

Now parents exploded, very much including the Asian community. It got more heated when it was discovered Ms. Collins had an old tweet accusing Asian-Americans of using "white supremacist thinking to assimilate and 'get ahead.'" She seemed rather a creepy and bigoted person to have in a position of such authority.

Even aside from that, parents who were up nights helping their children with homework, seeing that schoolwork was done and discipline learned, felt their effort was being discounted and their children abandoned to abstract notions of equity. It wasn't fair. It wasn't right. Kids have to be taught to earn their way through effort. Lotteries don't teach them that; lotteries teach them it's all luck.

Now the recall process took off.

It did not help that just before the pandemic, in 2019, the board had famously turned to censorship. There was a big, colorful series of Depression-era frescoes in a local high school. They'd been there since the 1930s and were commissioned by the Works Progress Administration of the New Deal, a stylized depiction of the founding of America that included slaves and American Indians. The board decided it was racist, cruel, reductive; there was the implication it was right-wing art. In fact the frescoes were the work of a Russian immigrant to America, Victor Arnautoff, who was a communist and trying to bring attention to the cruelty present in some of America's history. No matter, it was offensive, so the board decided to paint over the murals.

Art-sensitive San Francisco rose up: This is akin to book burning, you don't lay waste to art. The board then decided it wouldn't paint over the frescoes, merely conceal them behind barriers of some sort.

What was astonishing as you followed the story is what seemed the board members' shock at parental pushback. They seemed so detached from the normal hopes of normal people. They seemed honestly unaware of them. It was as if they were operating in some abstract universe in which their decisions demonstrated their praiseworthy anti-racist bona fides. But voters came to see their actions as a kind of woke progressive vandalism that cleverly avoided their central responsibility: to open the schools.

School boards somehow always seem to think they are immune from pushback, that their pronouncements will never be opposed because they can barely be understood.

But people have a way of seeing. If, during a pandemic lockdown, board members speak often and thoughtfully of the increased likelihood of the abuse of neglected children, one will get a sense of their motivation and heart. If instead they dilate on political issues that deflect, one will get a different, darker view of their motivation and heart.

That's why the three in San Francisco were fired.

What happened shows again that there is a real parents movement going on, and it is going to make a difference in our politics.

Democrats dismiss these issues as "culture-war distractions." They are not; they are about life at its most real, concrete, and immediate. That easy dismissal reveals the party's distance from the lives of its own constituents.

To think parents would sacrifice their children for your ideology, or an ideology coming from within your ranks that you refuse to stand up to, is political malpractice at a high level.

Joe Biden received 85 percent of the vote in San Francisco in 2020. Those board members just lost their seats by more than 70 percent. A cultural rebellion within the Democratic Party has begun.

THE KIDS ARE NOT ALL RIGHT

April 7, 2022

Journalists and people who think aloud for a living are often invited to gatherings where experts in various fields share what they know. These meetings often operate under Chatham House rules, in which you can write of the ideas presented but not directly quote speakers. At such a gathering this week I was especially struck by the talks on Big Tech, and since Congress is considering various regulatory bills I want to say what I gleaned.

First and most obviously, nobody understands the million current aspects of social-media sites. They raise questions ranging from the political (misinformation, disinformation, deliberate polarization, ideological bias) and the technological (hidden data harvesting) to the legal (antitrust law, First Amendment rights) and the moral and ethical (deliberately addicting users, the routine acquisition and selling of private information, pornography). It's all so big and complex. Mark Zuckerberg, who invented the social-media world we live in, appears to have thrown in the towel and fled to the metaverse, where things will no doubt become even more complex and bizarre. But what he calls a visionary next step looks very much like an escape attempt.

The breakthrough event in public understanding of social-media problems was the congressional testimony, last fall, of Facebook whistleblower Frances Haugen. She said Instagram, owned by Facebook parent Meta, was fully aware it was damaging the mental health of children and teenagers. She had proof, internal documents showing Instagram knew of studies demonstrating increased suicidal thoughts and eating disorders among young girls who used the site. Big Tech had failed at what Google, at the turn of this century, famously took as its motto: "Don't be evil." That wouldn't seem the most demanding mission, yet they all failed.

One thing that was strange and unreal about her celebrated testimony is that it was a revelation of what everybody already knew. Professionals in the field knew, think-tank observers knew, Big Tech knew it had addictive properties, they were put there deliberately to be addictive. It was part of the business model. Attentive parents knew as they watched their kids scroll. Ms. Haugen spoke of what she called "little feedback loops" in which "likes and comments and reshares" trigger "hits of dopamine to your friends so they will create more content." But now at least everyone else knows.

The difficulty at the heart of all Big Tech debate is how hard it is to get the facts, and how the facts keep changing. Transparency and disclosure are urgently required—how much information is being gathered about you each day, to whom is it sold, and for what purpose? The social-media sites don't want to tell you, or tell each other. The nature of the beast is opaque and fluid. How do you audit an algorithm? It's a moving river changing all the time. And the algorithms are proprietary. But constructive regulation must be based on clear information.

I asked a speaker if I was thinking correctly when I imagine algorithms: I see them as a series of waves, not necessarily in sequence, different in size, pushing my small skiff in this direction or that. No, she said, the algorithm isn't the wave, it's the water. It's the thing on which you sail. To go to a site is to choose to cast off.

Another speaker: When we speak of the internet we speak of "privacy rights." Companies are taking information they glean from your use of tech and without your permission selling it for purposes that aren't fully clear. This violates your privacy, but there's another way to look at it. Many of the devices you carry with you are pinging out exactly where you are. They know you got out of a car at Twenty-third and M. But your current location should belong to you. It is a private *property* issue when someone takes it from you. Because you belong to you. Making it an issue of property rights makes things clearer.

No one among the experts or participants had faith in Congress's ability to understand adequately or to move in a knowing and constructive way to curb Big Tech. The previous hearings have shown how out of their depth they are. The heads of Big Tech had been hauled in a few years ago and were supposed to break out in a sweat under heavy grilling, but they were pressed on petty irrelevancies and sucked up to, along the lines of *You started your business in a garage—only in America! Does Facebook charge for membership? No, Senator, we're totally free! Why doesn't my page load?* The hearings were a signal moment—the stakes were high and the inventors of Big Tech walked out more arrogant than ever. Because now they knew their opposition, their supposed regulators—the people's representatives!—were uninformed, almost determinedly so, and shallow. Big Tech had hired every lobbying shop in Washington, made generous contributions to organizations and candidates.

We'll see what happens on Capitol Hill. It would probably be best for America's worried parents to assume the cavalry isn't coming and take matters into their hands.

A participant suggested an at least partial solution that doesn't require technological sophistication and could be done with quick and huge public support.

Why can't we put a strict age limit on using social-media sites: You have to be eighteen to join TikTok, YouTube, Instagram? Why not? You're not allowed to drink at fourteen or drive at twelve; you can't vote at fifteen. Isn't there a public interest here?

Applying such control would empower parents who face "all the other kids are allowed" with an answer: "Because it's against the law."

When we know children are being harmed by something, why can't the state help? In theory this might challenge economic libertarians who agree with what Milton Friedman said fifty years ago, that it is the duty of companies to maximize shareholder value. Instagram makes massive profit from ads and influencers aimed at teenagers. But a counter and rising school of conservative thought would answer: Too bad. Our greater responsibility is to see to it that an entire generation of young people not be made shallow and mentally ill through addictive social-media use.

The nature and experience of childhood has been changed by social media in some very bad ways. Why can't we, as a nation, change this? We all have a share in this.

A participant here told a story of a friend, the mother of a large Virginia family who raised her kids closely and with limited use of social media. The mother took her children to shop for food. The woman at the checkout counter, who had been observing the family, asked the mother, "Do you homeschool your kids?" The mother wasn't sure of the spirit of the question but said, "Yes, I do. Why do you ask?" The checkout woman said, "Because they have children's eyes." And not the thousand-yard stare of the young always scrolling on their phones.

There were many different views expressed at the meetings but on this all seemed to agree, and things became animated.

SAVE CAPITALISM!

February 14, 2019

Let's think about the broader, less immediate meaning of our political era. This is how I read it and have read it for some time:

The Democratic Party is going hard left. There will be stops and starts but it's the general trajectory and will be for the foreseeable future. Pew Research sees the party lurching to the left since 2009; Gallup says the percentage of Democrats calling themselves liberal has jumped twenty-three points since 2000. But you don't need polls. More than seventy Democrats in the House, and a dozen in the Senate, have signed on to the Green New Deal, an extreme-to-the-point-of-absurdist plan that is yet serious: Its authors have staked out what they want in terms of environmental and economic policy, will try to win half or a quarter of it, and on victory will declare themselves to have been moderate all along. The next day they will continue to push for everything. The party's presidential hopefuls propose to do away with private medical insurance and abolish ICE. Three years ago Hillary Clinton would have called this extreme; today it is her party's emerging consensus.

The academy and our mass entertainment culture are entities of the left and will continue to push in that direction. Millennials, the biggest voting-age bloc in America, are to the left of the generations before them. Moderates are aging out. The progressives are young and will give their lives to politics: It's all they've ever known. It is a mistake to dismiss their leaders as goofballs who'll soon fall off the stage. They may or may not, but those who support and surround them are serious ideologues who mean to own the future.

None of this feels like a passing phase. It feels like the outline of a great political struggle that will be fought over the next ten years or more.

Two thoughts, in the broadest possible strokes, on how we got here:

The American establishment had to come to look very, very bad. Two long unwon wars destroyed the GOP's reputation for sobriety in foreign affairs, and the 2008 crash cratered its reputation for economic probity. Both disasters gave those inclined to turn from the status quo inspiration and arguments. Culturally, 2008 was especially resonant: The government bailed out its buddies and threw no one in jail, and the capitalists failed to defend the system that made them rich. They dummied up, hunkered down, and waited for it to pass.

Americans have long sort of accepted a kind of deal regarding leadership by various elites and establishments. The agreement was that if the elites more or less play by the rules, protect the integrity of the system, and care about the people, they can have their mansions. But when you begin to perceive that the great and mighty are not necessarily on your side, when they show no particular sense of responsibility to their fellow citizens, all bets are off. The compact is broken: They no longer get to have their mansions. They no longer get to be "the rich."

For most of the twentieth century the poor in America didn't hate the rich for their mansions; they *wanted* a mansion and thought they could get one if things turned their way. When you think the system's rigged, your attitude changes.

On the right the same wars, the same crash, and a different aspect. In the great issue of the 2016 campaign it became unmistakably clear that the GOP elite did not care in the least how the working class experienced immigration. The party already worried too much about border security—that's the lesson the elites took from Mitt Romney's loss in 2012, according to their famous autopsy. They appeared to look after their own needs, their own reputations: *We're not racist like people who worry about the border!* They were, as I've written, the protected, who looked down on those with rougher lives. The unprotected noticed, and began to sunder their relationship with establishments and elites.

Donald Trump came of that sundering. He was the perfect insult thrown in the establishment's face. *You're such losers we're hiring a reality-TV star to take your place. He'll be better than you.*

Conservatives regularly attend symposia to discuss the future of conservatism. Republicans in Washington stumble around trying to figure what to stand for beyond capitalizing on whatever zany thing some socialist said today.

But isn't their historical purpose *clear*? Their job—now and in the coming decade—is, in a supple, clever, and concerted way, to save the free-market system from those who would dismantle it. It is to preserve and defend the capitalism that made America a great thing in the world and that, for all its flaws and inequities, created and spread stupendous wealth. The natural job of conservatives is to conserve, in this case that great system.

I'll go whole hog here. We need a cleaned-up capitalism, not a weary, sighing, acceptance-of-man's-fallen-nature capitalism. Republicans and conservatives need a more capacious sense of what is needed in America now, including what their own voters need. The party needs a tax-and-spending reality that takes into account an understandable and prevalent mood of great need. They need to be moderate, peaceable, and tactful on social issues, but firm, too. This is where the left really is insane: As the earnest, dimwitted governor of Virginia thoughtfully pointed out, they do allow the full-term baby to be born, then make it comfortable as they debate whether it should be allowed to take its first breath or quietly expire on the table. A party that can't stand up against that doesn't deserve to exist.

All this must be done with a sense of how Americans on the ground are seeing things. What they see all around them is cultural catastrophe—drugs, the decline of faith, the splintering of all norms by which they'd lived, schools that don't teach and that leave their kids with a generalized anxiety. They want more help to deal with this. If you said, "We're going to have a national program to help our boys become good men," they would be for it, they would cheer.

If you said, "We're going to get serious and apply brains and money to what we all know is a mental-health crisis in America," they wouldn't care about the cost—and they'd be right not to care. They think as a people we've changed, our character has changed, and this dims our future. *Make things better on the ground now and we'll figure out the rest later.*

These are not quaint nostalgists pining for the past, they are realists looking at ruin. They know some future crisis will test whether we can hold together as a nation. Whatever holds us together now must be undergirded, expanded.

Much will depend on how the Republican Party handles this epic era, because the Democrats are not only going left, they will do it badly. They will lurch, they will be spurred by anger and abstractions, they will be destructive. They really would kill the goose that laid the golden egg, because they feel no loyalty to it.

Republicans, save that goose. Change yourselves and save capitalism.

You are thinking, "My goodness, that's what FDR said he was doing!"

Yes.

THE PRESIDENT HAS A PRESENTATION PROBLEM

April 21, 2022

I want to talk about Joe Biden and his unique problems presenting his presidency. You're aware of his political position and the polls. The latest from CNN has him at 39 percent approval. Public admiration began to plummet during the Afghanistan withdrawal. That disaster came as it was becoming clear the president was handing his party's progressive caucus functional control of his domestic agenda, which fell apart and never recovered.

James Carville the other night on MSNBC amusingly and almost persuasively said Democrats in the 2022 congressional elections should hit Republicans hard on their weirdo content—candidates who are both extreme and inane, conspiracists in the base. But the Democrats too have their weirdo quotient—extreme culture warriors, members of the Squad—and last summer the president appeared to have thrown in with them. That and Afghanistan were fateful for his position, and then came inflation.

But what struck me this week was a little-noticed poll from the NH Journal. It's always interesting to know what's going on in the first presidential primary state, but the Journal itself seemed startled by the answer to its question: If the 2024 election were held today and the candidates were Joe Biden versus Republican Governor Chris Sununu, who would you back? Mr. Sununu trounced the president 53 percent to 36 percent. Mr. Sununu is popular and that unusual thing, a vigorous moderate conservative who appears to have actual intellectual commitments. But Mr. Biden carried New Hampshire in 2020 with 53 percent. He's cratering.

All politics grows from policies, and policies are announced and argued for through presentation, including, crucially, speeches. Joe Biden has a presentation problem. This is worthy of note because his entire career has been about presentation, specifically representing a mood. In fifty years he has cycled through Dashing Youth, the Next JFK, Middle-Class Joe, and Late-Life Finder of His Inner Progressive. But the mood he represents now isn't a good one. It's there in the New Hampshire poll. Asked if they thought Biden was "physically and mentally up to the job" if there's a crisis, "not very/not at all" got 54 percent and "very/somewhat" 42 percent. Here we all use euphemisms: "slowing down," "not at the top of his game." If Mr. Biden's policies were popular, nobody would mind that he seems to be slowing. But they aren't.

So to the presentation problem. Here are some difficulties when he speaks.

When he stands at a podium and reads from a teleprompter, his mind seems to wander quickly from the meaning of what he's saying to the impression he's making. You can sort of see this, that he's always wondering how he's coming across. When he catches himself he tends to compensate by enacting emotion.

But the emotion he seems most publicly comfortable with is indignation. An example is his answer to a reporter's question in November about the administration's plans to compensate illegal-immigrant parents who'd been separated from their children at the border. Suddenly he was angry-faced; he raised his voice, increased his tempo, and started jabbing the air. "You lost your child. It's gone! You deserve some kind of compensation, no matter what the circumstances." Then, catching himself, he added mildly, "What that will be, I have no idea." He was trying to show presentness, engagement. But there's often an "angry old man yelling at clouds" aspect to this.

There are small tics that worked long ago. He often speaks as if we are fascinated by the family he came from and that formed him. Thus he speaks of the old neighborhood and lessons. *And my mother told me, Joey, don't comb your hair with buttered toast.* This was great for a Knights of Columbus pancake breakfast in Rehoboth Beach, Delaware, but not now. For all the mystique of the presidency, people hired you to do a job and want you to be clear and have a plan. They aren't obsessed with your family, they're obsessed with their family.

Mr. Biden tends to be extremely self-referential: "I'll give it to you straight, as I promised that I always would." Because I'm such a straight shooter. It's better to shoot straight and not always be bragging. He should lose "Lemme say that again." When you speak to America you don't have to repeat yourself for the slow. I don't think he's aware he often seems to be talking down. People will tolerate this from a politician when they think he's their moral or intellectual superior, but they push back when they don't, as in the polls.

The larger problem for the president is that in his most important prepared speeches there's a lot of extremely boring faux eloquence, big chunks of smooth roundedness, and nothing sticks. Last April to a joint session of Congress: "America is on the move again, turning peril into possibility, crisis into opportunity, setback into strength." This sounds as if it means something—it has the rhythm and sound of good thought—but it doesn't, really. It's the language of the sixty-second advertising spot, and America tunes it out. *Not from malice but from Alice.* It's the sound of the past forty or fifty years, meaning it's had its day.

Mr. Biden has an opportunity to do something new, reinvent his rhetorical approach. Why not, nothing else has worked. He should commit, when speaking, to Be Here Now. He should be straightforward and modest.

When I think of what is needed at this moment in history, my mind goes to the brisk factuality, the lack of emotionalism, of October 22, 1962. John F. Kennedy from his desk in the Oval Office offering eighteen minutes of fact and thought. "Good evening, my fellow citizens. This government, as promised, has maintained the closest surveillance of the Soviet military buildup on the island of Cuba. Within the past week, unmistakable evidence has established the fact that a series of offensive missile sites is now in preparation on that imprisoned island. . . . Having now confirmed and completed our evaluation of the evidence and our decision on a course of action, this government feels obliged to report this new crisis to you in fullest detail."

It was down to the bone, stark, and completely compelling. The military response he explained was persuasive because it was based in fact and clearly put interpretation. He provided complicated information: "The characteristics of these new missile sites indicate two distinct types of installations." You talk only to the intelligent this way; his listeners were aware of the compliment. He didn't stoop to them but assumed they'd reach to him.

He wasn't self-referential: He didn't say "as I promised," but "as promised," because putting himself in the forefront would be vulgar. It was "this government," not "my government." He said, "This nation is opposed to war. We are also true to our word." He was declaring the American position while putting the virtue of it on America, not himself.

You say, Well, that was a crisis, you cut to the chase in crisis. But our political moment is pretty much nonstop crises, and there are more than enough national platforms for emotionalism.

All politicians could learn from this approach. They have no idea how refreshing it would sound, how gratefully it would be received: "I'm not being patronized by my inferiors!" How people might listen again.

WHAT COMES AFTER ACHESON'S CREATION?

February 9, 2017

Let's look at a big, pressing question. Last fall at a defense forum a significant military figure was asked, If you could wave a magic wand, what is the one big thing you'd give the U.S. military right now?

We'd all been talking about the effects of the sequester and reform of the procurement system and I expected an answer along those lines. Instead he said, We need to know what the U.S. government wants from us. We need to know the overarching plan because if there's no higher plan we can't make plans to meet the plan.

This was freshly, bluntly put, and his answer came immediately, without pause.

The world is in crisis. The old order that more or less governed things after World War II has been swept away. The changed world that followed the fall of the Berlin Wall is also over.

We've been absorbing this for a while, since at least 2014, when Russia invaded Crimea. But what plan are we developing to approach the world as it is now?

I always notice that a day after a terrible tornado hits the Midwest the television crews swarm in and film the victims picking through what's left. People literally stand where their house was, their neighborhood was. In shock, they point at some flattened debris and say, "That was our living room." They rummage around, find a photo. "This was my son's wedding."

That's sort of what a lot of those interested in foreign policy have been doing in recent years—staring in shock at the wreckage.

But something has to be rebuilt. Everyone now has to be an architect, or a cement-pourer, or a master craftsman carpenter.

It's been instructive the past week to reread a small classic of statecraft, *Present at the Creation* by Dean Acheson, published in 1969. As undersecretary and then secretary of state he was involved in the creation of the postwar order.

After the war the world was in crisis, much of it in collapse. "The period was marked by the disappearance of world powers and empires, or their reduction to medium-sized states, and from this wreckage emerged a multiplicity of states . . . all of them largely undeveloped politically and economically. Overshadowing all loomed two dangers to all—the Soviet Union's new-found power and expansive imperialism, and the development of nuclear weapons." The Cold War had begun. China was in civil war, about to fall to communism. Europe's economy had been destroyed. Europe and Asia were "in a state of utter exhaustion and economic dislocation." The entire world seemed to be "disintegrating."

What came after the crisis was the Marshall Plan, in which the U.S., itself exhausted by the war, helped its allies, and enemies, survive and resist communism. The objective, as the Truman administration declared it, was not relief but revival—spending American money to bring back agriculture, industry, and trade. New financing was needed from Congress, in amounts then thought impossible—hundreds of millions that became billions.

It was an effort appropriate to its time. Apart from its essential good—millions didn't die of starvation, nations such as Greece did not fall to communism—it brought America more than half a century of the world's sometimes grudging but mostly enthusiastic admiration. They now knew we were not only a powerful nation but a great people. This was not unhelpful in times of crisis down the road.

It is exciting at a time like this to read of the development of a successful foreign-policy effort from conception to execution. And—how to say it?—Acheson's first-rate second-rateness is inspiring. This was not a deeply brilliant man, not a grand strategist, but more a manager who was a good judge of others' concepts. He could see facts—he had sturdy sight—and spy implications. He had the gift of natural confidence. He could also be clueless: One of his most respected aides was the Soviet spy Alger Hiss.

But Acheson was gutsy, willing to throw the long ball, and a first-rate appreciator of the gifts of others. He thought George Marshall, who preceded him as secretary of state, the greatest American military figure since

George Washington. He is moving on the subject of Harry Truman. You are lucky if you can love a president you serve, and he did. Unlike FDR, Truman was not devious but plain in his dealings; also unlike FDR, he was not cold at the core but available. After Truman left office, a friend of Acheson's, visiting the new White House, was told as a man went into the Oval Office, "Oh, he's going in to cheer up the president." Acheson's friend replied, "That's funny, in our day the president used to cheer us up."

Acheson: "Harry S. Truman was two men. One was the public figure—peppery, sometimes belligerent, often didactic, the 'give-'em-hell' Harry. The other was the patient, modest, considerate, and appreciative boss, helpful and understanding in all official matters, affectionate in any private worry or sorrow." Truman "learned from mistakes (though he seldom admitted them), and did not waste time bemoaning them."

What is inspiring about Acheson's first-rate second-rateness is that he's like a lot of those we have developing foreign policy right now.

Acheson, though he did not present it this way, provides useful lessons for future diplomats in future crises.

- *Everyone's in the dark looking for the switch.* When you're in the middle of history the meaning of things is usually unclear. "We all had far more than the familiar difficulty of determining the capabilities and intentions of those who inhabit the planet with us." In real time most things are obscure. "We groped after interpretations of [events], sometimes reversed lines of action based on earlier views, and hesitated before grasping what now seems obvious." "Only slowly did it dawn upon us that the whole world structure and order that we had inherited from the nineteenth century was gone."

- *Don't mess things up at the beginning.* Acheson's insight was that it wouldn't work to put forward the Marshall Plan and then try to sell it to the public. The way to go was to explain to Congress and the public the exact nature of the crisis. This, he believed, would shock both into facing facts. While they were doing that, a plan to deal with the crisis was being developed. "We could not afford a false start."

- *Be able to see your work soberly.* Keep notes so history will know what happened. "Our efforts for the most part left conditions better than we found them," Acheson says. Especially in Europe, which was dying and went on to live.

- *Cheer up.* Good things can come of bad times, great things from fiercely imperfect individuals.

- *Even though you'll wind up disappointed.* All diplomats in the end feel frustrated over missed opportunities and achievements that slipped away. "Alas, that is life. We cannot live our dreams."

Still to be answered: What is America's strategy now—our overarching vision, our big theme and intent? What are the priorities? How, now, to navigate the world?

That soldier needs an answer to his question: What do you need from us? What's the plan?

AMERICAN INSTITUTIONS ARE FRAILER THAN WE KNOW

May 31, 2018

I have been thinking about trust. All the polls show and have for some time what you already know: America's trust in its leaders and institutions has been falling for four decades. Trust in the federal government has never been lower. In 1958 Pew Research found that 73 percent trusted the government to do what is right "always" or "most of the time." That sounds healthy. As of 2017 that number was 18 percent. That's not.

Other institutions have suffered too—the church, the press, the professions. That's disturbing because those institutions often bolster our national life in highly personal ways. When government or law turns bad, they provide a place, a platform from which to stand, to make a case, to correct.

A problem that has so many parts and so much history—from Vietnam to Twitter bots—will not easily be solved. But there are things we can do individually to help America be more at peace with itself.

First, realize this isn't merely a problem but a crisis. When you say you believe in and trust democratic institutions, you are saying you believe in and trust democracy itself. When you don't, you don't. When a nation tells pollsters it's unable to trust its constituent parts it's telling pollsters it doesn't trust itself.

It's time to see our mighty institutions with their noble facades—the grand marble courthouses, the soaring cathedral—for what they are: secretly frail and in constant need of saving.

When you're young and starting out you imagine institutions are monoliths—big, impervious to your presence. Later, having spent time within, you know how human and flawed it all is, and how it's saved each day by the wisdom and patience—the quiet heroism—of a few. Be one of the few.

If you're young it would be good at this point to enter your profession with a premature sense of the frailty of everything.

Six years ago I was invited to speak to a small West Point class. Polls had come out showing that the U.S. military still retained the trust of the people, and this was much on my mind. I wondered if the cadets knew how much was riding on them.

I told them the institution they're about to enter was among the last standing, and one of their great jobs will be to keep it trustworthy.

Naturally maintaining their institution's moral stature was not the main focus of their minds. So I told them a story of a great army of the West, admired by all, that did something wrong, and then a series of things, and by the end, when it came out, as such things do, it broke that army's reputation in a way from which it never quite recovered. I was speaking of France and the Dreyfus affair. They had not heard of it.

There should be a course in it.

I urged them to conduct themselves so that such a thing could never happen in the U.S. Army. I don't think I left them rushing to download Émile Zola on their iPads. I do think they were hearing for the first time how much America depends on them not only for military expertise but to keep up the national morale.

In many ways we're too national in our thinking. Don't always be thinking up there. Be thinking here, where life takes place. In building trust think close to home. If your teenager judges an institution called Business in America by the billionaire hedge funder spouting inane thoughts on cable TV with a look on his face that says "See how original I am!" then capitalism is doomed. You can't make your teenager admire slippery, rapacious tech gods in Silicon Valley. But if your children understand business in America as modeled by you—as honorable men and women engaged in an honorable pursuit—then they will have respect for the institution of business. If for no other reason be honest in your dealings, be compassionate, and provide excellence.

Realize there's a difference between skepticism and cynicism, that one is constructive and the other childish.

Skepticism involves an intellectual exercise: You look at the grand sur-